NX 546. A3
STE

stepping stones

John Lee Hooker and Van Morrison at the Mississippi Delta, near Highway 51

stepping stones

the arts in ulster

1971–2001

edited by **Mark Carruthers**
and **Stephen Douds**

THE
BLACKSTAFF
PRESS
———
BELFAST

First published in 2001 by
The Blackstaff Press Limited
Wildflower Way, Apollo Road
Belfast BT12 6TA, Northern Ireland
with the assistance of
the Arts Council of Northern Ireland

Typeset by Techniset Typesetters, Newton-le-Willows, Merseyside

Printed in Ireland by Betaprint

A CIP catalogue record for this book
is available from the British Library

ISBN 0-85640-705-4

www.blackstaffpress.com

Contents

Acknowledgements

This book would not have been possible without the support and encouragement of a great many people. Anne Tannahill at Blackstaff Press was hugely enthusiastic about the project when we first approached her in June 2000 and her input throughout has always been positive. Marnie O'Neill at British Telecom was equally supportive when we sought financial backing and again her contribution to the book has been inestimable.

A number of people offered advice and support to us in recent months and to the following we are particularly grateful: Caroline Cooper, Marie-Clare Doris, June Gamble and Grainne Loughran from BBC Northern Ireland; Philip Hammond and Damian Smyth from the Arts Council of Northern Ireland; Michael Longley with whom we spoke at length in the early stages of the project and whose support ensured 'the apostolic succession';

Jan Branch, Paul McErlean, Hugh Morrison, John O'Farrell, Caroline Robinson and Barry Todd; Chris Hill, Jill Jennings, David Hammond, John T. Davis, Professor Seamus Deane, Walter McAuley, and Ed Curran, Editor of the *Belfast Telegraph* who provided support in sourcing appropriate illustrations. Our thanks also to Simon McWilliams for permission to use *Red and Blue Scaffolding* on the front cover. Wendy Dunbar, Aaron Kelly and Bronagh McVeigh at Blackstaff Press deserve special mention for their support and attention to detail throughout the editing process.

Our eleven contributors have laboured long and hard on their respective chapters and for that we are grateful. They met the often exacting demands placed upon them with unfailing good humour. They were, in turn, assisted and encouraged by a considerable number of people. Thanks on their behalf should be recorded to many of those already named above and to: the archivists at the Lyric Theatre and the Linen Hall Library; to Michael Alcorn, Edgar Boucher, Tony Carver, Donald Cullington, John Gray, Roy Johnston, Graham Nelson, David Openshaw and Irene Sandford. In addition to writing her own chapter, Grania McFadden often found herself acting as an unofficial sounding-board throughout this entire project and for this we are particularly indebted.

Finally, a special word of thanks should go to our respective families and close friends, for their support and understanding in recent months. We hope they feel our frequent disappearing acts have been worth it – we certainly do.

MARK CARRUTHERS and STEPHEN DOUDS
BELFAST, JULY 2001

Introduction

This book is built on firm foundations. They are foundations laid down fifty years ago when Sam Hanna Bell, John Hewitt and Nesca Robb compiled the original *Arts in Ulster* as part of Northern Ireland's contribution to the Festival of Britain celebrations. Twenty years later in 1971 Michael Longley, who was then working for the Arts Council of Northern Ireland, edited *Causeway*, a publication which updated the work of Hanna Bell et al. *Causeway*'s ten essayists captured the cultural flowering and optimism of the 1960s, while Michael Longley in his introduction, addressed the role of the artist in a society at war with itself. With characteristic prescience he observed that, 'too many critics seem to expect a harvest of paintings, poems, plays and novels to drop from the twisted branches of civil discord. They fail to realise that the artist needs time in which to allow the raw material of experience to settle to an imaginative depth where he can transform it ... he is not some sort of super-journalist commenting with unfaltering spontaneity on events immediately after they have happened'. The three decades since the publication of *Causeway* have afforded many artists the time to filter their experiences and produce those plays, poems, paintings and novels referred to so often in this book. It is our privilege to edit this third volume in the series; it is our pleasure to build our house on foundations of stone.

The years under review in *Stepping Stones* correspond more or less to the years of the Troubles, though this project was never intended to be specifically a study of the arts and the Troubles. Almost every essayist refers to the civil unrest in his or her chapter, very often chronicling the impact the violence had on the particular discipline in question. Inevitably it had more of a bearing on some areas than others. Our poets and playwrights tackled the subject often; our composers did not. Some of our painters did; many others did not. Many novelists mined the Troubles seam with vigour – some of them very badly – while others sought to tell their stories on a broader canvas. The truth is, of course, that whether or not a particular artist chose to examine 'the Ulster condition' in his or her work is not hugely important. What is important is that audiences – whether readers, listeners or viewers – should be reminded of the importance of the human voice and human experience. In the context of Northern Ireland and the past thirty years, that is perhaps what artists have contributed most – they have chronicled the individual stories. Their work has been a crucial counterpoint to the notion that society here has constituted nothing more than a collection of warring tribes, hell-bent on mutual destruction. The best of our poets, novelists, playwrights and composers, our painters, film-makers and actors have reminded us throughout of the individuals whose stories lie behind the headlines. As Bill Lazenbatt from the University of Ulster's English department observed in his editorial for *Writing Ulster* in 1999, 'we have been subjected for far too long in Ulster to the self-interested cant of a cacophony of political voices; perhaps we should reverse the exclusivity of Plato's Republic, banish the political and listen to the artists instead!'

Stepping Stones chronicles the last three decades of artistic endeavour in eleven chapters. We have devoted the first two chapters to drama. Ophelia Byrne considers, in some depth, the impact the violence of the early 1970s

had on the theatre community here. The escalating street violence, the introduction of internment without trial, Bloody Sunday, Bloody Friday – all had
serious repercussions for what was staged, where it was staged and who saw
it. After her initial exploration of that turbulent backdrop to the arts, she
examines the most significant venues and companies of the past three decades.
In the second essay on drama David Grant considers the major dramatists of
the period and their plays.

Frank Ormsby and Eamonn Hughes, tasked to review poetry and fiction
respectively, have produced astonishingly comprehensive surveys which
demonstrate the fertility of Northern Ireland as a source for both story and
story-teller. In these two disciplines in particular, writers from the north have
been especially successful, and the work of, for example, Seamus Heaney,
Michael Longley, Brian Moore and Jennifer Johnston is now widely known
and highly regarded internationally.

Musically there is much more to say than there was in 1971. As Joe McKee
records, classical music in Northern Ireland does not begin and end with the
Ulster Orchestra – vital though its contribution might be – and Tony McAuley in his chapter on traditional music and song summarises the rejuvenation
and revitalisation of a once moribund tradition. Completing a trio of
chapters on music, Stuart Bailie assesses the unexpectedly rich roll of successful rock and pop acts to have emerged in Northern Ireland from the Undertones to Van Morrison and Ash.

Images of this small community and its big problems have been beamed
across the world via television and film throughout the period under review.
In turn, that has attracted film-makers to Northern Ireland, often with
disappointing consequences for the international image of this community
and, more often than not, for the individual cinema-goer too. Mike Catto
charts that and the rise of a fledgling indigenous film industry in some detail,
while Martyn Anglesea summarises the steady achievements produced in the
visual arts with a breadth that takes the chapter beyond a mere catalogue of
painters.

Two final chapters, with less tangible subject matter than the others, complete the book. Ian Hill traces the developments in arts administration from
the Council for the Encouragement of Music and the Arts (CEMA) through to
the Arts Council of Northern Ireland (ACNI), and from the rise of the

National Lottery funding for the arts, to the creation of the Department of Culture, Arts and Leisure (DCAL). Grania McFadden has pored over countless cuttings files and back catalogues to establish just how the arts have been reported since 1971. Her examination of the internal media debate about how much space arts and culture deserve, in an essentially news-driven agenda, makes for absorbing reading.

In both previous volumes architecture was considered sufficiently important to merit inclusion; in fact *Causeway* carried two chapters on the subject. On this occasion, however, we have decided that the past thirty years have not produced enough work of substantial architectural significance to justify devoting a full chapter to the subject. This was not a decision taken lightly. Our research indicated that, in the first instance, much of the historical heritage is already adequately covered in the 1951 and 1971 publications and second, very little of real and enduring architectural worth has in fact been built within our particular time period. Regrettably, the artistic aspect of architecture still remains shamefully undervalued, perhaps even among some architects themselves, though more particularly on the part of those public and private sector companies and institutions which commission architects to design buildings for them.

There are, of course, some very notable exceptions to that. Victor Robinson's Waterfront Hall has rightly been celebrated as the jewel in the crown of Laganside's redevelopment, though that praise may be tarnished somewhat if it remains the only building of real architectural beauty in the area. Few other civic buildings have given Belfast, or indeed anywhere else in the north, such an embodiment of civic pride. Honourable mentions, however, should be made of Castlereagh Borough Council's new civic offices in south-east Belfast, the stunningly successful Market Place Theatre in Armagh and the extended Linen Centre in Lisburn, where a modern extension grafted on to a much older and classically handsome building, has created a freshness and originality few might have expected. Civic buildings aside, much of our architecture in the past generation has been humdrum and routine and in comparison with practitioners in other arts-related areas few, if any, Ulster architects would have any widespread public name recognition. One exception might well be Liam McCormick, who is best known for designing a number of strikingly modern catholic churches in counties Derry and Donegal.

As Northern Ireland's population has grown in the past thirty years, so too its housing stock has increased in volume. While public housing has always been designed with functionality as a high priority, the powers that be have nonetheless placed greater emphasis on aesthetics in recent years. There has been a welcome move away from housing families in high-rise hutches towards the construction of properly landscaped small-scale community developments instead. However, if much of what has happened in the public housing sector is to be welcomed, the same cannot be said for the private sector. Bungalow blight is now a major concern across much of rural Ulster, and the traditional agricultural vistas of the past have been seriously damaged by the multiplicity of 'haciendas on the hill'. Private developers too have a great deal to answer for. Their brief to architects is apparently to design what the builders think the paying customers want – hence the fascination with Georgiana and aspirational grandeur which makes for so much lacklustre private housing stock.

Architects would surely be happier to be given a freer rein. Perhaps in the next three decades the profession here will mirror the achievements of the very best architects in the Republic who, in the last thirty years, have established what amounts to a distinctive, contemporary Irish school of architecture which is known and admired internationally. Such a development would surely justify the devotion of a chapter to architecture in a fourth volume in this series thirty years hence.

Like architecture, dance does not merit a separate chapter in *Stepping Stones*. Again, this was not a decision taken without careful consideration and detailed discussion with several individuals prominent in the field. Dance is, of course, a respected and valuable aspect of any broad artistic mix, but over the past three decades it has remained something of a minority interest here despite valiant efforts to change that by the Arts Council and several dance teachers and enthusiasts. The innovative work of Patricia Mulholland, so much a feature of the 1950s and 1960s, is rightly remembered as a highpoint of local dance, as is the contribution made by the mesmeric émigré, Helen Lewis. It looked as if dance might put down lasting professional roots in the late 1980s when the Arts Council engaged the services of Royston Muldoom for several years to work with Ulster Youth Dance. The shows produced were generally judged successful, but the lack of any real development infrastructure, coupled with the absence of any genuinely appropriate dance venues and the usual problems of attracting financial support, combined to arrest the expansion of professional contemporary dance.

The network of traditional dance classes and competitions across the north today is probably as strong as it has ever been, and the popular appreciation of Irish dancing has been broadened on the world stage thanks to the soaring success of *Riverdance*. Similarly, ballet classes are taught to a large number of young people across the country, by several qualified and enthusiastic teachers. Gillian Revie, the Ulster-born ballerina who is currently First Soloist with the Royal Ballet Company in London, is, of course, an excellent role model for the would-be stars of tomorrow. All of this local dance activity is conducted on an amateur basis, however, and where dance has been singly unsuccessful is in putting down firm professional foundations. A 1997 dance audit, compiled by the Arts Council of Northern Ireland, reported a number of individuals and several professional or semi-professional groups working hard to expand interest in dance, but the fundamental problem of trying to unite several disparate elements into one coherent movement remains unresolved. According to current estimates, dance accounts for less than half of one percent of the Arts Council's annual funding allocations.

One trend present elsewhere in the United Kingdom, and equally true in Northern Ireland, has been the steady democratisation of the arts, a process which has changed the way the sector is viewed by government and by traditionally sceptical sections of the community. The continued rise of the community arts sector in the north has forced all arts practitioners to re-examine what they do, how they do it and crucially who they do it for. The fierce debate between the community arts sector and the so-called 'high' arts, which raged as the former began to make a real impact a decade ago, has now, to some extent, abated. Both parties to the dispute have apparently come to realise that they are in fact allies in the battle against the serried ranks of the non-believers however they may be defined. It is for that reason that we have resisted the temptation to devote a separate chapter to the community arts. Where such activities have been distinguished enough to merit mention or discussion, they appear in the relevant chapter. In short, we prefer to include community arts achievement on merit, rather than to make a special case for it. To employ watered down critical criteria on one isolated sector is surely to patronise it and those who work within it.

The experience of devolution could yet be the making of the arts in Northern Ireland. The shift from cultural cringe to cultural confidence is underway and perhaps now, as never before, the sector will receive the attention it deserves from government, attention which has been so demonstrably absent throughout much of the recent past. With hopes buoyed up that Belfast might just be a serious contender for European City of Culture in 2008, a major programme of education is now being launched. Local politicians need to know why the arts matter, and it is up to the arts community to be their persuader. The truth is, the arts have never dominated the public's consciousness here, and while many people can – and do – enthusiastically indulge their artistic cravings today, many others still feel the arts have no significant contribution to make to their everyday lives. Visual artists, actors, directors, writers and community arts organisations – in fact all those who benefit from public funding – now have an opportunity to start explaining why the arts and culture do count. The Department of Culture, Arts and Leisure has high ambitions for Northern Ireland and its cultural life, but no great art – whether it be a Derek Mahon poem, the lyrics of a Van Morrison song or a Brian Moore novel – was ever produced by committee, much less by a government department. While it may help promote local success abroad, DCAL is unlikely to be a catalyst for individual artistic activity.

When Sam Hanna Bell penned the introduction to the original *Arts in Ulster* he described himself, with characteristic self-effacement, as the carrier of the banderol or banner at the head of the procession. He saw himself as heralding the great parade of poets, painters and musicians, but he was, of course, an important part of the procession himself. So too was Michael Longley, his eminent successor, in 1971. As a perspicacious arts administrator then and a much-lauded poet today, he too has entered that procession of Ulster artists. We have largely been bystanders on that latter-day pageant, a vantage point afforded us in our work at the BBC where we have reported, debated and celebrated the arts in Ulster. When we first floated the idea of this book with some of our colleagues and friends in the arts sector, we quickly realised that many were of the view that such an artistic audit was, in fact, long overdue.

The title of this volume, *Stepping Stones*, was suggested by Seamus Heaney's Nobel lecture, *Crediting Poetry*, where he remarked, 'each point of arrival whether in one's poetry or one's life turned out to be a stepping stone rather than a destination'. Coincidentally, but equally significant, the title evokes Michael Longley's *Causeway*, upon which, of course, this book builds. The political resonance is there too in the title, suggesting the idea of a community negotiating the stepping stones from violence to peace – though as Heaney warns, the danger is in thinking we have arrived when, in fact, the crossing may have only just begun. Let the journey continue.

Fergal McElherron as Alan in the Replay production of Gary Mitchell's
That Driving Ambition, 1995

Theatre — companies and venues

OPHELIA BYRNE

It was scarcely believable in the circumstances, but there it sat. An Arts Dome. Space-age, visionary, glamorous and brightly-coloured, the construction rose gracefully on the banks of the Lagan, an aluminium and PVC 1971 wonder. Part of the Ulster '71 Festival, it would hold one of the 'most ambitious programmes of the arts yet staged here', and contribute to the biggest Grand Exhibition in the United Kingdom since the 1951 Festival of Britain. On Ulster '71 rested the hopes of a battered Stormont government seeking a great cultural public statement of confidence. Through its thirty-seven acre Expo-style site in Belfast's Botanic Gardens it was hoped would come thousands of visitors. It would galvanise a Troubles-beset society. It would symbolise the Ulster of the future. Those at least were the hopes. The reality was that from its opening would begin the serious countdown to disaster for the arts in Northern Ireland.

Nineteen seventy-one was the most pivotal year for Ulster theatre in the twentieth century. Not since its origins in 1902 did theatre undergo such seismic shifts; not in the three decades since has so much of significance been telescoped into a brief but turbulent twelve month period. That year marks the major fault line, with the period before and after it so acutely disjointed that it is only now, and with difficulty, that the theatre community has begun to rediscover its own tradition. It is for this reason that the 'year of the Dome' is so vital. To understand what happened to Ulster theatre in 1971 is to begin to understand what unfolded in the succeeding thirty years.

In early 1971 itself, however, this could hardly have seemed credible. The theatrical landscape was less than promising; indeed, by the opening of Ulster '71, the sector's decline already seemed well underway. This was highlighted by the much-vaunted programming of Ulster '71: though opera, ballet and music figured prominently, theatre was notably absent. No play, company or date was formally announced as part of the Ulster '71 programme, but after much grumbling from critics, a six-week season of stalwarts was finally staged by the Ulster Theatre Company. Though later productions such as *Oh What a Lovely War* were also adopted by festival organisers, much of the budget went on other artforms. 'Drama seems to have been given the cold shoulder', remarked the critic Gerald Rafferty. 'The world will think that Northern Ireland is a wilderness as far as theatre is concerned.'

The world in 1971 might have thought so with good reason. Writing for *Causeway,* a Festival publication on the arts in Ulster that year, author Sam Hanna Bell noted that the total number of new plays seen in Ulster in recent years was 'depressingly small'. Indeed, he continued, 'in the past twenty years there has often been a lack of playwrights and at times a complete absence of playhouses'. Belfast's Grand Opera House and the Hippodrome, both formerly theatres, were now for the main part cinemas, though each saw occasional drama performances. The Empire Theatre, home to music-hall and variety for many years, had been demolished in 1961. Occasional performances took place at the Grove Theatre on the Shore Road, but this was deemed an inflexible venue with poor acoustics for theatre.

Of the companies, Harold Goldblatt's touring Ulster Theatre Company alone professed a dedicated interest in new work, but in reality performed little that was original. Three professional companies had endured from the mid-twentieth century, each a Belfast-based producing company with its own venue. Two of these, the Ulster Group Theatre and the Arts Theatre, had strayed far from idealistic origins to become commercial homes of light entertainment. One company alone, the Lyric Players Theatre, still adhered to its original principles. Co-founded in 1951 by Cork woman Mary O'Malley and her husband Pearse, the Lyric was initially dedicated to presenting poetic drama and had a strong Irish orientation. By the early 1970s it had clearly become the most successful theatre company located in Northern Ireland, but was facing changes partly prompted by its acquisition of its new three hundred-seater Ridgeway Street venue. It had also existed for much of its pre-Troubles life as a private theatre. In general then, theatre by the time of Ulster '71 was largely regarded as being of marginal interest to a society of colour televisions, x-rated films and catsuits. Society had changed and theatre did not seem to be responding to the new challenges. Why then reward it with a central role in an Ulster '71 programme proudly promising: 'Mr Ulsterman . . . This is Your Life'?

Yet that this should be the case is ironic. If Ulster '71 programming made clear the poor standing of the sector, it also revealed the establishment attitudes which had helped make it that way. These principally concerned the areas of business and politics with which, traditionally, theatre in Northern Ireland has had a complex relationship. In the symbolic Ulster '71 Festival the core theme was 'Ulster Means Business'. The motto was 'By Our Skills We Live'. The glossy festival publication celebrated a 'people hard at work'. Given that the state was fighting for international economic survival, this is understandable. Yet for the arts, it is also telling. By the Ulster '71 benchmarks, the arts were notably not a skill by which one lived. Instead, in the glossy publicity brochure, they were placed in the 'Quality of Life' section with the countryside. Photographs of the Ulster Orchestra were accompanied by others of golf, fishing, waterfalls and mountains. Reinforcing this, while noting that individual cultural achievement in Ulster was 'impressive', the sparsely-worded brochure boasted that: 'There is hardly a town or village that does not have its drama group'. Culture and roses, landscape and scenery ranked together; drama was highlighted as a leisure pursuit, not a profession.

Such attitudes were hardly new. The battle to achieve state recognition of and support for local theatre had been long-standing; unlike its counterpart in the Republic of Ireland, northern theatre had not been in regular receipt of public funding throughout the twentieth century. Not until the late 1950s did funding begin to trickle through for local theatrical endeavours; until then, CEMA (the Council for the Encouragement of Music and the Arts) argued that funding was solely for professionals. In practice, this meant 'English and foreign artists' were supported, as Ulster practitioners were trapped in a hazy unfunded limbo between the amateur and the professional. Necessarily reliant on box office proceeds, they were often forced to take supplementary employment elsewhere and could not truly claim professional status. This double bind resulted in a public attitude that, in the words of playwright Bill Morrison in 1969, 'there is no worthwhile distinction between the professional artist and the enthusiastic amateur'. Another consequence of non-funding was a theatre characterised by caution. Throughout the mid-century it rarely engaged in ideological political debate about its own society. Reliant on door proceeds in a politically sensitive, relatively new state, it trod a careful line; if this left it open to charges of self-censorship and lack of artistic adventurousness, it nonetheless ensured its survival.

By the late 1950s, with the rise of other new media, the need for public funding had become incontrovertible. So too had the need for theatre to fully address its socio-political environs if it was to endure and be taken seriously by the wider community. The combination of the two was explosive. Two government-funded Ulster Group Theatre productions, *The Bonefire* by Gerard McLarnon and *Over the Bridge* by Sam Thompson, tackled the issue of sectarianism head-on; each caused a storm of controversy. The latter in particular became a cause célèbre for publicly exposing the narrow political parameters within which publicly funded theatre was expected to operate. The Ulster situation was to give 'local colour and no more', the Northern Ireland Governor informed the Group chairman; the play was very publicly pulled before going ahead as a triumphant independent production at the Empire Theatre.

Yet having been shown its political confines, theatre generally was left at an impasse. Despite the arrival in 1963 of the modernising government of Captain Terence O'Neill, and the replacement of CEMA by the more egalitarian Arts Council of Northern Ireland, theatre drifted demoralized through the 1960s. A report in the mid 1960s referred to high levels of emigration in the sector, to 'frustration and dissipation of effort' amongst those remaining, and to a business-oriented Ulster attitude deeply suspicious of public subsidy for artistic activities perceived 'not as an essential part of the fabric of community life, but as luxuries'. Despite this, funding was secured by some projects, but political conformity continued to be an issue. The most prominent example of this was the Lyric Theatre, which spent several years seeking public and private funding for a new building. The *Belfast Telegraph* amongst others noted that public goodwill towards the theatre 'apparently depends on an assurance of the theatre's pro-constitutional policy'; there lingered, said a Lyric-commissioned report, an 'erroneous belief that the theatre was in some way linked with politics.' Mary O'Malley had been a Labour councillor in the 1950s and had made speeches and gestures sharply critical of the unionist establishment; she herself noted that her 'very presence was a controversial one.' In addition, the National Anthem was not played at Lyric performances, the O'Malleys believing that to do so would affect the 'artistic independence' of the theatre. Elsewhere it was an integral part of many public functions, however, and some Lyric Trustees felt its absence contributed to a 'somewhat unhelpful' image of the theatre. Though the building was eventually completed and opened in 1968 with the support of the Arts Council of Northern Ireland and business and private sponsorship, the divergence of views on the anthem remained sufficiently sharp to cause a very public, if short-term, crisis at the theatre not long afterwards. Plans in the 1960s too to build a Civic Theatre in Northern Ireland eventually became embroiled in political debate. Political controversy, then, seemed to occur more often off stage during the 1960s rather than in the theatre itself; drama generally appeared the loser.

The most unfortunate consequence of serious underfunding and political tightrope walking in a highly sensitive society was theatre's inexperience by 1971 in addressing serious political issues. With occasional high-profile exceptions, Ulster theatre companies and writers had not specifically ideologically engaged with the political world around them in decades. The Lyric alone was now seeking to do so through programming, but, with its exception, theatre's general absence from Festival '71 programming probably indicated less its potential for danger and more its peripheral place in the world around it. By 1971 it was running dangerously close to becoming precisely what the Ulster '71 programme suggested it was: an add-on, a leisure pursuit, an agreeable presence and nothing more. Within months, this, as so much else, would be torn apart.

It was not, then, that the violence surrounding Internment Day in August 1971 caused the collapse of theatre in Ulster. It simply finished it off. At the beginning of the Troubles in 1968, the street disturbances had been perceived as ongoing difficulties. Even as the world around it increasingly slipped into further and deeper crisis, an optimism of sorts in the theatre community endured. So in 1969, though vigilantes took over the premises of the amateur Circle Theatre in Belfast's New Lodge Road during the August riots, this was seen as an isolated incident in a troubled area. The critics still wrote in confident terms about what was being offered by the various Belfast venues, and crucially, theatre-going continued.

By early 1970 the theatre situation was being discussed in less confident terms, but a typical round up in February still spoke of 'lots to choose from'. In June of that year however audience fall-offs were reported; in July, they were extremely low and the Grove Theatre closed. With a pub curfew in place that summer, and irregular bus services, it was reported that 'a climate of "expectancy of trouble" was being created', and that Northern Ireland was lapsing into 'virtual civil war'. The first major warning regarding theatre came in August 1970. The Arts Theatre manager Hubert Wilmot publicly declared that the venue had 'suffered severely from loss of audience in the past year due to the disturbances', and could only remain open if it received government assistance or if the street situation improved. A return to normality was considered the likely option. By the year's end, 1970 was designated a mixed experience. If patrons had not quite been 'tripping over each other to get to the box office', this was still only 'at times'. James Young, for example, was drawing full houses for Christmas performances at the Group Theatre; the future, while there was cause for concern, was still not entirely bleak.

Nineteen seventy-one was a different matter. Just three months into the year, organisers of the Belfast Music Festival and popular talent contest 'Stairway to Stardom' announced that the Troubles had badly hit their attendances. The violence worsened as Ulster '71 opened and shortly afterwards the London Festival Ballet cancelled its festival engagement, dancers having received threatening letters. Peter Montgomery, President of the Arts Council of Northern Ireland, thought the company 'might have been a bit braver'. In July dance halls reported a thirty to fifty per cent drop in business; people were reported to be reluctant to spend an evening in city centre Belfast. The Arts Theatre closed for the summer, stating its scheduled August re-opening would be dependent on 'whether the city is quiet or not'. The disturbances that July were described as exceptionally frightening, with ninety-four explosions in just four weeks. Then on 9 August internment was imposed: unprecedented violence followed.

The immediate impact was as might have been expected: attendances at cinemas and other entertainments fell off to practically nothing. With five thousand refugees and nineteen relief centres, Belfast was declared a 'ghost town'. From this point on, the arts and entertainment worlds moved rapidly towards shutdown. 'Events move with such speed now it is a struggle to keep up', declared the Chichester column of the *Belfast Telegraph*. On 21 August, 77 Sunset Strip Club was bombed; Miss Great Britain cancelled her visit to Belfast on 27 August. That same day London theatrical outfitters demanded unusually high indemnities before providing hats for *Oh What a Lovely War*. The first of September saw the bombing of the Talk of the Town cabaret club; 7 September brought news of the withdrawal of Ulster singers from the Waterford Festival of Light Opera. The next day an international design conference was cancelled, and on 9 September a Johnny Cash show was called off, Aiken Promotions reported to be forgetting 'all about Ulster Hall promotions for as long as the Troubles last'. Ulster '71 closed as planned on 11 September, reporters noting how artificial it now seemed 'considering the frightening escalation of history'. Cancellations now began for events the following year: on 30 September 1972 the Belfast Music Festival was cancelled for the first time since its 1908 foundation; so too was the Londonderry Feis of 1972. Scottish Opera and Opera For All visits were called off on 1 October, followed by the Ballyclare Musical Festival on 9 October. The Arts Theatre finally closed on 14 October, and James Young confirmed that the Group Theatre would not re-open, saying: 'All we need is a bit of peace and quiet and we'll be back in business'.

It was not to be. Unlike previous periods of disturbance, the announcements went on and on. The Grand Opera House issued notices that for the first time there would be an all-local cast in the annual pantomime, with 6pm evening shows to enable patrons to get home. Ulster Orchestra concerts were cancelled on 17 December and the Arts Council announced it had 'no plans for visiting ballet, drama or opera in the foreseeable future'. Late-night Christmas shopping was cancelled; four thousand troops accompanied Christmas shoppers around Belfast in one day alone. 'If it is true that the darkest hour precedes the dawn', noted the first *Belfast Telegraph* editorial of 1972, 'then Northern Ireland may hope for streaks of light in the sky in 1972'. Just twenty-nine days away lay Bloody Sunday.

On many levels the violence had devastating consequences. First, as one hotel manager summarised: 'No one is coming to Northern Ireland, the people of Northern Ireland aren't coming in to Belfast and the people of Belfast aren't coming in ...' Northern Ireland was internationally isolated. Though touring companies would eventually return, in the short-term they could no longer be absolutely relied upon to do so. External affirmation of Ulster's standing as a cultured society was not forthcoming. Consequently, in a comment memorable for its attitudes to local work, a *Belfast Telegraph* leader writer stated: 'If the outside world will not come and entertain us, then we must do the job ourselves ... The show must go on even if the stars cannot come.'

The Lyric excepted, the show was not going on. The theatres were dark, and with good reason. Bombers targetted not only shops and factories but also restaurants, cinemas and theatres; 1971 saw 73 pubs destroyed, with 4 clubs and 185 shops put out of business. And so, potential audiences splintered. In troubled areas, a pre-internment trend was compounded: people tended to stay in their own localities, with allegations that shebeens were doing a roaring trade. In less troubled city districts, people travelled out-of-town for entertainment. Portrush Summer Theatre had one of its best seasons ever; the Little Theatre continued in Bangor; amateur drama festivals survived in many provincial towns. Conversely, travel into Belfast from the rural hinterland was reported as minimal, with country coach parties simply refusing to attend theatre. The actor J.J. Murphy neatly summarised why the professional show could not go on: 'I understand why the security forces don't want thousands of people around the streets. But it takes thousands of people for me to stay in my job'. When could – or would – those thousands return?

Event organisers were uncertain, but now looking at a long-term forecast. The sheer scale of the violence had changed attitudes. After months of relentless bombing, the muted optimism was over. The convulsions of violence would continue, and some way of surviving would have to be found. 'This is the real Ulster '71', one editorial stated, 'and it is no use wishing it away'. Rapidly, a historical precedent was invoked: wartime London. The Prime Minister congratulated citizens for 'carrying on calmly and courageously', and specifically compared the Ulster spirit to that of the London Blitz. Continuing as normal was deemed a matter of patriotic duty, repeatedly spoken of as a way of beating the gunmen and terrorists.

Yet such 'normality' appeared to require a difficult doublethink, and the effort required to sustain such a veneer of normality in people's everyday lives was considerable. A *London Times* reporter specifically refuted the Blitz comparison, noting that in wartime London people had laughed a great deal while in Belfast people conveyed themselves as being deeply ashamed and gravely worried about their futures. The wartime spirit seemed more difficult to maintain when the IRA as well as the government were issuing posters stating 'Loose talk costs lives'. In the prevailing climate of fear and conservatism, establishment figures considered how wartime London had kept its spirits high. 'Somehow', columnists mused, 'Ulster must do the same'.

The arts were one way forward. By October, theatre found itself plucked from the margins by a society desperately seeking to affirm itself; suddenly, theatre became an editorial topic. The Arts Theatre closure was declared a 'psychological blow to the city' by Independent Unionist, Tom Caldwell, who put questions to the government on the issue. Cultural events were now deemed 'important', and the fact that the 'other, brighter side of life' was being 'swamped' was deplored. Theatre was one of the things 'which those in any civilised city take for granted', summarised the *Belfast Telegraph*. 'At no time has the Arts Council been more needed to give a welcome break' it continued. Thus bidden, theatre was given a clear-cut role: to provide sheer escapism and reassure society of its normality. The show would simply have to go on.

But what kind of show? Extending the pre-Troubles notion of the sector, the media began to speak of the arts as apolitical, as being less touchable by political violence than other sectors. Together with the countryside, they were discussed as being synonymous not only with civility, but with the unification of the community. The arts could show how 'easy it is for people to speak as one'; art forms were 'common to all'. Like the countryside, they could release tensions and overcome divisions. So one amateur drama group declared the aim of creating 'a more pleasant and relaxed atmosphere' in its area. Similarly, a cabaret company participating in a Ministry of Community Relations charity football game described itself as 'doing our bit for peace'. 'The entertainment world', one participant stressed, 'has always been noted for shunning sectarianism and bigotry . . . the only aim is to try and improve community relations in the province'.

And so theatre's former malaise seemed over. With newly imposed social functions, theatre might acceptably be a skill by which one lived; now, the theatre sector could assume a somewhat more mainstream role in society. It would bring people together from all political backgrounds. It would provide escapist entertainment. It would act as a morale booster. In the short-term crisis, fulfilling this societal remit would suffice for, even dynamise, the theatre sector. The long-term would be somewhat different. These social remits had the potential both to liberate and to shackle. Broadly interpreted, they could challenge both society and theatre in a rewarding way. Conversely, in an atmosphere of mistrust and vigilance, they could also impede the development of an art form already traditionally hidebound by politics.

For theatre to be required, for example, solely or even mainly to provide escapism and to act as a morale-booster might not be healthy for society or theatre. To work on a cross-community basis in an intensely fearful society could require the provision of bland entertainment, inoffensive to all, rather than genuinely challenging theatre work. And on the issue of art for art's sake – an idea about which Ulster had traditionally displayed discomfort – there had been no apparent attitudinal change. Troubles practitioners thus found themselves facing unspoken boundaries as surely as their mid-century predecessors. An intensely conservative society convulsed by sectarian violence would have its own ideas about what it found acceptable. Practitioners would find themselves almost entirely reliant on public funding: this would naturally bring its own emphases and pressures to bear. Political and sectarian tensions would now be admissable on stage, but only in a way making it easy for people to speak as one. By a different route, this could mean a re-emergence of local colour and no more; under these circumstances, would it be possible for this, the most public of the artforms, to do meaningful work?

Such issues would dog the theatre sector for the next thirty years. Largely unevaluated and unacknowledged, they have been a powerful undercurrent since 1971. As such, their contextualising presence is essential to a comprehension of theatre's evolution through the Troubles. In this there have been four discernable periods: survival, cautious re-emergence, the rise of the independents, and the creation of a 'scene'. The first period, survival, took place from 1971 to 1976, and tried to ensure that some form of drama continued despite the disturbances. Ironically, a good deal more was achieved. Two companies were selected to receive public money to enable theatre's survival: the Lyric, and the Arts Theatre Trust. Of the two, the non-commercial Lyric was immediately favoured, being described by the Arts Council as one of the 'keystones of community provision'.

The commercially-oriented Arts Theatre was a different matter. Indicating the kind of pressure being exerted on it, the Arts Council declared it had no 'brief to grant money to sustain public morale' and refused its emergency funding. Instead, to meet the actors' immediate employment needs, the Arts Council created the mobile educational drama unit Interplay Theatre. Based at the Arts Theatre, it would be managed by the Theatre Trust and administered by the former Arts manager Hubert Wilmot, with Denis Smyth as producer and director. By early 1972 small groups of performers were touring to schools' audiences across Northern Ireland with classic and documentary plays. 'It is not the same as a theatre', commented the critic Betty Lowry darkly, but nonetheless, Interplay did what most theatres throughout the 1960s had not done: it created a platform for new local voices in theatre. The productions also introduced phenomenal numbers of young people to the idea of seeing their own society presented dramatically. Production values were extremely high and pieces such as Stewart Love's *Titanic,* or Stewart Parker's *The Blue and the Gray,* were enthusiastically received by young people, adults and critics alike. By March 1973 Interplay had given 254 performances to 68,782 children.

As with many town halls and community centres across Northern Ireland, the Arts Theatre itself was severely bomb-damaged in September 1972. The Arts Council largely funded its repairs on the basis that it would have limited access to the space for its own promotions. It re-opened in November 1973 for use by the Belfast Festival at Queen's, and periodic productions occurred there over the next two years. Such assistance, the Arts Council made plain, was simply 'conceived to sustain the Trust through difficult times'. The Arts Theatre was expected to resume its programme of lighter entertainment without subsidy at an unspecified future date.

Meanwhile, the Lyric was both settling with difficulty into its new venue, and assuming its new role as a publicly funded 'keystone'. In principle this meant, in Conor O'Malley's words, 'aspiring to become an artistic con-science in the community'. In practice it meant the Lyric, by necessity, as-sumed ever-increasing responsibilities. Its core programming often featured works judged to be of particular relevance to contemporary public events, such as the staging of *Danton's Death* by Georg Büchner when the Stormont Parliament was suspended. More light-hearted work was not being presented elsewhere, however, and budgets were tight. Mary O'Malley thus began to mix more challenging productions with those which, like *The Importance of Being Earnest,* she saw as consistent with Lyric policy and yet popular enough to bring in an audience.

For the first time, too, the Lyric began to introduce new work on a peri-odic basis. This included *The Flats* (1970) by Belfast-born John Boyd, the first play staged locally on the current Troubles, and *We Do It for Love* by Patrick Galvin (1975). These were approvingly summarised at the time as plays evenly balanced in their attacks and presenting no answers. Since then, such works have been criticised for evasiveness, but it is salutary to remember their context. Galvin spoke of the opening night of his play as having 'an amazing atmosphere . . . You could have cut it with a knife. A young policeman who had been shot had been buried earlier in the day and I was really frightened. The reaction could have gone either way'. Theatre was surviving in an envir-onment of hostility, with leader writers noting a tendency for 'many people to retreat into their shells and wait until it is all over'. The Belfast Festival continued to successfully present an amount of non-local work annually despite everything, but locally it was more difficult. To speak directly in a society of doublethink was difficult enough; to re-present such a society immediately to itself was a formidable responsibility.

By the late 1970s, such duties began to be shared. The second phase, that of cautious re-emergence, began. Though resorting to Tilley lamps at times, the Lyric had closed only once. Local critics thought it had kept 'astounding' standards in the circumstances, but noted too that it 'would be stimulating to us all … to have more theatre'. Others agreed. A new Capital Provision for the Arts scheme was introduced, providing funding from central government for capital schemes initiated by District Councils. New venues such as Antrim's Clotworthy Arts Centre resulted. Funding was also provided by government to enable the Arts Council to take into public ownership the Matcham-designed Grand Opera House in 1976. It was hoped the large-scale venue might provide a range of entertainment and cultural experience in the unspecified future, and the purchase was seen by commentators as a 'considerable and highly imaginative act of faith'.

Belfast City Council, meanwhile, had also made a major commitment by investing in not one but two theatres. The Group Theatre was extensively refurbished and re-opened on 6 November 1976 as the home of amateur drama in Northern Ireland. The amateurs richly deserved the reward: they had played a major part in keeping theatre alive in the troubled Northern Ireland. The Arts Theatre, too, was refurbished with government capital grants after a package of financial support had been put together by the Arts and the City Councils. The venue was to present popular entertainment, with twelve weeks reserved annually for Arts Council events. The Arts Theatre re-opened on 16 December 1976, and thereafter the Ulster Actors' Company became its resident company. It undertook to present plays of popular appeal.

Outside Belfast the first purpose-built theatre opened in 1976, and for an experimental period the Riverside Theatre, sited on the campus of the New University of Ulster in Coleraine, was designated the new base of Interplay Theatre. It was also used for a wide range of events including plays, quiz shows, musicals, readings and performances by university and community groups. At last a venue scene of sorts seemed to be emerging; unfortunately, the effort required to sustain it was overwhelming. In 1977, after its move to Coleraine, Interplay's director and administrator resigned. While the company continued under new directorship until 1980, it was finally disbanded by the Arts Council and support was transferred to the independent company

Stage 80. Regrettably, this transfer coincided with a severe financial constriction for the Arts Council, and ultimately it had to withdraw its support. Stage 80, which had featured performers such as Marie Jones and Ian McElhinney as well as director Michael Poynor, struggled on and then folded. So too did the Ulster Actors' Company. Founded as Actors Wilde in 1975 by Patrick Galvin, John Anderson and Roy Heayberd, it had fulfilled its brief at the Arts Theatre with productions ranging from popular comedies to children's entertainment, variety and classics. Relying in the main for support from Belfast City Council, and only occasionally in receipt of Arts Council funds, it suffered severe financial problems in 1983. These it attributed to the unpredictable taste of the Ulster theatre-going public. Its residency ended and the Arts Theatre was offered for rent to other groups.

Such unpredictability made one particular ambition – the re-opening of the Grand Opera House – all the more ambitious. Nonetheless, after a government-backed refurbishment costing close to three million pounds, the magnificently restored one-thousand seater late-Victorian theatre opened its doors on 15 September 1980. Run by the Arts Council, the venue boasted near-capacity audiences on a regular basis in the first season. Soon, though, difficulties emerged. The tense political situation during the 1981 hunger strikes meant some companies cancelled visits. A decline in audiences was noted and attributed to the end of a honeymoon period. In April 1994 the Grand Opera House was leased to a Board of Trustees, the Arts Council finally of the view that it would operate more effectively as an independent entity.

Short-term attempts at winning audiences, then, certainly seemed most successful in this period. Without considerable subvention, running a venue was difficult. Town centres, while enjoying a stability of sorts, had not seen a real evening trade return; people understandably remained responsive to events on the ground, making audiences difficult to predict. The case of popular entertainment, the most unlikely to win arts subsidy, was particularly problematic. So too was the position of practitioners, for whom it was difficult to justify not going elsewhere to make a living. To survive in so inhospitable a climate demanded not just subsidy and an inspired programme, but also sheer dedication as well as, of course, talent.

These qualities were precisely what the new independent companies brought to Ulster in the next decade. During the 1980s a number of key independent theatre companies began to emerge, so that for the first time in decades a range of new voices could be heard simultaneously. The first was, famously, the Field Day Theatre Company. Founded in 1980 by actor Stephen Rea and playwright Brian Friel, its inaugural production, *Translations* by Brian Friel, proved a critical and popular sensation. As world critics arrived at the Guildhall in Derry, transformed with the backing of the City Council into a theatre, the opening night took on the status of a landmark event. The degree of excitement generated by the production bore testimony to the toll the Troubles had taken on society as a whole. Afterwards the ad hoc Field Day gathering was transformed into a Derry-based company. This would, throughout the 1980s, premiere controversial and challenging works including *Double Cross* by Thomas Kilroy (1986), and *Pentecost* by Stewart Parker (1987). To avoid the problems of others, Field Day deliberately remained a non-building based enterprise, undertaking extensive and well-supported tours throughout the island of Ireland. Ironically, this arrangement

Liam Neeson and Brenda Scallon in the Field Day production of Brian Friel's *Translations*, 1980

was later decreed to have its own disadvantages; long one-night stand tours were difficult to sustain, while the company's failure to fully impact on Derry was also blamed on its intermittent nature.

Field Day's major difficulty, however, has been judged to be its spread of activity, most notably its publishing ventures. In 1983 the company began issuing pamphlets designed to 'contribute to the solution of the present crisis by producing analyses of the established opinions, myths and stereotypes'. These pamphlets received a stormy reception, with critics such as Eavan Boland accusing them of promoting 'green nationalism and divided culture'. Some thought the pamphlets added to the resonances of the company's aims. Others, such as academic Marilyn Richtarik, believe that the largely unde-fined relationship between productions and pamphlets meant the plays were perceived and reviewed in a political context created by the pamphlets. Either way, the company for the first time provided a strong alternative to the Lyric, presenting serious new work with high production values. Field Day became a force of undoubted significance in theatre locally and interna-tionally, with productions becoming a much-anticipated annual event in Irish cities, towns and villages throughout the 1980s.

So too did the work of the second major independent company to emerge in the early 1980s, Charabanc. Founded in 1983 by Belfast actresses Marie Jones, Maureen McAuley, Eleanor Methven, Carol Scanlan (now Moore) and Brenda Winter, the company was born out of frustration at the paucity of good theatre roles for women. They determined to stage their own production, and local playwright Martin Lynch convinced them to write their own play. Not one, but a succession of new plays followed. These were written collectively and based on extensive research, with the company conducting many interviews and consulting with different communities. The resultant early works dealt with topics of local relevance, but had inter-national resonances. The first, *Lay Up Your Ends* (1983), was based on the strike of female Belfast millworkers in 1911. Directed by Pam Brighton and written with Martin Lynch, its success convinced Jones, Methven and Scanlan to continue. Six new plays were consecutively produced to considerable acclaim: *Oul Delf and False Teeth* (1984); *Now You're Talkin'* (1985); *Gold in the Streets* (1986); *The Girls in the Big Picture* (1986) and *Somewhere Over the Balcony* (1987). All were devised by the company, but

Jones' responsibility for the final writing process was reflected in her full billing as the writer of the plays from *The Girls in the Big Picture* onwards.

Charabanc did pioneering work in creating a new and comprehensive touring circuit which included rural and urban communities. Audiences ranged from 'farmers and ex-mill women to the arts festival crowds', and critical opinion was in general extremely positive. Common to all reviews were references to 'incisively unsentimental humour', and to tight ensemble playing. These elements were subsequently tested in much overseas touring by Charabanc, where again the responses were on balance extremely favourable. The company reached the late 1980s on an artistic high note but in a precarious financial position. Funded on a project-by-project basis, maintaining its vital touring and research work was a constant struggle.

In difficulties too were the Arts and Riverside Theatres. The popular programmes at both had not resulted in financial stability and so the Arts Council, while it could not substantially increase its funding to them, designed a vehicle for 'collaborative and joint programming' to be jointly managed by both theatres. This was Theatre Ulster – not, the Council stressed, a new theatre company, but a mechanism to enable both houses to achieve maximum benefit from slender resources. A small number of productions would be staged annually at the two theatres including Irish and international classics such as Alan Ayckbourn's *How the Other Half Lives* and Sam Hanna Bell's *That Woman at Rathard*. After playing the 'home' venues, the productions would travel through the emerging network of new theatre spaces, including the new Ardhowen Theatre in Enniskillen. Opened in May 1986, its programming mixed tours from companies like Field Day and Charabanc together with visiting mid-scale companies such as Paines Plough. A small touring circuit of designated venues was finally starting to emerge.

Against this backdrop of expansion, the Lyric Theatre continued throughout the 1980s with its mixed programming of new work and popular Irish and international classics. Increasingly, under a succession of artistic directors, it became difficult to discern a perceptible, long-term vision. Instead, the Lyric appeared to be evolving into a contemporary repertory company, and its already populist direction was accentuated. There were more musicals, adaptations of classic novels and classic comedies, though there were also more examples of notable new writing. Graham Reid, Christina Reid and

Martin Lynch became writers-in-residence, while new plays were also contributed by writers such as Jennifer Johnston, Robin Glendinning and Eugene McCabe.

Yet as with the other full-time houses, the Lyric was achieving lower than anticipated box office income. Towards the end of the 1980s this resulted in a crisis. In April 1987 the theatre closed for an 'indefinite period'; by then, the Arts Theatre also looked shaky. Its five-year funding arrangement with Belfast City Council ended in 1987; an interim period of uncertainty existed before the Council entered into another agreement. Meanwhile, Charabanc too had temporarily postponed operations; short of funds, it pleaded 'creative exhaustion', and members embarked on individual work. The third phase – the emergence of the independent companies – had apparently drawn to a close. This had brought the local theatre sector through pioneering first steps, from simply surviving to presenting a broad range of works from, of and about its own society. Now it was time to move on again.

A new generation quickly grasped the torch. The late 1980s saw a flurry of activity with the formation of several new companies, the opening of dynamic venues such as Belfast's Old Museum Arts Centre and an explosion of new plays. Credit for at least some of this can be attributed to the youth drama movement. Begun in 1978, the Youth Drama Scheme had developed regional access to drama for young people and trained leaders in drama skills. The first Ulster Youth Theatre production took place in 1983 and large-scale productions took place annually thereafter under the guidance successively of Michael Poynor, Nick Philippou and David Grant. Many of the current generation of local performers are ex-UYT members; certainly, together with Queen's Dramsoc, it was part of the formative experience of many of those who were involved in the early days of the Belfast-based Tinderbox Theatre Company.

Tinderbox originated in 1988 with founding members including Tim Loane, Lalor Roddy and Stephen Wright. Since then, it has had the aim of promoting contemporary writing and in particular, new plays by Irish writers. The company has since focused on presenting such work at various stages of development, including readings, plays-in-progress and full productions. This has been greatly facilitated by its annual Festival of New Writing, inaugurated in 1989. Tinderbox has also undertaken extensive touring, bringing new and relevant plays to urban and rural audiences. Overall, it has been deemed one of the most exciting companies to emerge in the recent past, having fully staged or given reading to over thirty new pieces for the stage since 1988. Productions such as Stewart Parker's *Pentecost* (1994), Joe Crilly's *Second Hand Thunder* (1998), *Language Roulette* by Daragh Carville (1996), a co-production with Field Day of Stewart Parker's *Northern Star* (1998) and most recently *Convictions* (2000), have won a raft of local and national awards.

New work is also the focus of Replay Theatre Company. Founded in 1988 under the artistic directorship of Brenda Winter, it aims to provide both a high quality theatre experience for young people and a range of learning opportunities for schools. It has fulfilled these aims admirably, and commissioned an astonishing amount of new material in the process. Most productions have been of original work, and Replay has given platform to writers such as Gary Mitchell (*That Driving Ambition,* 1995) and Damian Gorman (*Ground Control to Davy Mental,* 1992). The range of topics dealt with in the company's work includes the history of Belfast, Irish emigration, Jewish

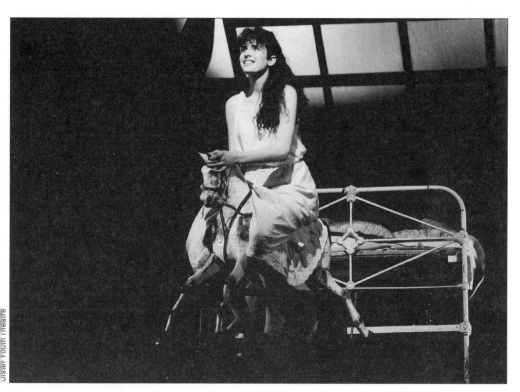

Susan Lynch as Juliet in the Ulster Youth Theatre production of *Romeo and Juliet*, 1987

Annie Farr and Conleth Hill in the Tinderbox and Field Day co-production of Stewart Parker's *Northern Star* at Rosemary Street Presbyterian Church, Belfast. The production marked the bicentenary of the 1798 rebellion.

immigration, alcohol abuse and punishment beatings. The company has also created living history projects on museum and historical sites.

Big Telly, Northern Ireland's only permanent, professional, regionally based theatre company, was created in 1987. Established by three graduates of Kent University – Kate Batts, Jill Holmes and Zoë Seaton – the company was based at Flowerfield Arts Centre in Portstewart, and has often premiered its work at the nearby Riverside Theatre in Coleraine. Temporarily relocated to the town hall in Portstewart, it has produced work by international writers such as Dario Fo and Eugene Ionesco, but has become best known for its new devised work in a distinctively multimedia style (*Metamorphosis*, 1996; *To Hell With Faust*, 1998). The company undertakes extensive tours, and has a strong commitment to arts for young people and to community involvement.

In the early 1990s, yet more enterprises emerged. The playwright Martin Lynch banded together with director Joe Devlin in 1991 to found Point Fields, a company dedicated to new writing. Productions included *Rinty* by

Stephen Rea (Lenny) and Eileen Pollock (Marian) in Stewart Parker's *Pentecost*

Martin Lynch (1990), *Winners, Losers and Non-Runners* by Owen McCafferty (1992), *Justice* by Hugh Murphy (1992) and *Lengthening Shadows* by Graham Reid (1995). In 1991 too Dubbeljoint Productions was formed by Pam Brighton, Marie Jones and Mark Lambert. It aimed to create and stage accessible plays with an appeal across the island of Ireland. Many of its productions of Jones's work particularly became hugely successful, including an adaptation of Gogol's *The Government Inspector* (1993), *A Night in November* (1994) and *Women on the Verge of* HRT (1995). More recently Dubbeljoint has worked with the community theatre company JustUs. Their devised presentations of single-identity work such as *Binlids* (1997) and *Forced Upon Us* (2000) have proved controversial. Not 'seeking a balance' in themselves, as were so many of the Troubles plays, these works have sought to portray the experiences of predominantly nationalist west Belfast.

Meanwhile Prime Cut Productions – originally known as Mad Cow – was founded in 1992 by Jackie Doyle, Aidan Lacey, Simon Magill and Stuart Marshall to produce the work of international playwrights yet to be given a local showcase. This has resulted in highly acclaimed productions of works such as Trevor Griffiths' *Who Shall Be Happy?* (1994), Ariel Dorfman's *Death and the Maiden* (1995) and Michel Marc Bouchard's *Coronation Voyage* (2000). Other companies include Aisling Ghear, the first professional Irish language theatre company, and Centre Stage, which, guided by Roma Tomelty and Colin Carnegie, regularly produces Ulster and international classics. Michael Poynor's Ulster Theatre Company has become best known for its highly successful musicals and pantomimes, while Paddy Scully's Belfast Theatre Company continues to produce new and contemporary writing. Derry-based Ridiculusmus established its initial reputation on quirky interpretations of the work of Flann O'Brien, while the now-defunct O'Casey Company devoted itself to presenting the works of Sean O'Casey. Under the artistic directorship of Karl Wallace, Kabosh, founded in 1994, has carved out a particularly exciting niche, with a daring, physical style of theatre exemplified by Owen McCafferty's celebrated *Mojo-Mickeybo* (1998) and the quirky devised work *Chair* (2000).

Not all of the bodies from earlier phases endured. One casualty in the early 1990s was Charabanc. Having re-grouped in 1988, the company principally presented extant plays on topics as diverse as the lives of lives of Ku Klux Klan

Stanley Townsend and Kulvinder Ghir in the Prime Cut production of *Who Shall Be Happy?*

wives in 1960s Alabama (*The Stick Wife* by Daragh Cloud, 1989) or women farmhands in Scotland (*Bondagers* by Sue Glover, 1991). By 1995, after twenty-two productions, the company decided it was time to 'get off the bus'. So too, did its counterpart Field Day, in practice if not formally. As the company prepared its *Anthology of Irish Writing*, there was a commensurate decline in the number of plays produced. Full productions took place up to 1991, and again in 1995, but from then nothing was heard until a co-production with Tinderbox of Stewart Parker's *Northern Star* in 1998. Unlike Charabanc, the company officially remains suspended rather than disbanded; like Charabanc, its legacy has been vital. These companies blazed a trail for theatre in its evolution from simple survival. Each brought theatre to new audiences, cleared a path for the new independent theatre sector, employed a generation of actors and, of course, generated an impressive amount of challenging new work. Between them, they proved not only that independent theatre could exist in Northern Ireland, but that it could exist with an international reputation and some style.

Building-based organisations also experienced a tumultuous time from the early 1980s into the 1990s. The Grand Opera House was bombed twice in 1991 and 1993, and sustained extensive, though reparable, damage. Despite this it has since become one of the most successful entertainment managements in Northern Ireland, attracting large audiences for opera, ballet, pantomime, musicals and popular drama. The Lyric's history has been more chequered. The only building-based theatre producing management in Northern Ireland, it suffered a severe box office decline in 1989/90, forcing significant programme changes. In the 1990s the Lyric's Board of Trustees adopted a series of measures aimed at eliminating the theatre's debts and increasing production budgets. As the venue moved towards a period of financial stability, it undertook in 1993 to promote increased accessibility. This, stated the Arts Council, was to ensure 'there is a place in the dramatic repertoire for the authentic voice of the people of the province'. Lyric programmes began to feature co-productions and guest residencies; in recent years these have dominated its stage. This may be because the Lyric's Troubles-originated repertory programming has served its purpose. Theatre has survived, and the Lyric is now fifty. The many roles it assumed of necessity have increasingly been colonised by the independents. The Lyric now has the opportunity to again find its own vision, and to explore what new roles are required of it by society and the theatre community. The end of another phase has come.

For now, at a time of 'not peace, not war', theatre faces new challenges and new opportunities. Audience figures have been increasing; new entertainment spaces such as Belfast's Waterfront Hall and Odyssey Arena, have opened. Tellingly, older venues such as the Arts Theatre, kept alive by

The Market Place Theatre and Arts Centre, Armagh, opened 2000

funders during the Troubles, have been closed. A regional network of purpose-built theatres is emerging from the Arts Council's *To The Millennium* initiatives. Fine spaces at Lisburn, Armagh and Cookstown are already open; Omagh will follow soon. Derry sees its long-awaited Millennium Forum, as well as a new arts centre, open in 2001.

New training opportunities have also evolved: as well as the drama degree at the University of Ulster, young people can also study drama at Queen's University Belfast. A Higher National Diploma in Performing Arts is available too at the Belfast Institute of Further and Higher Education. Due to a heartening increase in independent youth drama and theatre groups during the 1990s, the Arts Council of Northern Ireland has devolved youth theatre responsibility to the Ulster Association of Youth Drama, an independent membership-led umbrella organisation. Independent companies continue to be founded, albeit at a less hectic rate than in the early 1990s. There is an Arts Minister and a dedicated government department in place at Stormont. After a century in which new writing predominantly placed itself in an Irish context, voices such as Gary Mitchell's are emerging with confidence from the working-class protestant and unionist community. Building on the groundbreaking 1970s work of Fr Des Wilson and Martin Lynch, community theatre is now a vibrant force in Northern Ireland, as exemplified by the ground-breaking *Wedding Community Play* (1999). Playwrights such as Owen McCafferty, Daragh Carville and Nicola McCartney have emerged.

Arguably, theatre's greatest achievement in this period has been its regeneration after years of stagnation. Yet curiously many of the questions first posed for professional theatre in 1971 remain. The answers the Troubles provided are now increasingly irrelevant to a society moving towards a post-conflict environment. In a global village, indigenous theatre is no longer needed to fill the escapist 'and finally . . .' slot in the news agenda. The traditional social remit has increasingly been assumed by the community sector. The cross-community role is already being challenged by companies such as Dubbeljoint and Justus. And art for art's sake continues to be questioned, this time from funders demanding quantifiable links between the professional arts and community development.

The issue of theatre's role in society, then, has been sidestepped rather than resolved by the Troubles. It remains uncertain whether theatre is truly a skill by which one can acceptably live in this society, and whether it is an art form genuinely respected in all its incarnations by the community. It also remains to be seen whether companies and practitioners can find for themselves a relevant and distinctive voice in the post-Troubles era, and can find resources within themselves as a community to fight for their recognition. Otherwise, capital developments notwithstanding, theatre may drift off course once again. Belfast is bidding to become European Capital of Culture in 2008. Will the option for theatre this time around be the 'wilderness', the short season of stalwarts? Or will theatre want, and be allowed, to symbolise the Ulster of the future? There are uncomfortable echoes of the 'year of the Dome' about at present. Theatre and society need to make some choices – and fast.

Theatre – the playwrights and their plays

DAVID GRANT

S peaking in September 2000 at the official opening of the fine new extension to the Linen Hall Library, Seamus Heaney referred to the era of the
library's foundation in the 1790s as a 'moment of possibility' for Belfast. He
went on to recall how, after the promise of the 1960s, the 1970s brought on a
time of darkening. The curtain had risen, a few actors had stepped forth, and
then the lights went out. His chosen imagery was all too relevant to our
present purpose. Re-reading Sam Hanna Bell's account of theatre in
Northern Ireland in the 1971 edition of *Causeway*, it is hard not to be struck,
for all its efforts at an upbeat tone, by an underlying eddy of pessimism.

There seems an obvious equation between the eruption of violence and the
decline of theatre in Northern Ireland in the early 1970s, but in fact, the
Troubles simply accelerated an already inexorable trend. Hanna Bell

Brian Friel

acknowledges the difficulties of sustaining a programme of serious drama in a city of Belfast's size and cultural disposition. But he begins and ends his survey of theatre in Northern Ireland in the 1950s and 1960s by repeating the plea of David Kennedy in *The Arts in Ulster* (1951), for a 'true development' in which the region's young writers would return to the theatre and provide new plays for Belfast's two new playhouses.

Of these two playhouses the Arts Theatre has now closed and the Lyric Theatre has enjoyed an uneven history. Nevertheless, it has been responsible for the premieres of a high proportion of the plays referred to in these pages and the dearth of playwrights so evident in 1970 has given way to a fertile environment for new writing for the stage. Indeed, the millennium year's dramatic highlight, Tinderbox Theatre Company's *Convictions*, a site-specific production set in the disused Crumlin Road Courthouse, was able to call on a by no means exhaustive list of seven regularly produced local dramatists. Marie Jones, Owen McCafferty, Gary Mitchell, Daragh Carville, Nicola McCartney, Damian Gorman and Martin Lynch all contributed short plays to the production. Each has steered a different course into the limelight, but together they illustrate a resurgence in the theatre life of Northern Ireland that would have been impossible to predict in the early 1970s. And significantly their work was not in this instance presented in one of the 'new playhouses', but in a derelict shell of a building, resonant with recent history.

In at least one detail, however, Sam Hanna Bell's 1971 account did prove prophetic. Amid accounts of fading theatre companies he mentions a reading at the Lyric Theatre of John Boyd's play *The Flats* having been so well received that it was scheduled for full production later that year. And in doing so Hanna Bell heralds the harbinger of what a decade later would come to be known as 'Troubles drama'. One of the great ironies of the last thirty years is that the political turmoil which is usually seen as having rung the death knell of local theatre may, in fact, have been its salvation.

Viewed with hindsight, *The Flats* seems quite naive. But it was the first play to explore the essentially working-class roots of the recent Troubles, and as such it blazed a trail for the generation of playwrights including Martin Lynch, Graham Reid and Christina Reid, which was to dominate Belfast theatre at the turn of the next decade. The play shows one day in the life of a catholic family at risk from protestant intimidation, under the watchful eye of a British soldier. It ends, in an echo of O'Casey's *The Shadow of a Gunman*, with the death of the young female lead. Contemporary reviews acknowledge its schematic form and the difficulty of rendering such immediate events as effective drama, but the play found a ready audience and, after a successful first run, an extension was quickly scheduled later in the same season.

Despite its success, *The Flats* was to prove a rarity in its attempt through drama to cast light on the pervasive madness that surrounded Belfast in the early 1970s. Perhaps there was enough drama on the streets. Whatever the reason, such new plays as the Lyric selected for its programme in this period tended to avoid direct local relevance. While the programme in the early 1970s certainly reflected its founder Mary O'Malley's concern that it be first and foremost a writers' theatre, the range of playwrights also indicated her interest in it being an Irish rather than simply a Belfast theatre.

Joe O'Donnell, whose play *The Lads* was produced in 1972, was from Limerick and had worked as an actor with the celebrated actor-manager who gave Pinter his first break, Anew McMaster, before moving into television as a cameraman and then a director. The play is set in Dublin and its politics are entirely sexual. In 1977 the novelist Edna O'Brien's play *The Gathering,* about a stormy family reunion, reflected her own upbringing in county Clare, while Dubliner Frank Dunne's *The Rise and Fall of Barney Kerrigan,* a trivial comedy about an Irish actor's fleeting flirtation with fame produced in the same year, was set in the writer's native city. Ennis-born Tom Coffey's *It Would Be Funny If It Weren't So Bloody Ridiculous* (1975) was even further removed from a Belfast audience's general preoccupation with escalating violence. Set on a raft in some post-apocalyptical world, it struck an uneasy balance between naturalism and the theatre of the absurd. Its most memorable character was the Chronicler – played by the ubiquitous Louis Roulston – who struggled to maintain some semblance of order amid the chaos. Perhaps it spoke to a largely university-based audience of their own predicament.

Little by little, though, Belfast themes and a Belfast voice did gain more of a foothold. Wilson John Haire's *Within Two Shadows* about the children of a marriage divided by religion and class – a perennial theme in Ulster drama going back at least as far as St John Ervine's *Mixed Marriage* in 1911 – opened the Lyric's 1972-3 season. The play had already enjoyed a successful production at London's Royal Court, and Belfast-born Haire, who was himself the child of a mixed marriage, promised to become an important contributor to the Lyric stage – though in the end two plays he wrote for the Lyric under a Leverhulme Fellowship were never produced. *Nightfall to Belfast* by Patrick Galvin, a Cork man, produced in 1973, also had an overt Troubles context. Neither play seems to have been able to match the raw impact of *The Flats* and both drew lukewarm reviews.

These tentative skirmishes with pressing local issues were far outnumbered by plays on other themes. John Boyd's *The Farm* (1972) in its obsession with the ownership of land provided a northern version of John B. Keane's *The Field*, but it was never intended to be a rural counterpart to *The Flats* and had no direct bearing on the continuing political unrest. Nineteen seventy-

Alwyn James, Lyric Players Theatre

Stella McCusker (left) as Mrs Castle, Leila Webster (centre) as Mrs Ellis and Fionnuala O'Shannon as Mrs Ryan in *We Do It For Love* by Patrick Galvin at the Lyric Theatre, Belfast, 1975

four saw a clear move away from any attempt directly to address the roots of the political crisis, with John Boyd adopting a deliberately middle-class context for his play *Guests*, and Patrick Galvin – now writer-in-residence at the Lyric – contributing what was described at the time as an Irish *Exorcist* in the form of *The Last Burning*, based on the notorious witch-burning in Clonmel in 1895.

Then in 1975, almost out of the blue, the Lyric enjoyed what remains its greatest ever box office success (100.77 per cent of capacity!) with Patrick Galvin's *We Do It for Love*. Belfast audiences suddenly showed themselves ready to begin to address their common predicament through the medium of drama and, significantly, the play was a comedy – though not in the eyes of all its beholders. Outsiders were aghast at the uproarious response to jokes aimed directly at the violence. But in 1975, while suspect devices throughout the city were doing so literally, in a packed Lyric Theatre the laughter – figuratively – lifted the roof. The playing style was robust. Boldly drawn characters were unashamedly stereotypical. There was a lively use of music, and the linking character of Micky Marley was a familiar sight around Belfast with his home-made roundabout. The real and surreal became blurred, much as seemed to be happening in everyday life.

We Do It for Love proved a hard act to follow. John Boyd's *The Street* (1977), a piece of 1930s nostalgia, was well received by the Belfast critics, but the *Irish Times* regretted the absence of the incisive social comment that had characterised *The Flats*. The next year the black comedy *Europe* by Brendan Behan's brother Dominic, although set in Belfast, failed to strike the same chords as Galvin's great hit which was successfully revived in the same year.

Among the many writers produced at the Lyric in this period, two names predominate – Patrick Galvin and John Boyd, the theatre's Literary Adviser. They were to continue to be presented regularly on Ridgeway Street, with the frequency of productions of Boyd's work – *Facing North* in 1979, *Speranza's Boy* in 1981 in the same season as Galvin's *My Silver Bird*, *Summer Class* in 1986 and the whimsical *Round the Big Clock* in 1992 – giving rise to a widespread feeling that the literary management of the theatre was in a stranglehold. But though the Lyric's board seemed sometimes to adopt an ostrich attitude to the steady change in Belfast's cultural climate, the next decade

Martin Lynch, playwright and community arts advocate

was to present the theatre with profound challenges.

Nineteen eighty is an important date in this short history. It saw the re-opening of Belfast's Grand Opera House, an event which triggered the revitalisation of the city centre, and prompted the first visit of the Royal Shakespeare Company to the Belfast Festival. The green shoots that signalled a revitalised cultural life were beginning to emerge, most potently in Derry, with the foundation by Brian Friel and Stephen Rea of Field Day Theatre Company, and in Belfast through the programming at the Lyric of Martin Lynch's *Dockers*. While the international impact of Field Day has been immense, the emergence of Martin Lynch as an established playwright was no less significant for the future development of drama in Northern Ireland.

It was not long after the publication of *Causeway* in 1971 that Lynch started to write plays for his local theatre group. We have become familiar now with the idea of community drama, but at that time Lynch's work with the Turf Lodge Theatre Fellowship, creating plays that spoke of local experiences, was truly ground-breaking. Eventually his work began to reach a wider audience at the Group Theatre where it came to the attention of Sam McCready, an early member of the Lyric Theatre, and soon all too briefly to be responsible for its artistic programme. Lynch is quick to acknowledge his debt to

McCready's dramaturgical skills, and the growth in his own sense of self-worth when he was appointed writer-in-residence at the Lyric. He was also greatly influenced by the success of *We Do It For Love*.

Although bracketed with the 'Troubles plays'which followed it onto the Lyric stage, *Dockers* is set in 1962, well before the onset of the recent Troubles – but it explores the sectarianism that gave rise to them. The first production of *Dockers* struck a chord with both the Lyric's traditional middle-class audience and the substantial new working-class audience which it attracted to Ridgeway Street in significant numbers for the first time, and it played to ninety-four per cent of capacity over its four week run. This record was matched by Lynch's next three plays, *The Interrogation of Ambrose Fogarty* (1982), *Castles in the Air* (1983) – originally staged by the Turf Lodge Theatre Fellowship under the more memorable title, *A Roof Under Our Heads* – and *Minstrel Boys* (1985). Christina Reid's *Tea in a China Cup* (1983) enjoyed simi-

Chris Hill, Lyric Players Theatre

Joe McPartland as Razor and Adrian Dunbar as Bap in *Castles in the Air* by Martin Lynch, Lyric Theatre, Belfast, 1983

lar success. Meanwhile Graham Reid, fresh from his success in Dublin with *The Death of Humpty Dumpty*, had also joined the Lyric fold with eighty-five per cent business for the school-based drama *The Hidden Curriculum* (1982).

The audience figures are significant. They are the clearest evidence of the extent to which these fresh new plays overturned the received wisdom that new drama did not sell. The Northern Ireland public clearly had an appetite for plays that could speak to them of their own lives and they were prepared to turn out in large numbers to prove the point. Sam Hanna Bell quotes an audience survey from the late 1960s indicating that only ten per cent of Northern Ireland's theatre audience was interested in serious drama, the rest preferring musicals and thrillers. His tone was despairing. Yet here, after a decade of terrorist attrition, members of the public were rediscovering how live drama could be a unique forum for finding out about themselves.

This was unquestionably the Lyric's golden age. In the 1982-3 season there were no fewer than four full productions of new plays, with *The Hidden Curriculum* receiving a second run. The following season was equally dominated by new work with Graham Reid's *Remembrance* and Stewart Parker's *Northern Star* in the autumn of 1984 followed by Daniel Magee's *Horseman Pass By* early in the following year. *Northern Star*, which would be memorably revived in 1998 by Field Day and Tinderbox theatre companies in the atmospheric setting of Rosemary Street Presbyterian Church, merits special mention for its stylistic daring. The play chronicles the final hours of Henry Joy McCracken as he awaits arrest and execution, each scene being played in the style of a different Anglo-Irish dramatist. Credit for much of this achievement must be given to Leon Rubin who came from the RSC to become Artistic Director at the Lyric in 1982. His successor, Patrick Sandford, took over in 1984 and although equally committed to new writing, he came up against increasing resistance from a theatre board whose members were rumoured to be uneasy at the 'unliterary' nature of so much of the new work in what was, after all, a 'Poet's Theatre'.

Although in 1985-6 there were three new plays, two were by visiting companies – Field Day with Thomas Kilroy's *Double Cross* and Paines Plough which had drawn away the talents of Christina Reid for the premiere production of *Joyriders*. Sandford left at the end of the season, no doubt exhausted by the struggle, and the theatre went into decline. In the next eight years the theatre was to have no fewer than four Artistic Directors and produce only nine new plays. Despite a belated gesture in the form of Theresa Donnelly's wartime romp *Put Out That Light* in 1993, the Lyric lost its claim to be the natural home of the local voice.

Of the new plays staged at the Lyric in this period, *Pygmies in the Ruins* (1991) by Ron Hutchinson, deserves special acknowledgement. The split time frame set 1991 Belfast alongside its late Victorian past and asked the question – 'how could all this mercantile promise have gone so wrong?' Originally from Lisburn, Hutchinson is a prolific screenwriter and was for a time writer-in-residence with the Royal Shakespeare Company. His best-known stage play is the interrogation drama *Rat in the Skull* which received a first class independent production in Belfast in 1987 following its Royal Court premiere in 1984.

The likelihood of playwrights from Northern Ireland receiving their first production elsewhere is often held up as an implicit criticism of local theatre. While the support for new writing here has certainly been uneven, it is surely fairer to see this as evidence of the extraordinary quality of local dramatists. Why would Belfast-born Anne Devlin, for instance, prefer the much less visible platform of a Belfast premiere to first productions at the Liverpool Playhouse and the Royal Shakespeare Company respectively for her plays *Ourselves Alone* (1985) and *After Easter* (1994)? Gary Mitchell's more recent meteoric rise flowed from high profile productions at the Abbey and Royal Court, whereas his first stage production, *Independent Voice* (1993), by Tinder-box Theatre Company in Belfast's Old Museum Arts Centre, went largely unnoticed further afield.

Robin Glendinning, whose play *Mumbo Jumbo* won the Mobil Playwriting Competition and was premiered at Manchester's Royal Exchange in 1986, is another local writer first recognised away from home. A subsequent production of *Mumbo Jumbo* at the Lyric in 1987 was followed by *Culture Vultures* in the following year. But his work seemed to connect more readily with an English audience, and his next play *Donnyboy* was again premiered at the Royal Exchange in 1990, only to be given an Irish production by Tinder-box the following year.

Perhaps the audience's appetite for self-examination had been sated. Perhaps the bewitching normalisation of an 'acceptable level of violence' had numbed our capacity to question. Or perhaps it was the challenge from a growing independent theatre sector, which had emerged with the foundation of Charabanc in 1983, that was causing the Lyric to lose confidence in its commitment to new work. *Charlie Gorilla* (1989) by John McClelland, a zoological fantasy, was a bold piece of programming, but it seemed to sit uncomfortably on the Lyric stage. Robert Ellison's ill-fated *Rough Beginnings* (1991), despite the youthful energy on stage, was critically panned.

Both productions seem with hindsight to have represented an attempt to respond to the threat from the new independent theatre companies by playing them at their own game. Perhaps it was too soon to contemplate partnerships with these companies, as Robin Midgley was to do as the Lyric's new Artistic Director a few years later. But the writers who had been the engine of the Lyric in the early 1980s had now dispersed. Martin Lynch was firmly in the independent camp. Graham Reid had long been lured away by television, and the Lyric's production of *The Belle of Belfast City* (1989) by Christina Reid – by now resident in England – which sought to reflect on an outside perspective of Northern Ireland, failed to communicate to local audiences.

In the early 1980s Graham Reid and Christina Reid had provided a working-class protestant counterpart to Martin Lynch's catholic perspective. As Christina's *Tea in a China Cup* made clear, working-class people on both sides of the divide had more in common than divided them. This largely biographical play movingly and amusingly recalled how a protestant mother – a role brought powerfully to life by Stella McCusker – failed to come to terms with her catholic neighbours becoming better off and clung to the fragile gentility of her remaining fine china – a kind of east Belfast equivalent of Tennessee Williams' Amanda Wingfield.

The sense of betrayal felt by working-class protestants was also at the heart of Graham Reid's *The Hidden Curriculum*. Two recent school leavers return to visit their former teacher and one of them proceeds to educate him about how little he really knows about the lives of his pupils, dominated as they are by paramilitary repression. When the play was revived at the Lyric Theatre in 1994, although the educational context had changed considerably, the play's treatment of paramilitarism seemed all too topical at a time when the number of murders by loyalists was for the first time exceeding those committed by republicans.

The changing sense of protestant identity in Northern Ireland in the face of increasingly rapid political change has been one of the strongest themes in recent local writing for the theatre. And what emerges is a far from monolithic image. Instead, different dramatists have contributed to a much more pluralist understanding of protestantism. The world portrayed by Christina Reid, though poignant, seems much less harsh than Graham Reid's, or that of his more recent counterpart, Gary Mitchell. And Mitchell's portrayal of 1990s Rathcoole seems both more isolated and politically sophisticated than Graham Reid's Shankill Road in the early 1980s. At a recent seminar, Susan McKay, author of *Northern Protestants: An Unsettled People,* presented a bleak picture of a cultureless protestantism, and was challenged by Christina Reid, who felt this did not fairly represent her own experience. But as Reid pointed out, a defining aspect of her own experience was that she grew up in a largely female environment. It seems to be the combination of protestantism and maleness that proves so inimical to art.

A complementary standpoint is to be found in the work of Robin Glendinning, who is unusual among these writers in reflecting on a mainly middle-class experience. The setting for his play, *Mumbo Jumbo* was a school not entirely unlike Campbell College, which prepared the sons of gentlemen to take their places in society. The central character is the son of a judge. But even here there is dissent. His friend is well-to-do enough for a public school education, but rebels against the overt colonialism of his education. In a powerful speech to his temporarily incapacitated teacher, he articulates this frustration in a way that would surely have been familiar to the working-class boys in Graham Reid's *The Hidden Curriculum.* Glendinning's masterpiece, *The Summer House,* which was premiered by the Druid Theatre Company in Galway in 1994, and given its first Belfast production by Michael Poynor's Ulster Theatre Company as part of the 1995 Belfast Festival, broadens this theme to include the increasing bewilderment of the inheritors of the Ascendancy. Eva Ross is the last survivor in the Big House. By her own account, her family has done much for the small village community they have lived to serve. She cannot understand the disintegration of the old order. Glendinning often uses illness as a metaphor within his work, and here the progress of the old lady's cancer parallels the collapse of traditional landed unionism, as anger slowly gives way to acceptance.

An alternative view of the 'big house' is provided by Jennifer's Johnston's three plays, *Indian Summer* (1983), *How Many Miles to Babylon* (1993) and *Desert Lullaby* (1996). Despite their dark themes these plays inhabit a detached and lyrical world, far removed from the earthy preoccupations of the other Lyric playwrights. *How Many Miles to Babylon*, with its Great War setting and powerful climax, where a young upper-class officer feels compelled to kill his batman to save him from a firing squad, counterpoints another play set in the same period, which has succeeded in placing on the stage the complex conundrum of the Ulster protestant identity. That play is, of course, Frank McGuinness' *Observe the Sons of Ulster Marching Towards the Somme.*

By common consent this play, though written from the external perspective of a Donegal catholic and set at a defining moment in the modern Ulster protestant experience, came closest to unravelling its mysteries. Again, it is its pluralism in terms of locality and class that proves the key to understanding its success. Its eight diverse characters from Belfast, Derry, Coleraine and Enniskillen encompass many of the different facets of their kind.

Observe the Sons of Ulster Marching Towards the Somme by Frank McGuinness, Lyric Theatre production, 1990

Jill Jennings, Lyric Players Theatre

McGuinness' secret is to concentrate on the humanity of the characters rather than on their allegiances. He succeeds in the same way with *Carthaginians* (1988), where an equally diverse group of individuals – catholics, this time – gather in a Derry graveyard to exorcise their painful memories of Bloody Sunday, and again in *Someone To Watch Over Me* (1992) about an American, an Englishman and an Irishman held hostage in the Middle East. Since the Abbey Theatre produced his first play, *Factory Girls*, in 1982, McGuinness's output has been prolific, encompassing the intellectual complexity of *Innocence* (Gate Theatre, 1986), *Mary and Lizzie* (RSC, 1989), and *Mutabilitie* (Royal National Theatre, 1997), and the more domestic themes underlying *The Breadman* (Gate Theatre, 1990), *The Bird Sanctuary* (Abbey Theatre, 1994) and *Dolly West's Kitchen* (Abbey Theatre, 1999). McGuinness continues to be the most versatile and challenging of modern Irish dramatists.

Even McGuinness's colossal achievement, however, is overshadowed by the range and depth of the work of Brian Friel. Sam Hanna Bell acknowledged Friel in 1971 as an important voice in Northern Ireland theatre, but after his first radio plays were produced by the BBC in Belfast, Friel invariably chose to premiere his work in Dublin, or in the case of *Faith Healer* (1979), in New York. The Lyric produced a revival of *Gentle Island* in 1972, Liam Neeson appeared memorably as Private Gar to John Hewitt's Public in the theatre's production of *Philadelphia, Here I Come!* in 1976 and *Crystal and Fox* was staged in 1980. Meanwhile, Dublin enjoyed a steady stream of new plays – *Volunteers* in 1975, *Living Quarters* in 1977 and the Chekhovian *Aristocrats* in 1979 – all adding to the world's understanding of Ballybeg – their common setting in County Donegal – and of itself. Only *Freedom of the City* (1973), a lightly veiled response to Bloody Sunday, could be described as overtly political – an exceptional response to extraordinary events. But when it was announced that Friel had teamed up with the actor Stephen Rea to form Field Day Theatre Company and that the company's base was to be in Derry, the political subtext was already evident.

When the company produced *Translations* in 1980, it was a landmark event, not just because it introduced an important new production base into theatre in Northern Ireland, but also because the play itself had all the hallmarks of a future classic. The play was written from a nationalist standpoint, but its subtle blend of historical drama and love story intricately balanced issues of identity with broader reflections on humanity. Two scenes stand strongest in the memory – the bilingual love scene where the young English soldier, Yolland, and an Irish girl, Maire, struggle to understand each other in the absence of a common language, and second, Yolland's Irish friend Owen's ironic attempts to justify the renaming of Irish place names in English, during which the absurdity of the process is audible in the clash of name on name. Stephen Rea brilliantly captured Owen's internal struggle between his appetite for progress and his residual loyalty to his cultural heritage.

Translations was followed, appropriately enough given Friel's affinities with Chekhov, by the playwright's own version of *Three Sisters* (1981). *The Communication Cord*, a farcical subversion of *Translations* followed in 1982. But plans in 1983 to stage David Rudkin's intricate verse play *The Saxon Shore* in which the collapse of the Roman Empire serves as a parallel for modern Ulster did not come to fruition. Although not resident in Northern Ireland, Rudkin grew up here, and his best-known play *Ashes*, which received a Belfast production by Michael Poynor's Stage 80 in 1980, is concerned with the impact on a married couple of their differing Northern Irish roots. The same company produced Martin Lynch's *Crack Up* in 1993.

In 1984 Field Day again produced new work in an imaginative double bill of Tom Paulin's *The Riot Act - Antigone* transposed to modern Ireland – and *High Time*, Derek Mahon's jaunty version of Molière's *School for Husbands*. The powerful starkness of the former provided an effective complement to the madcap energy of the latter. Thomas Kilroy's *Double Cross* followed in 1986, offering Stephen Rea the glorious double role of Brendan Bracken (Churchill's propaganda chief) and William Joyce (Lord Haw-Haw). Then in 1986, Field Day enjoyed its greatest success since *Translations* with Stewart Parker's *Pentecost*.

Parker had come to prominence in 1975 with *Spokesong*, a musical play about John Boyd Dunlop, the inventor of the pneumatic tyre, with incidental references to the crucial political events in the Ireland of the late nineteenth century. Despite its quintessentially Belfast theme, and concerted attempts to produce it in his native city, it eventually received its premiere as part of the Dublin Theatre Festival, transferring to London the following year, where it won Parker the *Evening Standard* Drama Award for Most Promising Playwright.

Playwright Stewart Parker (left) with actor Joe McPartland
during a break in rehearsals, 1975

There had been interest in Stewart Parker's work from the Lyric in the late 1960s but this had come to nothing. In common with another Belfast writer, Stewart Love – author of *The Titanic* and *The Potata Blight* – he contributed a number of short new plays to the work of the theatre-in-education company Interplay, then under the direction of Denis Smyth, including *The Blue and the Gray* about the American Civil War. But it was to be 1982 before *Kingdom Come*, a Caribbean musical, would receive a mainstream production in his home city when it became the Lyric's contribution to that year's Belfast Festival.

Widely regarded as his best play, *Pentecost* is set during the Ulster Workers' Council Strike in 1974. Four friends in their late twenties and early thirties find themselves trapped in a terrace house by the collapse of law and order around them. Above all else, *Pentecost* is about a yearning for redemption. Perhaps for this reason it enjoyed two important revivals in the early 1990s; one by Belfast's Tinderbox Theatre Company just after the loyalist ceasefire that followed the first IRA ceasefire in 1994; the other, eighteen months later by the Dublin-based Rough Magic and directed by Parker's niece Lynne, shortly after the IRA ceasefire had collapsed. If it is the hallmark of great drama to be able to connect with the moment, regardless of when or where it is produced, *Pentecost* passed this test. I can clearly recall the overwhelming sense of optimism engendered by the play's moving last scene when I saw the Tinderbox production, and the corresponding sense of apprehension that accompanied a visit to Rough Magic's. The central character, Marian, ends the play with a moving plea for reconciliation, which rings in the ears long after the audience has left the theatre. Perhaps this is why the production has always made such an impact. A recurring criticism of the early 'Troubles plays' was that they pathologised the situation – though they asked the right questions, they failed to offer any answers. *Pentecost*, almost uniquely, seemed to point a way forward.

Sadly, Stewart Parker's premature death in 1988 meant that he did not live to see the recent marked improvement in the political situation. But he has continued to be remembered through the annual awards to playwrights that bear his name. Many of the recipients have been northern writers, most of whom have benefited from the remarkable development of a lively independent theatre sector in Northern Ireland, the lack of which Parker so regretted when he himself was starting to write.

The pioneers of independent theatre in Northern Ireland were those who founded Charabanc Theatre Company, but the collaborative nature of their work makes it problematic how best to place them into an article about 'playwrights'. Set in the 1930s and based on interviews with women who had worked in Belfast's linen mills, their first play, *Lay Up Your Ends,* evoked a world of inequality, where the bosses ruled and where women came out bottom of the heap. The company developed an ensemble playing style, with each actor playing a multitude of characters, and as had happened with Martin Lynch's work at the Lyric, the local audiences flocked in. Subsequent attempts to repeat the format with *Oul Delf and False Teeth* (1984), about the war years, and *Now Yer Talking* (1985), about the cynicism of the reconciliation industry, were less successful, but with *Gold in the Streets*, a piece about emigration, *The Girls in the Big Picture*, about the claustrophobia of rural life – both produced in 1986 – and *Somewhere Over the Balcony* (1987) set in the notorious Divis Flats, Charabanc really returned to form. By now though, while the plays were still written collaboratively, Marie Jones had emerged as the key author. As she herself has disarmingly put it: 'When we started

Playwright Marie Jones photographed in her native east Belfast

off we were all in this bus and we needed a driver. So I had a go at driving the bus. After the first few trips, suddenly I was a bus driver!'

In 1990 the company returned to an interview-based approach with *The Hamster Wheel*, a play about the inadequacies of the health service, and the problems inherent in a collaborative process of defining authorship resurfaced. Although Marie Jones wrote two further short plays, *The Blind Fiddler of Glenadauch* and *Weddins, Wee'ins and Wakes* for the company, her career was starting to move in other directions, and Charabanc began to work with a wider range of writers. These included Andrew Hinds – until then best known as a director – who wrote and directed the family drama *October Song* in 1992 and Sue Ashby, whose play about domestic violence, *A Wife, a Dog and a Maple Tree*, was produced in 1993.

By the time Charabanc was wound up in 1995, Marie Jones had left the company to pursue a freelance writing career, renewing her association with Pam Brighton – the director of *Lay Up Your Ends* – in the new Dubbeljoint Theatre Company. For Dubbeljoint she wrote *Hang All the Harpers* with Shane Connaughton (1991), *Eddie Bottom's Dream* (1996), *Christmas Eve Can Kill You* (1991), *A Night in November* (1994) and *Women on the Verge of* HRT

(1995) and also contributed a host of new plays to Replay, the theatre-in-education company set up in 1988 by another Charabanc founding-member, Brenda Winter. These included the company's first production, *Under Napoleon's Nose*, *It's a Waste of Time Tracy* (1989), *The Cow, the Ship and the Indian* and *Don't Look Down* (1991), *Hiring Days* (1992) and *Yours Truly* (1993). In recent years, Jones has widened the number of companies she has worked with to include the Tinderbox Theatre Company – *Ruby* (2000), the story of the Belfast singer, Ruby Murray – and the Lyric, which produced the outstandingly successful revival of *Stones in His Pockets* (1999) which transferred to London and Broadway, and won Marie Jones the 2001 Olivier Award for Best New Comedy in the West End.

The emergence of all these new independent theatre companies such as Dubbeljoint, Tinderbox and Replay, has been one of Charabanc's most important legacies. The belief that actors could indeed take charge of their own destinies led in the late 1980s and early 1990s to the establishment of a

Jill Jennings, Lyric Players Theatre

Conleth Hill (left) and Sean Campion in *Stones in His Pockets* by Marie Jones at the Lyric Theatre, Belfast, 1999

plethora of initiatives. Not all were committed predominantly to new writing, but the Portstewart-based Big Telly Theatre Company devised *Onions Make You Cry* in 1988 and *Fish* in 2000, and Prime Cut – formerly Mad Cow – premiered Trevor Griffiths' play about Danton, *Who Should be Happy?* in 1995. Two companies made new writing a speciality, however – Tinderbox and the now defunct Point Fields. The latter was set up by Martin Lynch and Joe Devlin in the early 1990s expressly to encourage the emergence of new playwrights. Besides producing full productions of Lynch's *Rinty* (1990) and *Justice* (1992) by Hugh Murphy, it also promoted two developmental programmes under the banner *Angels with Split Voices* which gave timely encouragement to Owen McCafferty and Gary Mitchell, two writers currently attracting great attention both at home and abroad.

Owen McCafferty's monologue, *The Waiting List*, performed by Lalor Roddy for Point Fields in 1994, encompasses two otherwise distinct strands within his work. Plays like *I Won't Dance, Don't Ask Me* – premiered by Sean Caffrey's Who the Hell Theatre Company in 1993 – and the as yet unproduced *Tonto's Way* are written as intricate monologues. But *The Waiting List* also contained the seeds of a more dynamic style, which was to give rise to plays like *Freefalling*, a road-movie for the stage (1996), and the award-winning *Mojo-Mickeybo* (1998) which vividly portrayed the friendship of two children in the 1960s whose innocence is destroyed by the changing times. These two plays, which were produced by Kabosh Productions, and *Shoot the Crow* premiered by Druid Theatre Company in 1997, have established McCafferty as one of the names to watch for in the next decade. This fact has not been lost on the Royal National Theatre which has recently offered McCafferty a major commission. With a background in philosophy, he is one of a new post 'Troubles drama' generation of local writers – Damian Gorman, Nicola McCartney, John McClelland and Daragh Carville would be others – who are growing increasingly impatient with the narrow remit often allowed to Irish writers by commissioning managements outside Ireland.

Gary Mitchell's star is also in the ascendant. He sits much more comfortably within traditional definitions of the Ulster playwright. A skilled story-teller, he has become fêted as the voice of the beleaguered working-class protestant, but what sets his work apart from, say, Graham Reid's, is his focus on unhealed wounds left behind by the decades of violence and the ongoing peace process. At the height of the Troubles there was an immediacy to the violence, but now it is furtive and festering. The claustrophobia and intensity implicit in the title of *In a Little World of Our Own* – premiered on the Abbey's Peacock stage under the inspired direction of Conall Morrison in 1997 – characterises all Mitchell's work. This play shows us the destructive power of lingering hatreds in a domestic setting, a theme developed in *Trust* (1999). *As The Beast Sleeps* extends that to the world of fringe loyalist politics, while *The Force of Change* (2000) explores the effect of recent changes on the RUC. Most of Mitchell's mainstream theatre work has been premiered at the Abbey or the Royal Court. Interestingly, the two exceptions have been uncharacteristic plays – the punk musical *Energy* produced by the Playhouse in Derry in 1999 and the historical drama *Tearing the Loom*, commissioned by the Lyric to mark the bicentenary of the United Irishmen's ill-fated uprising in 1798.

Tinderbox's contribution to the development of new work has also been considerable. Apart from first Northern Ireland productions of important plays by local writers – Stewart Parker's *Catchpenny Twist* (1990), Robin Glendinning's *Donnyboy* (1991), Frank McGuinness's *Someone to Watch Over Me* (1995) and Brian Friel's *Faith Healer* (1996) – the company has also premiered many new plays including *Into the Heartland* (1998) by John McClelland, *Second Hand Thunder* (1998) and *On McQuillan's Hill* (1999) by Joe Crilly, and *Language Roulette* (1996) and *Dumped* (1997) by Daragh Carville.

Language Roulette has special significance in that it toured widely, including visits to the Traverse Theatre in Edinburgh and the Bush Theatre in London. Set around a return visit to his home town by a young man clearly distanced from his peers by the experience of having lived abroad, the play has a youth-fulness which sets it apart from much of the other writing considered on these pages. Its outward-looking approach gives hope that Northern Ireland theatre is ready to move on to address new themes and a wider audience. Carville's most recent play, *Observatory*, which was produced at the Peacock Theatre in 1998, extends this notion by combining his home town of Armagh with a science fiction storyline. By contrast, Lurgan-born Joe Crilly's plays are rooted in the soil, exploring the murky depths of small-town intrigue.

One of Tinderbox's more unusual productions was Ken Bourke's *Galloping Buck Jones*, an intricately plotted historical farce in which the same actor – Tim Loane – played both the hero and the villain and had to avoid meeting himself in the final act. The production was also unusual in being presented as a co-production with the Lyric Theatre. This joint venture – together with a co-production with Point Fields of *Pictures of Tomorrow*, Martin Lynch's fine play about veterans of the Spanish Civil War facing up to the collapse of socialism – was one of the first initiatives of Robin Midgley on his appointment as Artistic Director of the Lyric in 1994. He inherited a theatre suffering the consequences of constantly changing leadership which had resulted in it becoming cut off from the rapidly developing cultural renaissance around it, and his first step was to try to open the theatre up again to creative partnerships. Exceptionally, he managed to secure the rights from the Royal Shakespeare Company to *After Easter*, a new play by Anne Devlin, while it was still in the RSC's repertoire, and presented it along with Owen McCafferty's short play *The Private Picture Show*, as the Lyric's contribution to the 1994 Belfast Festival.

Midgley also attracted Graham Reid back to the theatre with a new play, *Lengthening Shadows* (commissioned by Point Fields) in 1995, about the legacy of terrorism beneath the respectability of a well-to-do protestant family. The late Birdy Sweeney gave a memorable performance in Michael Harding's *Where the Heart Is* in the same year. Midgley then commissioned a piece from Bill Morrison, who, despite his Northern Ireland origins and a prolific record as a dramatist in England, had never been produced in Belfast. He responded with a biographical play, *Drive On* (1996). But the old problem of sustaining an audience for new plays amid mounting competition from other companies and other media undermined the theatre's commitment to new writing.

Robin Midgley succeeded in breathing renewed life into the theatre, but at the end of his five year directorship a painful process of re-evaluation took place under the auspices of the National Lottery's Advancement Programme. The advent of the National Lottery has had a huge impact on the development of new work by providing for it significant financial resources. But this has created a real danger of the supply of new plays outstripping audience demand. Yet despite this bleak reality, the Advancement review concluded that the only way forward was to continue to prioritise the development of new writing. To begin with this policy worked well, with five new plays being presented from 1998–2000. These included *Iph . . .* (1999) by Colin Teevan, *Marching On* by Gary Mitchell (2000) and *The Butterfly of Killybegs* (2000) by Brian Foster. At a preliminary reading of Foster's play no less than five local playwrights were present. There was a tremendous sense of renewed energy. But the drain on the theatre's resources, even with additional financial support from the National Lottery, proved too much to sustain.

It may well be that the days of building-based production in Belfast are numbered. There is no lack of artistic initiative as evidenced by the energetic work of the smaller independent companies, but as Tinderbox's award-winning courthouse project, *Convictions* (2000), made clear, there is a demand for theatre constantly to reinvent itself. One such example of reinvention is evident in the latest plays of Brian Friel. Since *Making History* in 1988 – his last play for Field Day – he has moved away from historical themes towards a renewed preoccupation with close personal relationships. While Field Day went on to premiere *Saint Oscar* by Terry Eagleton in 1989 and Seamus Heaney's first play, *The Cure at Troy*, in 1990, Friel has written what amounts to a whole new cycle of plays including the phenomenally successful *Dancing at Lughnasa* at the Abbey (1990), *Wonderful Tennessee* (Abbey, 1991), *Molly Sweeney* (Gate Theatre, 1994) and *Give Me Your Answer, Do!* (Abbey, 1997). When the Lyric staged this last play in 1999 as part of the celebrations for Friel's seventieth birthday, its assertion of the need for a 'necessary uncertainty' had a clear resonance for the prevailing political situation as well as for theatre itself. The theatre, like the wider community, must be prepared to embrace change – what Heaney dubbed the 'moment of possibility'. Friel is a monument to the potential of local work to take its place on the world stage.

Important recent productions produced outside the north but with significant northern resonance have included two plays with border settings – *Hubert Murray's Widow* by Michael Harding and the Druid Theatre Company's outstanding production of Vincent Woods' *At the Black Pig's Dyke* (both in 1993) which combined 'Troubles drama' with the ancient mumming tradition in a way that was stylistically little short of revolutionary. As the peace seeps in, it is salutary to remember that some of the deepest wounds are to be found at the edges of the region. *Frank Pig Says Hello*, adapted by Joe O'Byrne from *The Butcher Boy* by Pat McCabe must also be mentioned in this border context, not least because it paved the way for a succession of tight-knit, highly physical two-handers such as *Mojo-Mickeybo* and *Stones in His Pockets*. Mention must also be made of Rough Magic's production of Donal O'Kelly's *The Dogs* (1992), an elaborate allegory of northern politics and an *Animal Farm* for modern Ireland – and Nicola McCartney's *Heritage* (1998). Brought up in Northern Ireland, McCartney has worked mainly in Scotland, but has recently returned as writer-in-residence at the University of Ulster.

Acknowledgement should be given to the wealth of new writing emerging from the youth and community field. Mention has been made of the Replay Theatre Company in connection with Marie Jones. But the company has also worked extensively with other writers, including John Rooney, Brenda Winter, Gary Mitchell, John McClelland, Rebecca Bartlett, and Damian Gorman. A body of twenty-two plays makes Replay the most productive local originator of new work after the Lyric. This is an impressive achievement, and one that has been of immeasurable value to the wider theatre community. Damian Gorman has also benefitted from the support of the Catholic Church which commissioned his moving quartet of plays for Christmas, *Broken Nails*, presented in Belfast's Saint Peter's Cathedral in 1988, and from the independent Fallen Angels Theatre Company, which produced his modern fable, *The Man in the Moon* in 1992. Nor should the Ulster Youth Theatre's *Stations* (1989) be forgotten, in which six writers – Frank McGuinness, Jennifer Johnston, Michael Longley, Robin Glendinning, Damian Gorman and Mark Brennan – wrote short plays to accompany a performance of Seamus Heaney's long poem, *Station Island*. The UYT also commissioned the darkly comic *Goodnight Strabane* from Gerard Stembridge in 1992. He then went on to write *Family Album* for the young people's theatre company, Virtual Reality, the following year.

The huge growth of community theatre, due not least to the committed advocacy of Martin Lynch, has led to a blurring of the distinction between community and professional drama. Plays like *Moths* (1992) and *Bunjoor Mucker* (1993), which Lynch wrote expressly for the Citywide Community Theatre and Saint Patrick's Training School respectively, seem easy to define,

Theatre – the playwrights and their plays 51

but the epic *Stone Chair* at the Grand Opera House in 1992 strained the descriptive boundaries. More recently, Dubbeljoint's productions of the collaboratively written *Binlids* (1997) and Brenda Murphy and Christine Poland's *Forced Upon Us* (1999) with the prisoners' wives' group, Justus, have raised even more profound questions of definition. The latter play, which addressed the difficult issue of policing, generated a level of controversy unknown since the days of Sam Thompson and *Over the Bridge*.

In the crowded landscape of late twentieth-century Northern Ireland drama, the following landmarks loom large. *The Flats* established that the theatre has a role in helping us to understand the madness that often surrounds us; *We Do It for Love* taught us the importance of laughing at ourselves; *Translations* reminded us of our place on the world stage – that the world is round; while *Dockers*, *The Hidden Curriculum* and *Tea in a China Cup* reassured us that it is also flat – that in an increasingly global world the theatre still has a role in allowing us to gauge our own horizons. *Lay Up Your Ends* combined the local and the global and opened up a whole world of new opportunities for local writers and practitioners. *Observe the Sons of Ulster* . . . showed us that theatre, as well as asking questions, can provide some of the answers, and *Pentecost* gave us renewed hope in the future. Three recent successes have shown how diverse that future can still be. *In a Little World of Our Own* has reaffirmed the theatre's capacity to look in; *Language Roulette* encourages us to look out; and *Stones in his Pockets* has demonstrated once again that good work which speaks to its own audience can still reach out to the wider world. Northern Ireland's playwrights need to seize this new sense of confidence to break free of the often limiting expectations of commissioners, funders and producers, to tell the stories they want to tell in the way they want to tell them.

Poetry

FRANK ORMSBY

Introducing *The Penguin Book of Contemporary British Poetry* (1982), an anthology in which the work of six Northern Irish poets is included, Blake Morrison and Andrew Motion singled out Seamus Heaney as the 'most important new poet of the past fifteen years' and commented: 'So impressive is recent Northern Irish poetry . . . that it is not surprising to find discussions of English poetry so often having to take place in its shadow.' It is certainly true that the period since the mid 1960s has been a remarkably fertile one for poetry in Northern Ireland with successive generations of poets not only consistently producing poetry of a high order, but providing creative continuity where poetry had previously been fitful and sporadic. The poets themselves have been properly wary of terms like 'renaissance' and have resisted categorisation as a group or school, while benefitting from the existence of such a community – both through the fruitful poetic exchange that it makes possible and the challenge it poses to younger poets to learn from their formidable elders and emerge from their shadow.

The broad outlines of the period under consideration are already well known to readers of poetry. Louis MacNeice, who died in 1963, continued to exert a strong influence – most clearly visible in the work of Derek Mahon, Michael Longley and Paul Muldoon – and poets such as John Hewitt, Roy McFadden and Robert Greacen, initially associated with the 1940s, had a new lease of poetic life. John Montague consolidated an already considerable reputation. An exceptionally gifted quartet, Seamus Heaney, Michael Longley, Derek Mahon and James Simmons, most of them associated with the writers' group founded by Philip Hobsbaum at Queen's University in the early 1960s, published their first collections at the end of the decade, and in the 1970s another exceptional generation of poets made their presence felt, among them Paul Muldoon, Tom Paulin, Ciaran Carson and Medbh McGuckian.

Any survey of Northern Irish poetry in the last thirty years must take into account the pervasive impact of the current phase of the Troubles. Writing of the poetry of Seamus Heaney and Derek Mahon, Seamus Deane has argued that in their efforts 'to come to grips with destructive energies, they attempt to demonstrate a way of turning them towards creativity' and goes on: 'Their sponsorship is not simply for the sake of art; it is for the energies embodied in art which have been diminished or destroyed elsewhere.' The poets of the 1940s and 1950s had already reflected, in varying degrees, long-standing cultural, religious and political divisions in the north and for the survivors of that generation and their successors, the Troubles were an immediate, devastating and challenging reality. Many of these poets have commented directly, or indirectly, on questions of poetic responsibility and the aesthetic dilemmas posed by the conflict. Heaney writes that after 1968 'the problems of poetry moved from being simply a matter of achieving the satisfactory verbal icon to being a search for images and symbols adequate to our predicament'. Longley, recording how Northern Irish writers were sometimes accused of exploitation if they took the Troubles as their subject and evasion if they did not, acknowledges that a poet 'would be inhuman if he did not respond to tragic events in his own community' but insists also that: 'The

Belfast Telegraph

John Hewitt in characteristic pose

artist needs time to allow the raw material of experience to settle to an imaginative depth'. Medbh McGuckian uses as epigraph to her collection *Captain Lavender* (1994) a statement made by Picasso in 1944: 'I have not painted the war ... but I have no doubt that the war is in the paintings I have done', implying how deeply and unquantifiably such a complex of conditions and circumstances in a particular time and place may run in the poetic bloodstream.

John Hewitt is widely acknowledged as the most influential of the 1940s generation. Edna Longley has described how his 'cross-sectarian ideal of regionalism [not] only energised writers, painters and general cultural activity during the post-war period [but] recovered ancestral voices and provided some of the basis for a second take-off in the sixties'. This process may also have worked in reverse. Stimulated partly, perhaps, by the success of their younger contemporaries, Hewitt and a number of other 1940s poets re-emerged in the late 1960s and early 1970s. Hewitt's *Collected Poems 1932–1967* appeared in 1968 and in November 1970 he accompanied John Montague on a reading tour of Northern Ireland, sponsored by the Arts Council and titled *The Planter and the Gael*.

In 1971 he returned to Belfast from Coventry and in the remaining fifteen years of his life his many publications included eight collections of poems. Though Hewitt continued to produce new work during this period, his creative emphasis was on the revision and recasting of earlier poems, published and unpublished, and on salvaging material from his manuscript notebooks. *Time Enough* (1976) and *The Rain Dance* (1978), for example, are both described as 'Poems New and Revised' and *Freehold and Other Poems* (1986) collects for the first time in book form his verse play *The Bloody Brae* (written in 1936) and a long poem written in the 1940s. *Kites in Spring: A Belfast Boyhood* (1980) is an autobiographical collection in sonnet form in which he reconstructs an area and a way of life changed radically and partly destroyed by the Troubles. Hewitt's central themes – the troubled interaction of past and present in Ulster, the complexities of 'protestant' identity – acquired a new context and resonance, as did his key writings on regionalism, published shortly after his death in book form as *Ancestral Voices: The Selected Prose of John Hewitt* (ed. Tom Clyde, 1987). The inauguration of the John Hewitt International Summer School in 1988 and the publication of *The Collected Poems of John Hewitt* (1991) have further strengthened the reputation and influence of a poet whose writings and ideas 'underlie current approaches to "cultural diversity" in Northern Ireland' (Edna Longley).

Hewitt's younger contemporary, Roy McFadden, who, though he had continued to write, had not published a book-length collection since *The Heart's Townland* (1947), also re-surfaced with *The Garryowen* (1971) and continued to produce collections throughut the 1970s and 1980s, including *The Selected Roy McFadden* (ed. John Boyd, 1983). McFadden extended his range considerably, particularly in collections such as *A Watching Brief* (1979), *Letters to the Hinterland* (1986) and *After Seymour's Funeral* (1990). As is the case in Hewitt's later work, these volumes present retrospective portraits of people and places, though McFadden also draws on his professional life as a solicitor, a subject area unique in Irish poetry. His *Collected Poems 1943–1995* (1996), published shortly before his death, represents a creative life spanning over fifty years.

Robert Greacen, too, who had not published a book of poems since *The Undying Day* (1948), reappeared in print with *A Garland for Captain Fox* (1975), an unusual, satirical volume, in which the eponymous Fox features as a shady customer about whom we know little and suspect much. Greacen's

John Montague, 1986

A Bright Mask: New and Selected Poems appeared in 1985 and his *Collected Poems 1944–1994* was issued in 1995, another monument to the achievements of the 1940s and after in Northern Irish poetry.

Norman Dugdale (1921–1995) published all four of his individual collections between 1970 and 1991 and his *Collected Poems 1970–1995* appeared posthumously in 1997. There have been six collections from Padraic Fiacc within the period, as well as two 'selected' editions of his work. Louis MacNeice's *Collected Poems* has remained in print since 1966 and his *Selected Poems* was re-issued in 1988 and again in 2000, edited by Michael Longley.

By the early 1970s John Montague's collections *Poisoned Lands* (1961), *A Chosen Light* (1967) and *Tides* (1971) had established his reputation as a laureate of change and continuity in rural Ireland, an accomplished love poet and a writer whose work reflected a sophisticated awareness of contemporary European and American verse. The appearance in 1972 of his epic *The Rough Field* on which he had worked for almost a decade, confirmed his stature as a leading Irish poet. He writes of having 'a kind of vision in the medieval sense, of (his) home area, the unhappiness of its historical destiny'. The poem is, then, partly a lament for the decline of rural tradition and the loss of community, partly an angry record of sectarianism and oppression, partly a celebration of survival and adaptation. Montague's sense of 'The pattern history weaves/From one small backward place' is movingly evident, both in personal evocations of his aunt Brigid in 'The Leaping Fire' section and of his father's exile in Brooklyn in 'The Fault' and in more public utterances such as those in the section titled 'A Severed Head', with its emphasis on lost traditions and the imposition of the English language on the native Irish. The humour of 'Hymn to the New Omagh Road' and the declamatory style of 'A New Siege', which parallels the siege of protestant Derry in 1690 with the siege of the catholic Bogside in 1969, demonstrate further the range and variety of a meditation which, in addition to the success of particular lyrics within it, has a haunting cumulative impact.

Montague structures *The Rough Field* in sections, sometimes recycling poems which had appeared as separate lyrics in previous books. These techniques form the structural basis of Montague's next three collections. As its title suggests, *A Slow Dance* has a ritualistic quality, invoking cycles of birth and death, joy and grief, sometimes through formal incantation, sometimes through fine individual lyrics such as 'Small Secrets', 'Falls Funeral', 'Dowager' and 'Windharp', which compares the sounds of Ireland to:

> a hand ceaselessly
> combing and stroking
> the landscape, till
> the valley gleams
> like the pile upon
> a mountain pony's coat.

There is a compelling sense in Montague's books of poetry as a restless, psychic journeying into the personal and communal selves, often in order to seek healing through the exploration of old wounds. The personal journey has, perhaps, its most sustained expression in *The Great Cloak* (1978) and *The Dead Kingdom* (1984). The first of these charts movingly the disintegration of a marriage, the growth of a new relationship and the experience of fatherhood. A number of the poems have Irish settings, and the epigraph 'As my Province burns/I sing of love, hoping to give that fiery/Wheel a shove', suggests that one energising force in the collection is a desire to affirm the universals of the personal life in a time of political turmoil.

In *The Dead Kingdom* the journeys are both literal and psychic. The poet travels from Cork, through the midlands to Fermanagh–South Tyrone to visit his dying mother and, later, for her funeral, but also through Ulster's troubled past and present and into the traumas of family history. In partcular, Montague's experience of being 'given away to be fostered' by aunts at the age of four and the painfully fragmented nature of his relationship with his parents surges to the surface in sad, raw, unforgettable lyrics such as 'The Silver Flask' and 'A Flowering Absence'. Later collections, *Mount Eagle* (1988), *Time in Armagh* (1993) and *Smashing the Piano* (1999), build upon and develop Montague's central concerns. *Time in Armagh*, for example, exorcises the pain of a repressive catholic education and *Smashing the Piano* shows the ageing poet continuing to seek a final equilibrium between joy and grief, discord and harmony, rootedness and dislocation.

James Simmons' manifesto for his magazine *The Honest Ulsterman*, founded in 1968, declared that the publication would attempt to 'rescue Literature from the Academics and folk art from the world of fashion' and asked for 'clarity, feeling and humour' to be added to 'high seriousness'. Such considerations remained central to Simmons' own poetry, which promoted the strengths and values of more popular, accessible forms such as ballad and folk song as a counter to what he perceived as the élitism of influential modern poets like T.S. Eliot. Simmons' priorities were apparent again in, for example, 'Didn't He Ramble' (*The Long Summer Still to Come*, 1973), a robust, loving act of homage to jazz and blues as embodying 'Profundity without the po-face/Of court and bourgeois modes':

> ... the word of life, if such a thing existed,
> was there on record among the rubbish listed

in the catalogues of Brunswick and HMV,
healing the split in sensibility.
Tough reasonableness and lyric
grace together, in poor man's dialect.

Not only did Simmons, himself a songwriter and singer, love the music, he told us, but also 'the men who made/the music', in all their creativity and fallibility. Indeed a sympathetic and often ironic awareness of such fallibility was one of the most engaging positives in Simmons' poetry, particularly when he wrote of the complex joys and disasters of love, sex, marriage, adultery, divorce and of relationships within the family. From 'Ballad of a Marriage' (*Ballad of a Marriage*, 1966), in part an unsparing scrutiny of jealousy and its effects, in part a record of how more tender, workable relationships can

BBC Northern Ireland

James Simmons (left) and writer Harry Barton photographed in Derry in 1972 for the BBC radio series *Why Doesn't Someone Explain?* Simmons wrote 'Claudy' for the series. Barton wrote many radio plays for the BBC and created the popular 1970s satirical character Mr Mooney, whom Barton described as 'a ten thousand year old political leprechaun who smells as strongly as his politics'.

evolve, through 'Meditations in Time of Divorce' (*Constantly Singing*, 1980), to the love poems centring on a new relationship and a third marriage in *Mainstream* (1995) and *The Company of Children* (1999), Simmons was Irish poetry's most candid explorer of these areas of human experience. The explorations can be tenderly lyrical, painfully probing, bawdy and humorous, challenging puritanical assumptions, reflecting an ironic sense of human absurdity – including the poet's own – and a refusal to be disenchanted. Even in the valedictory 'Goodbye, Sally' (*Energy to Burn*, 1971) the speaker, though anticipating loss, exclaims: 'God, but I'm lucky too,/the way I've muddled through/to ecstasy so often'.

There was, however, a darker, more angry note in Simmons' poems about political and sectarian murder. Typically, one of his best Troubles poems, 'Claudy' (*West Strand Visions*, 1974), is also a song. It presents the victims of the atrocity by name as they go about their daily lives, then the carnage as the car bomb explodes, and ends with the controlled bitterness of:

> Meanwhile to Dungiven the killers have gone,
> and they're finding it hard to get through on the phone.

The ballad form's apparent lack of artifice, its almost colloquial directness of statement, give the poem a powerful immediacy, an emotional charge that seems extra-poetic, though the form is handled with unobtrusive skill.

Effective in different ways is the title poem in *From the Irish* (1985), a collection in which Simmons adapted freely from classic poetry of the Gaelic tradition; here he moves with withering irony from the world of Celtic mythology to that of the proxy bomber, forcing us in the process to reconsider a particular concept of 'heroism' and its consequences. Michael Longley wrote in 1971 that Simmons' work was 'still seriously underestimated'. Thirty years later the same comment might be made. Here was a poet who, at his best, had a verve and intimacy and gravitas which has not yet been adequately acknowledged. His death, in June 2001, robbed Irish poetry of one of its most dashing and cherishable presences.

Simmons was one of the poets who attended and read at meetings of Philip Hobsbaum's writers' group in the early 1960s. The first member of that group to publish in book form was Seamus Heaney. *Death of a Naturalist* (1966), with its fresh, sensuous explorations of Heaney's boyhood on a farm in county Derry, won instant acclaim. This collection and its successor, *Door into the Dark* (1969), recreate the formative power of a pre-articulate or pre-literate world in rich, muscular rhythms and diction. Their central metaphor is of poetry as a 'dig' towards understanding, not only of self and immediate community, but of the Irish past and its shaping influence on the present. In all his subsequent collections Heaney returns to the springs of his inspiration while simultaneously extending his range, so that his *oeuvre* is characterised by powerful individual poems and a cumulative range and depth few other poets can match. *Wintering Out* (1972) includes memorable poems of landscape and place. Most significantly, however, the collection reflects the outbreak of the Troubles and shows the first fruits of Heaney's search for 'images and symbols adequate to our predicament'. In 'The Other Side' he writes from direct personal experience of sectarian and political division and evokes a tentative but powerful impulse towards reconciliation. 'The Tollund Man', on the other hand, draws on Heaney's reading of P.V. Glob's study *The Bog People* (1969) about the sacrificial victims of Iron Age fertility rites in Scandanavia, to suggest imaginative parallels between that society's religion centred on territory and aspects of republican mythology in contemporary Ireland.

These poems prefigure the two-section structure of *North* (1975), which attracted widespread attention – positive and negative – as a Troubles collection. The opening section employs the mythic approach of 'The Tollund Man', with a particular focus again on the bog people. 'Punishment', for example, progresses from a portrait of an Iron Age adultress, executed and buried in bogland, to the tarring and feathering of catholic girls for fraternising with British soldiers and explores Heaney's own ambivalence in relation to such tribal mores. Elsewhere, he posits the potentially assuaging power of ritual – whether it be the domestic and work customs of 'Mossbawn: Two Poems in Dedication for Mary Heaney' at the beginning of the volume or the imagined rituals of 'Funeral Rites' – against 'neighbourly murder', the violent realities of history. The second section of *North* culminates in the sequence 'Singing School', an autoiographical record of growing up in Northern Ireland, 'Fostered alike by beauty and by fear', as the epigraph from Wordsworth has it. The book ends with the anxious intensity of 'Exposure', in which Heaney, an inner émigré' now living in Wicklow, ponders his responsibilities as a poet, vulnerably unsure of the road he has taken and haunted by the possibility of lost opportunities.

The shadow of the Troubles continues to fall across Heaney's subsequent collections, but not disablingly so. *Field Work* (1979), though it contains a series of moving elegies for the victims of violence, including friends and a relative of the poet, is markedly less sombre than *North*. The central sequence of *Station Island* (1984) finds Heaney weighing his 'responsible tristia' again; the poet, on a pilgrimage to St Patrick's Purgatory at Lough Derg, converses with a number of literary and family ghosts who question and challenge him about his responsibilities and priorities. The decisive voice seems to be that of James Joyce, who elevates creative freedom and adventure over the pull of tribal allegiances. The final section is itself an imaginative flight in which Heaney speaks through the persona of the mad king-poet Sweeney, free from his obligations but lonely and guilty in his freedom. Dante's presence in both *Field Work* and *Station Island* shows Heaney's increasing interest in European poetry, a development evident again in *The Haw Lantern* (1987), where some key poems reflect the inspiration of Eastern European poets such as Czeslaw Milosz and Zbigniew Herbert. The volume is notable also for the sequence 'Clearances', eight sonnets in memory of the poet's mother and a number of poems – 'The Mud Vision' and 'Parable Island', for example – which point towards Heaney's next collection, *Seeing Things* (1991). As the title suggests, the poet here combines the attention to the textures of the palpable world that has always been one of his strengths with a liberating impulse to 'credit marvels'. Heaney's most recent books *The Spirit Level* (1996) and *Electric Light* (2001), as well as his translation of the Anglo–Saxon epic *Beowulf* (2000), all published after the award of the Nobel Prize for Literature in 1995, reflect the thrusting continuity of his work, as well as what the critic Helen Vendler called his 'vigilant willingness to change'. As Heaney himself remarked in his Nobel Lecture, each 'point of arrival' in his writing has 'turned out to be a stepping stone rather than a destination'.

Three years after Heaney published *Death of a Naturalist*, Michael Longley's first collection, *No Continuing City*, appeared. Longley had begun writing as an undergraduate at Trinity College in Dublin and on his return to Belfast in the 1960s became, like Simmons and Heaney, a participant in Hobsbaum's writers' group. One of Longley's richest sources of inspiration is the Great

The poet Michael Longley pictured in the late 1970s

War, experienced first at an immediate family level through the anecdotes of his soldier father who had looked 'death and nightmare in the Face' at the Battle of the Somme and afterwards, then imaginatively through the poetry and prose of poetic soldier fathers such as Wilfred Owen, Edward Thomas, Siegfried Sassoon, Isaac Rosenberg and Charles Sorley. The poem 'In Memoriam' (*No Continuing City*, 1969) in which the crosses in the war cemeteries 'sink roots' into the poet's mind, initiates an elegiac mode which runs through most of Longley's collections. Many of these 'war' poems, while registering destruction and loss, tactfully affirm the survival of the creative impulse, both human and natural, and the endangered, doubly-precious persistence of the ordinary. 'The War Graves', for example, with its 'blizzard of headstones', presents also the field mice smuggling seeds into the ruins and the fragile persistence of the celandine, 'the flower that outwits winter'.

After the outbreak of the Troubles, Longley's poems of the First – and Second – World War take on an additional, local dimension, the most explicit expression of which is found in 'Wounds' (*An Exploded View*, 1973), one of the most harrowingly particular and universal of his elegies. Here, his

father's memories of the Ulster Division at the Somme – its courage, its prejudices, its teenage dead – and the fact that his father's death many years after
the war was partly a result of his wounds, modulates into a lament for soldier
and civilian victims of violence in Northern Ireland. Indeed, the focus of
Longley's Troubles poetry is consistently on the victims and, in particular,
on the destruction of domestic and familial securities. Like Heaney, Simmons
and Mahon, to whom he has addressed verse letters *(An Exploded View)*,
Longley has a life-enhancing sense of how the human values embodied in
poetry, though in danger of being drowned by the 'stereophonic nightmare
of the Shankill and the Falls', nevertheless persist.

   Another vital strand in Longley's work derives from his love of classical
literature. His grounding in Greek and Roman poetry has not only influenced the structures and rhythms of his poems – he is a master both of the
epigrammatic short poem and of the single-sentence poem which may run
to twenty lines or more – but extended his range and perspective. From the
formal dramatic monologues in *No Continuing City* ('Circe', 'Persephone' and
'Narcissus', for example) to the more colloquial 'versions' in *The Weather in
Japan* (2000), episodes and images from *The Iliad* and *The Odyssey* and Roman
poets such as Tibullus and Ovid resonate throughout Longley's work.
Several of his most powerful Troubles poems are filtered with immense
artistry through Homer, so that they are simultaneously immediate and
oblique. In 'The Helmet' (*The Ghost Orchid*, 1995) a violent heritage is
rendered all the more terrible for being presented in family and spiritual
contexts, as Hector bequeaths his helmet to his son and prays that the boy
'might grow up bloodier than him', and in the sonnet 'Ceasefire' (*The Ghost
Orchid*) Achilles, the slayer of Hector, and Hector's father Priam, unite to
clean the body for burial, Priam having made the unthinkable leap:

> I get down on my knees and do what must be done
> And kiss Achilles' hand, the killer of my son.

The poems described here indicate the complex interweaving of themes in
Longley's poetry. Yet another vivid strand is to be found in his poems set in
the west of Ireland. The celandine in the war cemetery and the field mice
among the ruins have natural, fertile links with the flora and fauna of the
Burren and County Mayo. These places have been an integral part of

Longley's poetic landscape since 'Leaving Inishmore' (*No Continuing City*) and, in particular, 'The West' (*An Exploded View*), in which the poet's remote cottage becomes 'home from home', contrasting with, but not remote from, home in troubled Belfast. In 'The Ice-Cream Man' (*Gorse Fires*, 1991), about a sectarian murder, Longley invokes 'all the wild flowers of the Burren' that he had seen in one day as a kind of charm, a consoling litany of the beautiful and vital to set against violent death. The energies of *Gorse Fires, The Ghost Orchid* and *The Weather in Japan* are, to a significant degree, the energies of animal, bird and insect. Whether focusing on an Amish rug or paying homage to Fats Waller and Bix Beiderbeck, or addressing the subject of the Holocaust, Longley has established himself as one of the most delicate, benign and cherishable of the Ulster poets. His international standing was further recognised in January 2001 when he received the T.S. Eliot Prize and Hawthornden Prize and was awarded the Queen's Gold Medal for Poetry.

Like Longley, Derek Mahon was born in Belfast of a protestant middle-class background and educated at Trinity College Dublin. Of the poets who emerged at the end of the 1960s, he is perhaps the most 'urban'. Mahon's ambivalent attitude to Belfast, Ulster protestantism and the middle classes is one striking aspect of his first two collections, the startingly achieved *Night-Crossing* (1968), published when he was only twenty-seven, and *Lives* (1972). The poet declares at the end of 'In Belfast' (*Night-Crossing*) that the kitchen-houses and 'echoing back-streets of this desperate city' demand more than 'casual' interest or pity. 'Ecclesiastes' *(Lives)* blasts the messianic self-righteousness of puritan fundamentalism in Ulster and the bleakness of the society it has produced.

Already in this poem there is a sense of the divisions and injustices – 'close one eye and be king' – that will help to precipitate the Troubles and in *Lives* and subsequent collections Mahon makes his own impassioned journeys over the nightmare ground. Like virtually all of his contemporaries he calls his own position and the relevance or effectiveness of art into question. The title poem in *The Snow Party* (1975) juxtaposes, in a Japanese setting, the formal domesticities and social/aesthetic rituals of tea-drinking and snow-viewing in Nagoya with the brutalities of life elsewhere and the reader is left to decide whether the 'silence/In the houses of Nagoya' represents an abrogation of public responsibility by the poet Basho and his friends or the heartening survival of civilised normalities. This poem is followed immediately by 'The Last of the Fire Kings' in which the speaker declares himself 'through with history' and yearns to escape from the demands of the 'fire-loving/People'. One of Mahon's most complex poems on these subjects is 'Rage for Order' in which poetry is at first viewed as self-indulgent, 'a dying art,/an eddy of semantic scruples/in an unstructurable sea', but which ends with the concession that its 'Germinal ironies' may be vital and necessary in the enterprise of rebuilding. Mahon's portrayal of the bourgeoisie is sometimes humorously, sometimes bitingly satirical. 'Glengormley' (*Night-Crossing*) opens:

> Wonders are many and none is more wonderful than man
> who has tamed the terrier, trimmed the hedge
> and grasped the principle of the watering-can.

'After Cavafy' (*Lives*), which begins by anticipating the arrival of the barbarians, ends with a sense that they may already be within the walls, concealed behind talk 'Of fitted carpets/central/ Heating and automatic gear-change'.

Given the alienated, disenchanted note struck in such poems, it is not surprising to find Mahon attracted to writers and artists on the margins of society or in exile, tormented victims and survivors. The protagonists in his poems are often isolated individuals speaking from exposed coastal locations or in the aftermath of unspecified global disasters, or as the ghosts of defunct civilisations. One of Mahon's finest poems, the much-anthologised 'A Disused Shed in Co. Wexford', opens with global images of abandoned places, then focuses on the shed of the title, with its forgotten mushrooms growing towards the keyole which is the 'one star in their firmament'. In a poem of commanding gravity they come to represent victims such as 'powdery prisoners of the old regime' and the 'Lost people of Treblinka and Pompeii', crying out for rescue and salvation. Mahon conveys both the bleak extremity of their plight and the desperate passion with which they persist towards the deliverance which may or may not be granted. The poem is a reminder that the darkness which is pervasive in Mahon's poetry is never overwhelming, light never entirely absent.

Mahon's mastery of the longer poem is evident in the early verse letter 'Beyond Howth Head' (*Lives*) and his most recent collections are, for the most part, more relaxed and expansive. The title sequence in *The Hudson Letter* (1995) treats the theme of exile in the urban maelstrom of Manhattan. Parental guilt, anxieties and hopes are nakedly evident in addresses to the poet's son and daughter and there is a vulnerable groping towards positives by which his children and others might live. *The Yellow Book* (1997) is a fin de siècle meditation which explores, in twenty sections, the subject of cultural decadence in a wide range of settings, but also the lives and values of exceptional individuals such as Wilde and Schopenhauer. 'Death in Bangor' – retitled 'A Bangor Requiem' in the reissue of Mahon's *Selected Poems* (2000) – is an elegy for the poet's mother and a revisiting of his Belfast boyhood. The whole sequence is reminiscent of MacNeice's *Autumn Journal* in its blend of the autobiographical, the cultural and the historical and the latest reminder of the effortless cosmopolitan range which is one of Mahon's strengths. Mahon's *Collected Poems* (2000) provide ample evidence of why Michael Longley has hailed him as 'our bravest and most stylish wielder of the singing line' and John Montague asserted: 'From an age as bloody and chaotic as the Elizabethan his poems are among those certain to survive.'

The outstanding poet of the generation which followed Simmons, Heaney, Longley and Mahon is Paul Muldoon, who has to date produced eight book-length collections, two 'selected' volumes and a *Poems 1968– 1998* (2001), which is virtually a 'collected' edition of his work. He is widely acknowledged as an influence on British and Irish poetry since the late 1970s. Muldoon's first two collections, *New Weather* (1973) and *Mules* (1977), introduce many characteristic features of his poetry, features which recur and develop in endlessly inventive and subtle ways throughout his work. The landscape, history and mythology of the Armagh–Tyrone border area where he grew up are already nourishing presences, but luminously renewed and universalised. There is a strong sense, both explicit and implicit, of the individual identity as perpetually unfinished business, an ongoing process of exploration and re-adjustment. Closely allied to this is the way Muldoon begins to reflect a complex engagement with Ireland's violent history and, like his predecessors, with the role of the poet in a troubled society. Technically too Muldoon sets about transforming the traditional, partcularly in the way he revitalises cliché and begins to experiment with, for example, rhyme and the sonnet form. Other significant features are his interest in parable and narrative

Paul Muldoon in his days as a BBC radio producer,
Belfast circa 1980

and his fascination with American culture, particularly the folklore of the American Indian.

Muldoon has commended Robert Frost's 'mischievous, sly, multi-layered quality under the surface', and the phrase might be used to describe his own work. In 'The Weepies' (*Why Brownlee Left*, 1980) a gang of boys who attend the local cinema, expecting the usual Saturday western, are embarrassed to have their masculine solidarity shattered by altogether messier human realities. The poem not only charts an emotional landmark for the boys, it constitutes a serio-humorous attack on the 'no surrender' mentality, the macho posturing that blights human development, personally and politically. In 'Aisling' (*Quoof*, 1983) Muldoon reworks the 'aisling' or 'vision' poem of Gaelic literature. The seductive beauty encountered might be a goddess or some promiscuous female promising abundance but threatening venereal disease and starvation. Similarly, the grim realities of hunger-strikes are set against the idealised Ireland of romantic nationalism. The speaker escapes infection and the hunger-striker calls off his fast, but the poem leaves us pondering the potentially deceptive nature of certain ideals and the need for vigilance. The collection *Why Brownlee Left*, in which one central theme relates to journeys, quests, roads not taken, other possible lives, culminates in 'Immram', a sly adaptation of the eighth century Gaelic epic 'Immram Mael Duin' – the 'Voyage of Muldoon' – crossed with a parody of Raymond Chandler to produce a bizarre, entertaining story of a young man's search for information about his parents.

Muldoon's whirlwind narrative style is on show again in the dark humour of 'The More a Man Has, the More a Man Wants' (*Quoof*), 'loosely based on the Trickster cycle of the Winnebago Indians', in which we accompany the shape-shifting protagonist Gallogly, a terrorist on the run, on his fantastical and nightmarish adventures in a world of violence, particularly that of the Troubles. In this world, reality and identity are dangerously and often hilariously, elusive. Muldoon's individual 'search for images and symbols adequate to our predicament' leads him into art, literature, mythology and the visions and dislocations of hallucinogenic experience. So apparently inexhaustible are Muldoon's resources as a poet, that the publication of his *Poems 1968–1998* at the age of fifty, amounts not only to an impressive retrospective but a tantalising promise of riches in store.

Like Muldoon, Tom Paulin came to public notice through Faber and Faber's *Introductions* series of anthologies. The title of his first collection, *A State of Justice* (1977) and its opening poem 'States', a meditation on the complex organisation of society and the nature of law and order, establish the preoccupations which have earned him a reputation as the most directly 'political' of the Northern Irish poets. In both *A State of Justice* and *The Strange Museum* (1980), Paulin explores the idea of the state as a potential embodiment of order and enlightenment but also as potentially an instrument of oppression, in poems that range from Northern Ireland to Muslim and eastern European dictatorships. The locations are frequently grim, claustrophobic places in which human and political behaviour is dominated by a lethal, self-righteous desire for retribution. Though the people in such poems tend to be victims or survivors, the bleakness of Paulin's vision in *A State of Justice* and *The Strange Museum* is alleviated by intimations of purity and promise. The waters that 'might be kind', referred to in the poem 'A Just State', find their counterpart in, for example, the speaker's vision at the end of

'Dawros Parish Church' of 'A silent water beyond society'. Again, in 'A New Society' (*A State of Justice*), there is a cautious but heartfelt imagining of 'an order that's unaggressively civilian'.

The Strange Museum is energised by a tension between the hunger for an original purity and the impossibility of ever attaining it. The hunger, the pursuit, the quest is, in itself, positive and enabling. The title poem has the speaker escaping from an oppressive place to wake in a 'tennis suburb' where there is 'a grey tenderness' and he anticipates the return of a woman who is 'the season beyond winter, the first freshness'. There are also poems in *The Strange Museum* such as 'The Garden of Self-Delight' and the sequence 'The Other Voice', in which the hunger for what Paulin called, in interview, a 'living form that expresses the spirit' draws the poet towards the seductive concept of art for art's sake, an attraction that conflicts with the obligations prompted by politics and public events.

One of the apostles of art for art's sake, the Russian poet Osip Mandelstam, who is a powerful presence at the end of 'The Other Voice', appears again in 'The Book of Juniper' in Paulin's next collection, *The Liberty Tree* (1983). Nevertheess, in this book and its successor, *Fivemiletown* (1987), there is a decisive movement back towards the public and political. Taken together, these collections constitute an intense scrutiny of protestant inheritance and identity, both in Northern Irish and European contexts. *The Liberty Tree* is, on one level, a loving quest for the radical, free-thinking, dissenting presbyterianism which flourished in the North of Ireland in the late eighteenth century. Paulin mourns the loss of that protestant enlightenment – so important also to John Hewitt – and what he sees as its debasement in present-day Northern Ireland. The poem 'Desertmartin' is Paulin's most ferocious assault to date on the crippling influence of fundamentalist religions; the 'free strenuous spirit' of presbyterianism has changed to a 'servile defiance that whines and shrieks/For the bondage of the letter'.

The fractured loyalties of a culture waving a flag it 'loves and hates', which appeared first as a theme in the poem 'Settlers' (*A State of Justice*), is central to the collection *Fivemiletown*. The northern unionists' sense of betrayal at the suspension of Stormont and the signing of the Anglo-Irish Agreement is sympathetically portrayed in poems such as 'Sure I'm a Cheat Aren't We All?', 'An Ulster Unionist Walks the Streets of London' and 'The Defenestration of Hillsborough', in the last of which the speaker bluntly defines the 'choice' facing unionism – 'either to jump or get pushed'. The defenestration image is one of a number which links the experience of Northern Irish protestants to the history of protestant Europe, particularly during the Thirty Years War. The collection ends with an ambitious longer poem, 'The Caravans on Luneburg Heath', in which the main subjects are the role of writers – and language – in time of conflict and the lessons that may be learned from history. In the final section the poet goes, as it were, back to school to be 'born again', to have his education revised in the light of what has been explored in the poem.

The preoccupations and obsessions of these four collections persist into Paulin's most recent books, *Walking a Line* (1994) and *The Wind Dog* (1999). However, these volumes are, on the whole, less directly public, more personal than his earlier work. His fascination with Ulster dialect, Hiberno-English, and language generally animates both collections. There is a sense of the poet at play with words. The long poem which gives its title to *The Wind Dog*, originally written for radio, dramatises the drunkenness of words and sounds being various and their early and lasting impact on the poet. Paulin is yet another Northern Irish writer who has, to adapt an image from Heaney's 'North', lain down in the word-hoard and created out of it a tough music unmistakably his own.

Ciaran Carson is another archaeologist of language, indeed of several languages. His first collection, *The New Estate* (1976), is an accomplished debut, both in its range of subjects and its skilful use of traditional forms and techniques. Yet there are very few poems that anticipate Carson's re-emergence eleven years later, in *The Irish For No* (1987), as a poet of immense originality and power, qualities confirmed and extended in *Belfast Confetti* (1989). In these two collections the city of Belfast and the impact of the Troubles become central subjects. Carson also makes extensive use for the first time of the long, flexible line characteristic of his poetry, influenced partly by the practice of the American poet C.K. Williams, partly by the seventeen-syllable *haiku* form and partly by tradtional storytelling techniques. 'Dresden', the opening poem in *The Irish For No*, enacts the rich, funny digressions and circumlocutions of the oral tradition, before focusing on the ostensible subject – the impact on 'Horse Boyle' of his part in the bombing of Dresden:

> As he remembered it, long afterwards, he could hear, or almost
>   hear
> Between the rapid desultory thunderclaps, a thousand tinkling
>   echoes –
> All across the map of Dresden, store-rooms full of china shivered,
>   teetered
> And collapsed, an avalanche of porcelain, slushing and cascading:
>   cherubs,
> Shepherdesses, figurines of Hope and Peace and Victory, delicate
>   bone fragments.

The bombing of a city and its people, the fragility of art in wartime, the loss of childhood securities are themes which permeate this collection and its successor. The rear-gunner's perception of Dresden as a map echoes the line 'The city is a map of the city' in an earlier poem, 'The Bomb Disposal', and points forward to the extensive use of map imagery in Carson's Belfast poems to convey the labyrinthine nature of the city and the way it changes daily to create a nightmarish atmosphere of dislocation in a familiar place. 'Turn Again' (*Belfast Confetti*) presents the Belfast that exists only in map form – the bridge that was never built, the projected streets that never existed. Another version of the city occurs in the recollections of the Falls Road Club of Adelaide, Australia ('The Exiles' Club', *The Irish For No*) who have spent years reconstructing 'the whole of the Falls Road' and are now working on details such as the Nemo Cafe menu and 'the entire contents of Paddy Lavery's pawnshop'. The severed hand image from 'Dresden' recurs ominously also, as, for example, the Red Hand of Ulster in 'Bloody Hand' (*Belfast Confetti*) and in '33333' (*The Irish For No*), where the speaker thinks 'I know this place like the back of my hand, except/My hand is cut off at the wrist.'

Carson's city is a place of code-named undercover operations, 'the lazy swivelling eye of the security camera', the murder victim identified by his teeth-marks in an apple, where your shadow might be a harmless nothing or another self, a figure following you or the haunting past. Though viewed with a sharply unsentimental eye, it is not, however, relentlessly frightening or repellent. There are healing, regenerative forces at work too, however menaced. In 'Night Out' (*Belfast Confetti*) the revels described are 'punctuated through and through by rounds of drink, of bullets, of applause', and in 'The Knee' (*Belfast Confetti*) the victim of a punishment shooting takes his son on his 'other knee', one learning to walk, the other learning to walk again, images of the future's precarious potential. Furthermore, Carson's poems about his postman father are moving homage to the dignity, wisdom and stature of the 'ordinary'. These books reflect Carson's interest in etymology and show him wittily alive to the richness of language itself. This aspect of his work is increasingly to the fore in *First Language* (1993), *Opera et Cetera* (1996) and *The Twelfth of Never* (1998), as well as in *The Alexandrine Plan* (1998), versions of sonnets by Baudelaire, Mallarme and Rimbaud. Carson's originality lies in his gift for catching the texture of city life and in the way he has extended, collection by collection, the possibilities of narrative poetry. He is a poet who revels in the minutiae of everyday life, transmuting them into something rare and wonderful.

Muldoon, Paulin and Carson have all been accused of obscurity, inaccessibility and 'an over-dependence on allusion'. Medbh McGuckian's first two collections, *The Flower Master* (1982) and *Venus and the Rain* (1984), though widely praised for their originality, have drawn similar responses. Her poems resist paraphrase in that logical argument and narrative is eschewed in favour of images and symbols. The speakers in the poems are often anonymous or unidentifiable, the pronouns sometimes used so ambiguously and the syntax so convoluted, as to dislocate the reader. Kevin Barry has attempted to define McGuckian's procedures by describing how her poems 'work like a yeast, growing within their own process of writing' and Seamus Heaney speaks of her language moving 'amphibiously between the dreamlife and her actual domestic and historical experience as a woman in late twentieth century Ireland.'

There is a sense in all of McGuckian's collections of a woman poet working within a predominantly male poetic tradition, consciously adapting and subverting it in ways that mark an independent, elusive sensibility at work. 'Mr McGregor's Garden' (*The Flower Master*), for example, is a dramatic monologue in which Beatrix Potter expresses a playful dominance over the male animals which inspire her stories, and 'The Flitting' in the same collection, dramatises movements – as the title suggests – from an almost passive

Poet Medbh McGuckian

subordination to the male world, domestically, towards a vulnerable definition of self.

Throughout these early collections there are intimations of discovery and
initiation and sometimes a longing for experience and maturity. In 'The
Flower Master' the rituals of flower-arranging become subtle emblems and
symbols that suggest preparation for lovemaking and, possibly, pregnancy:

> This black container calls for sloes, sweet
> sultan, dainty nipplewort, in honour
> of a special guest who, summoned to the
> tea ceremony, must stoop to our low doorway,
> our fontanelle, the trout's dimpled feet.

Other poems address the conflicting demands of poetry, marriage, motherhood. In 'The Sofa', for example, the speaker is aware that romance has been
replaced by something more mundane and has a sense of being dispersed and
marginalised: 'Somewhere/ A curtain rising wonders where I am, /My books
sleep, pretending to forget me'. In 'Venus and the Rain' McGuckian

establishes both a tension and a balance between the positive associations of the planet Venus with love, womanhood, fertility, and its negative aspects as a distant, uninhabited place, sometimes tantalisingly visible, sometimes mysterious and obscured, and in doing so evokes the complex nature of womanliness and of the relationship between men and women.

In subsequent collections McGuckian pursues and develops the themes and strategies of her earlier work. The relationship of a poet to his or her place and the potentially limiting aspects of womanhood are again addressed in *On Ballycastle Beach* in which contrasting images of rootedness or fixity and travel, flight or movement recur. In this collection, Osip Mandelstam – already a vital presence in the work of Seamus Heaney and Tom Paulin – is a central figure, particularly in the poem 'The Dream Language of Fergus', where McGuckian incorporates phrases from Mandelstam's critical writings into the fabric of her poem, not exactly as quotations, but in contexts which alter or add to their original meaning.

McGuckian's poetry has an increasingly international dimension. In addition to Mandelstam, Tsvetaeva and Rilke are discernible influences, particularly in *Marconi's Cottage* (1991). Here, again, the focus is predominantly on the conflicts and fulfilments of female experience, especially in relation to the demands of motherhood and poetry. More recently, in *Captain Lavender* (1994), McGuckian has written about the death of her father, though, characteristically, these poems bear little resemblance to conventional elegies. In the same collection there is a series of poems which seem to approach the politics of Northern Ireland more directly than in previous work, though even in these there are few concessions to the reader. *Shelmalier* (1998) extends this direction in her poetry. Like Paulin's *Liberty Tree* and a number of poems in Carson's *The Twelfth of Never*, it is prompted by the rebellion of 1798 and is, in the main, a set of historical elegies with a strong historical application. The gnomic, intensely private McGuckian is still in evidence but beginning, perhaps to find her way towards less oblique, more accessible forms of utterance.

This survey has focused on ten leading Northern Irish poets of the last three decades and has mentioned several others. The canvas is, of course, broader and more detailed than such a focus suggests. By my reckoning there are about fifty other poets born or living in Northern Ireland who have published book-length collections since the 1960s. An alphabetical list would include Alan Alexander, Michael Brophy, George Buchanan, Sam Burnside, Brendan Cleary, C.H. Dallat, Gerald Dawe, Seamus Deane, Andrew Elliott, James Ellis, Michael Foley, Sam Gardiner, Denis Greig, Sean Haldane, Sam Harrison, Francis Harvey, John Hughes, Fred Johnston, Robert Johnstone, James Keery, Tom Matthews, Leon McAuley, Peter McDonald, George McWhirter, Martin Mooney, Tom Morgan, Paul Murray, Pól Ó Muirí, Frank Ormsby, William Peskett, Victor Price, Damian Quinn, Adrian Rice, Damian Smyth, Shaun Traynor, Anthony Weir and Patrick Williams. Among poets of other nationalities who have lived and written here since the mid 1960s are Chris Agee (American) and Gerry Hull, Andrew Waterman and Paul Wilkins (all English).

When the present writer edited the second edition of *Poets from the North of Ireland* (1990), the only notable woman poet to have published in book form was Medbh McGuckian; ten years later there are collections in print by Jean Bleakney, Colette Bryce, Catherine Byron, Ruth Carr, Moyra Donaldson, Janice Fitzpatrick-Simmons (American), Anne-Marie Fyfe, Kerry Hardie, Tess Hurson, Eilis Martin, Ann McKay, Sinead Morrissey, Joan Newmann, Kate Newmann, Carol Rumens (English), Janet Shepperson (Scottish), Sabine Wichert (German) and Ann Zell (American). Numerous other poets, male and female, have published in pamphlet form or been represented in anthologies. Furthermore, there is an active community of poets writing in Irish, many of them included in Greagoir Ó Duill's 1986 anthology *Filíocht Uladh 1960–1985*.

The vitality of Northern Irish poetry owes much to publishers such as Blackstaff Press, founded in 1971, and more recently to Lagan Press, Lapwing Publications, Abbey Press and Summer Palace Press. A host of small magazines has provided outlets for poetry and criticism, in particular *The Honest Ulsterman*, which has appeared regularly since 1968. The development and dissemination of poetry has been further enhanced by a number of annual festivals, the most prominent being the Belfast Festival at Queen's, the Aspects festival in Bangor and the Between the Lines festival, also based in Belfast. The English Society at Queen's University and many other organisations have promoted poetry readings, as has the Arts Council of Northern Ireland's Writers in Schools initiative. The Arts Council has also funded poetry-reading tours of the province and provided financial support for publishers and bursaries for poets.

Northern Irish poets are now regularly included on examination syllabuses and literature courses at universities. Queen's University and the University of Ulster employ writers-in-residence in both English and Irish. The Poets' House, founded by James and Janice Simmons, offered – in conjunction with the University of Lancaster – the first M.A. in Creative Writing available in Northern Ireland and Queen's University introduced a similar degree course in the year 2000. Writers' groups and creative writing classes have flourished in recent years in arts centres, community centres, prisons and elsewhere and the Creative Writers' Network has come into existence as a co-ordinating body. The volume and quality of poetry has, in addition, begun to generate

Pressens Bild, Stockholm

Seamus Heaney is awarded the Nobel Prize for Literature

a corpus of poetry criticism, not only by poets such as Seamus Heaney, Tom Paulin, Seamus Deane, Gerald Dawe and Peter McDonald, but by numerous academics in Irish, British, European and American universities.

The quantity of poetry being produced is not, of course, a guarantee of quality and it has been suggested that a golden age of Northern Irish poetry may now be entering its twilight. This seems a premature judgement in the sense that many of the poets examined here – though the youngest are already in their fifties – continue to demonstrate that their creative energies are far from exhausted. It is, however, also true that no startling new planets have swum into our ken since the arrival of McGuckian in the early eighties. To say that most recent practitioners are, as yet, located in the foothills, rather than on the slopes of Parnassus, is not to deny possibility or preclude develop-ment. Whatever the future, Northern Ireland is likely to figure in literary history as a place where, at the end of the twentieth century and the begin-ning of the twenty-first, richly and nourishingly and in ways no one could have expected, poetry happened.

Fiction

EAMONN HUGHES

Fiction and Northern Ireland are alike in resisting easy definition. Definitions, or at least some questions about them, are however necessary given the potential scope of this survey. Some comparative statistics illustrate the point. John Boyd's 1951 survey of a century of Ulster prose referred to some sixty-six books by twenty-eight writers; John Cronin, covering 1950–1971, mentioned twenty-seven books by ten authors. By my count – and that of the political collection in the Linen Hall Library – the period 1971–2000 produced nearly six hundred novels by at least two hundred writers. While we will not reach a final definition of either fiction or Northern Ireland here, the questions raised by considering definition can be illuminating. The central question is, of course, what is Northern Irish fiction?

Given that political violence is the dominant subject matter of most of these novels, it is not surprising that the majority of them are thrillers or crime narratives, and that these are the dominant forms of fiction about the north. It is tempting, when confronted by instances such as Andrew Lane's just functionally literate and risibly improbable *The Ulsterman* (1979) or Jonathan Kebbe's grossly misogynistic and stereotypical *The Armalite Maiden* (1990) to take refuge in the handy phrase, 'Troubles trash' and dismiss such works out of hand, especially as they are produced by non-Northern Irish writers. However such a response would close down some important questions. On the basis that exclusion, though it would make life easier, would also make it less interesting, we cannot dismiss the phenomenon of 'Troubles trash' out of hand.

The thriller is for the most part a circular and enclosed form which represents Northern Ireland as a fated place, doomed to inevitable and enduring violence. At its best, however, the thriller can be a subtle moral and political genre dealing with questions which extend beyond glamorised treatments of political violence. It is therefore a form which has been used or adapted by a number of Northern Irish writers from Benedict Kiely in *Proxopera* (1977) through Bernard MacLaverty in *Cal* (1983), to Brian Moore in *Lies of Silence* (1990), not to mention more straightforward uses by Eugene McEldowney in, for example, *A Kind of Homecoming* (1994), and Keith Baker in *Inheritance*, 1996 and the comic thrillers of Colin Bateman. Even when not used directly its predominance makes it an influence and a context which must be taken into account. The work of younger writers, such as Deirdre Madden, Glenn Patterson and Robert McLiam Wilson, is often concerned to dismiss stereotypes and conventions about Northern Ireland established within thrillers: the satiric energies of *Eureka Street* (1996) are fuelled in part by Wilson's gleeful demolition of such conventions, while the muted quality of Madden's work stands opposed to the thriller's frequent hysteria.

The sheer quantity of fiction from recent years serves some useful purposes. Poetry is seen to be the dominant form of writing about the north and fiction is regarded, as it has always been in Irish writing generally, as the poor relation. Fiction's ability to depict an entire society may well have worked against it at a time when society was not willing to think too deeply about itself. The growing reputation of younger as well as established novelists seems to indicate that society is now more willing to listen, literally so given the growth of literary festivals and readings, which were previously the domain of poets. However, there is a danger that such quantity might also be seen to support the contention that fiction as a major form, both north and south, is a new phenomenon. Before considering the Troubles novel it is therefore useful to consider what was happening in fiction in 1971. There are a number of indicators that change was underway. St John Ervine, novelist and playwright, died in 1971. Other significant, if overlooked, careers had at this point come to an end: Anne Crone, writer of three novels including *Bridie Steen* (1949) died in 1972 and Janet McNeill's chronicles of quiet desperation among the protestant middle class had recently been completed.

There are also, however, certain markers of continuity in evidence in 1971. Sam Hanna Bell himself – convenor of the original *Arts in Ulster* symposium – is generally associated with the 1940s and 1950s and his first, and perhaps

Writer and broadcaster Sam Hanna Bell in the days when presenters dressed for the occasion

best novel, *December Bride* (1951), was written then. Its depiction of the break-down of a traditional way of life casts a long shadow, especially when we realise that as a novelist, Bell was only halfway through his career in 1971. He would publish two more novels after that date. Benedict Kiely, who in *Poor Scholar* (1947) did much to establish the reputation of one of the first Ulster novelists, William Carleton, and in *Modern Irish Fiction* (1950) wrote one of the still comparatively few studies of Irish fiction, had also moved through at least two phases of novel writing by this period. His early realist works such as *Land Without Stars* (1946) and *In A Harbour Green* (1949) had given place to more fantastical, folk tale influenced fictions such as *The Cards of the Gambler* (1953) and *Dogs Enjoy the Morning* (1968). Brian Moore was in the middle of a long career and already showing signs of following the same trajectory, from early realist work such as *Judith Hearne* (1955) to the more parable-like work starting with *Catholics* in 1972. Maurice Leitch's *The Liberty Lad* (1963) and *Poor Lazarus* (1969) had already established him as a young novelist of promise.

Such continuities not only counter the critics' sense of the discontinuity of recent fiction but also establish a framework within which to view the seemingly overwhelming force of the Troubles as they emerge at this time. It is of course the Troubles, a conflict of definitions, which force us to raise questions of definition. These questions take two forms (sometimes over-lapping): the first is a question about the importance of origin and the boundaries that we might wish to place round the 'North of Ireland', while the second has to do with what we might want to classify as fiction. Do we exclude what might be called the border writers, which could take in such figures as Eugene McCabe, Shane Connaughton and Patrick McCabe? What about writers such as Francis Stuart, born in Australia but from an Antrim family, though never resident in the north except for childhood holidays? So do we include him as a northern writer in the same way that we might include the northern-born Benedict Kiely and Patrick Boyle, though both based themselves in the south? Or do we establish a category which might include them alongside writers from the south who have taken the Troubles for their subject?

This in turn becomes a question about what stories the Northern Irish novel can and should tell. To include all six hundred or so novels of the past thirty years as Northern Irish fiction is on the one hand to be expansive and inclusive. It allows for the porosity of the borders around Northern Ireland and constructs it as an open rather than a closed place. It allows for the inclusion of writers from a variety of backgrounds within the ambit of Northern Irish fiction. This is itself salutary in revealing that recent fiction has broken with the regionalist concerns of earlier generations as expressed by Shan F. Bullock or Sam Hanna Bell.

On the other hand this inclusiveness implies that the major and perhaps only story to be told about Northern Ireland in this period is the story of the Troubles, for this is the story that has attracted the majority of these writers. We can acknowledge as an advantage of this the way in which fiction has provided multiple viewpoints on this story. It has been seen from the perspective of republicanism in work by Danny Morrison (*West Belfast* 1989) and Ronan Bennett (*The Second Prison* 1991); from that of unionism in the work of Maurice Leitch (*Silver's City* 1981), Roy Bradford (*The Last Ditch* 1981) and Andrew Lane (*The Ulsterman* 1979); from an army perspective by Alan Judd (*A Breed of Heroes* 1981) and A.F.N. Clarke (*Contact* 1983); from an RUC perspective by Blair McMahon (*Nights in Armour* 1993) and Eugene McEldowney (*A Kind of Homecoming* 1994); from the secret agent's perspective by Gerald Seymour (*Harry's Game* 1975) or Reg Gadney (*Just When We Are Safest* 1995); from a woman's viewpoint by Mary Beckett (*Give Them Stones* 1987), Mary Costello (*Titanic Town* 1992), Briege Duffaud (*A Wreath upon the Dead* 1993); from the perspective of the working class (John Morrow, *The Confessions of Proinsias O'Toole* 1977); and from that of the middle class (Benedict Kiely, *Proxopera* 1977). As the reader may have gathered this list could be continued indefinitely, but two points are worth making about it.

The first point, perhaps perversely, since I started by saying that in the face of so much fiction we needed to find ways to delimit the field, is the question of work which does not exist, of dogs that, as Sherlock Holmes once put it, didn't bark in the night. Certain perspectives are missing from the above list: both southern Irish and English perspectives – if we exclude the thriller and crime fiction – are extraordinarily rare. The northern novel of the last thirty years has continued to fit into the broader tradition of the Irish novel; the southern novel, with precious few exceptions, has long since given up any kind of territorial claim on the north. Francis Stuart, always in any case a self-proclaimed exception to every rule and, at some level a northerner by dint of his background, takes the north as subject matter in the phantasmagorical *A Hole in the Head* (1997) – in which a fictional homecoming of a kind for Emily Brontë is staged – and the only slightly less strange *Memorial* (1973). Apart from Stuart and some work by Terence de Vere White (*The Distance and the Dark* 1973), Kevin Casey (*Dreams of Revenge* 1977) and Edna O'Brien (*House of Splendid Isolation* 1994), writers from the south have confined themselves to factual or documentary works – Dervla Murphy's *A Place Apart* (1978), Colm Tóibín's *Walking the Border* (1987) and Carlo Gebler's *The Glass Curtain* (1991) though Gebler, along with Jennifer Johnston is that rarity – a southern-born writer now resident in the north. In such novels from the south as do exist, the typical narrative is of an individual for whom the north and its Troubles are less a set of distinct circumstances which have an impact on them, and more a metaphor for their own troubled psychology.

Such indifference is not the prerogative of southern writers only. Given that the Troubles have been arguably the single major political and ethical crisis within the British state over the last thirty-five years, one might have expected some gestures towards it on the part of serious British novelists, but the silence is deafening. Since it is seemingly compulsory for English poets to write Belfast poems, and poets as different as Tony Harrison and the current Poet Laureate Andrew Motion have both done so – raising in passing the question of whether or not the Poet Laureate should produce a peace process poem – the absence of Northern Ireland from the pages of serious British fiction is all the stranger. The political novel as written by Benjamin Disraeli or Anthony Trollope is now not much written. Though if Trollope, a writer of political novels who recognised that Ireland had a part to play in British politics, has contemporary heirs they would probably be thriller writers such as John Le Carré and P.D. James. Their work can be read as explorations of the institutions and political structures of the British state and yet neither have written about Northern Ireland. This situation is ironical given that Christopher Harvie's *The Centre of Things: Political Fiction in Britain from Disraeli to the Present* (1991) identifies as 'the last great English political novel' the Chester Nimmo trilogy, written by the Derry-born and occasionally Donegal-domiciled, Joyce Cary. The political novel since then has died a death, apart perhaps from Douglas Hurd's thriller *Vote to Kill* (1975).

This is not however a British failure only. The political novel has been startlingly absent from Irish fiction and Northern Irish fiction is consonant with this. There are perhaps specific reasons for such an absence. Narrowly defined political issues make their presence felt in the pages of thrillers but usually only in the closing pages when shadowy figures in shadier corridors of power institute a cover-up, as is the case in both Keith Baker's *Inheritance* and Colin Bateman's *Divorcing Jack* (1995), but there are no novels which take as their subject the political discussions and debates which have continued over the whole period of the Troubles.

Fiction has instead concentrated on the more visible and glamorous, or at least attention-grabbing, working out of those politics on the streets. In such work comment usually takes the form of an outright and rather pious rejection of violence which can actually be offensive in that the speed and force of the recoil suggests less a rejection of violence and more an expression of distaste with the north as a whole or an effort to distance oneself from culpability. Even those who might have been expected to engage with this form – whether from loyalist and unionist or republican and nationalist backgrounds – have surprisingly given up the politicisation of the conflict in favour instead of suggesting the necessity, even inevitability of violence. Political figures then are rarely, if ever, centre stage in the pages of northern fiction, though this may be more to do with the poor material that they offer to novelists than with the failure of fiction. If fiction depends on uncertainty and dialogue, our politicians, representing certainty and monologue, are fiction's antithesis.

Regardless of the multiplicity of points of view represented in the list above, the story remains the same. A violently divided society, doomed to its fate with, more often than not, a pair of individuals whose love transcends the division, but ends in inevitable tragedy. The Troubles then loom large as a story and writers have been enjoined to engage with it. That many, if not most, of the novels which have done so come under the heading of 'Troubles trash', and can therefore be said to be exploitative rather than engaged, requires us to consider other possibilities. I would suggest that the difference between engagement and exploitation – a difference that admittedly depends on the perspective of the accuser – can very often be seen to depend on whether or not the writer sees the Troubles as the whole or only story of Northern Ireland. Writers who do not see the Troubles in this way are often accused of evasion.

If this is the case are the many writers who have chosen locations outside the north of the present moment – Brian Moore, Ian Cochrane, Glenn Patterson, Robert McLiam Wilson, Ronan Bennett, Carlo Gebler and others – who do not take the 'Troubles as subject', then to be called simply evasive? One possibility is that we need not take such works literally; we may need to consider the possibility of analogy. So various locations and times used by northern writers may be analogies for Northern Ireland. But there is a danger here.

The Troubles have not unnaturally dominated our thinking, but this may have been to an excessive degree. In consequence a self-consciousness, even narcissism has affected us: wherever we look we see ourselves. In literary terms this has led to analogy hunting, the tendency to see everything as a version of or metaphor for the Troubles. Though often justifiable, this view should not function to exclude all other possibilities. As the Troubles recede – and part of the point of this survey is, one hopes, to exercise hindsight – novels which have concentrated exclusively on the Troubles will become historical curios. Novels which have been read as being about the Troubles may be freed for other readings. Stories about ill-matched lovers, in other words need not be read within the familiar love-across-the-barricades paradigm. Perhaps such novels are actually just doing what novels have always done, exploring relationships and how they are affected by matters of class, gender, sexuality, politics and/or religious beliefs. After all, relationships and the impact of such factors on them, have long been important fictional topics.

Equally novels about other places do not necessarily have to be related back to the Troubles. Perhaps their authors were more concerned with how other societies conducted themselves than with finding analogues which confirm our own sense of ourselves. Maybe Brian Moore was trying to write about the intersection of politics and religion in say, *The Colour of Blood* or *The Statement* because, as for Graham Greene and Robert Stone, it is an interesting subject, rather than because it happens to be a subject of particular relevance to Northern Ireland. The same might be said about Ronan

Bennett's novels about central America and Africa. Given the degree of introspection in this society, amounting to a self-absorbed disregard for other places and issues, one solution might well be to give up a claim to such novels, and indeed to extend that abstinence. Instead of claiming that 'Troubles trash', regardless of the origins of its writers, is northern writing, we might reverse our analogical logic and point out that it is the north which is being used analogically in such writing: thriller writers are not interested in the north except insofar as it provides a plausible locale for the enduring battle of good and evil which is their real subject. Definition of what makes a novel northern then is not merely an academic question: how many writers can dance on a mere six counties? The issue of definition leads to those questions of socio-political psychology – how do we see ourselves? – that are at the heart of the novel.

In other words the tendency to read all novels as being about the Troubles may actually already be, and should in the future prove to be even more, reductive. The importance of this point is that it may in fact help to put the Troubles in their place. Political violence is difficult to avoid and one responsibility of the writer is to enable us to think about it. However, it is the journalist's role to help us to think within the immediate context – and too many commentators would enforce this role on novelists in the name of engagement. The novelist, like Louis MacNeice's poet, should be concerned with news that will stay news. Looking back at work from the 1950s and 1960s, even work which now seems rather dated because it is too caught up in its moment, we can see signs in novels by McNeill, Kiely, Moore, Bell and Leitch of the need for change. Despite society seeming comfortably stable for many, the permafrost that had held Northern Ireland in stasis for so long had to thaw. These novels reflect both the need for and anxiety about change. Regret about what might be lost in urbanisation, increased physical and social mobility, and modernity more generally marks many of them but the best still see change as necessary. The typical narrative of 1960s Northern Irish fiction was of an individual being crushed by the stultifying pressure of a monolithic society or resisting it at all costs. In itself this precludes looking back nostalgically to some supposed pre-Troubles idyll. The best work of more recent years has avoided turning the Troubles into a similarly crushing monolith. Novels from the 1970s, 1980s and 1990s – at least the best of them

– are the same in being able to see that wishing for some apparently idyllic moment before the Troubles is a lost cause. Instead there is a need to locate the Troubles as one strand in a more complex set of stories. Hence the necessity of realising that there are other stories to be told about Northern Ireland.

This keeps us in the area of definition for a while yet, as one of the most central of these other stories is that of leave-taking. Most writers whom we might wish to claim as Northern Irish have left Northern Ireland both biographically and fictionally. While many have also returned – more often fictionally than biographically – we can see this as another instance of continuity, a way in which, even though sometimes enforced in one way or another by the Troubles, such leave-takings fit into the older and broader traditions of movement and migration. It is worth emphasising such a theme for the way in which in the face of the stasis so often found in Troubles-oriented writing it suggests that some forms of mobility are possible. Insofar as leave-taking is about movement it can be seen as the first step, both literally and figuratively, to the other themes that I would wish to highlight. Movement is in the first instance often away from the country and to the city, and the rise of the urban novel is one of the most significant phenomena of recent years. In turn this movement to the city is part of the even broader narrative of the opposition of tradition and modernity which underscores much writing, an opposition made all the more pointed by the increasing influence of globalisation which allows so many writers to use locations other than Northern Ireland. With these themes in mind we can finally turn to consider some individual writers.

As already noted, so firmly is Sam Hanna Bell related to the 1940s and 1950s that it comes as a surprise to find that half of his career as a novelist falls within the period under review. The necessary breakdown of tradition found in *December Bride* leads him to an urban setting for both *The Hollow Ball* (1961) and *A Man Flourishing* (1973) so that in Bell's work we find the sense of movement, urbanisation and the opposition of tradition and modernity. In *A Man Flourishing*, which deals with the consequences of the failure of the United Irishmen's rebellion in 1798, Bell remains clear-sighted about the sinister aspects of the city but arrival in Belfast is no longer simply a matter of trauma and loss as it had been for the generation of, say, Michael McLaverty, in which Belfast was seen as a hellish alternative to the Edenic lost fields. Bell then, in line with his pioneering work in so many fields, can be seen as the forerunner of one of the more significant movements in the period. His sense that even the alienation of urban life may be beneficial in marking a new form of society continues an interest in social (even socialist) history. His final novel *Across the Narrow Sea* (1987) loops back to the origins of present day Northern Ireland in a tale of the early seventeenth century which brings us back to the origins of the Echlin family in Ravara. The historical setting of both novels can be seen as a return to a moment of possibility rather than an acceptance of inevitable outcomes. In these novels then, Bell is to be seen not as a hangover from a previous generation, but rather as someone setting out the co-ordinates within which much northern fiction will function as writers come to grips with the fact of the urban as a specific aspect of northern experience.

Bell's work, with its moral seriousness and commitment to history from below, may seem to be a world away from that of John Morrow, but they share a commitment to the urban working class which enables Morrow to produce a voice which has not been heard often enough in fiction over the period: scabrous, witty, in gleefully deliberate bad taste and utterly at home in the bars, bookies' shops and backstreets of Belfast. Morrow's is a voice against piety which can be heard in the pubs and streets but which has been strangely absent from fiction, an absence which suggests that all too often a self-censorship in the name of piety has affected writers, leading to a number of novels which convey the discomfort and even despair of the novelist without ever transforming it into anything more. Such novels express only that pious condemnation which is the preserve of the politician and journalist, and never therefore offer what fiction is ideally suited to offer, which is a sense of the social and political complexities of the situation. That Morrow, whether in the short stories of *Northern Myths and Other Stories* (1979) or the novels *The Confessions of Proinsias O'Toole* (1979) and *The Essex Factor* (1982), is able to deal with political violence in Northern Ireland as an almost farcical state of affairs could be given a Marxist spin – the Troubles are history re-peated as farce.

More importantly, Morrow's humour shows that he was fulfilling one of the novelist's most important functions and listening to his society: that such joking reactions were common even in the darkest days of the 1970s is something that might now be forgotten if we were to attend to the over-whelmingly pious tones of public commentators and too much fiction. Morrow's work therefore has an importance; it is also wildly funny. Given the sexual innuendo-laden quality of much of Morrow's fiction it might seem odd to place him beside another overlooked writer who is remembered, if at all, as a feminist voice. There is, however, in terms of tone of voice and the confident construction of a linguistic universe which owes much to actual speech without simply being a direct copy, common ground between Morrow and Frances Molloy. *No Mate for the Magpie* (1985) is a one-off novel – though followed some years later by a collection of short stories, *Women are the Scourge of the Earth* (1998) – from a writer who died very much prematurely in 1991. Its story of Ann McGlone's odyssey from Derry to Dublin and beyond is told in a fully formed and richly dialectal voice of the kind which would later be found in Patrick McCabe's *The Butcher Boy* or, ranging further afield, Irvine Welsh's *Trainspotting*. While considering voices against piety, Michael Foley's *The Passion of Jamesie Coyle* (1978) is worth mentioning for its imagination of Christ's second coming in Derry. His more recent *The Road to Notown* (1996) is a roman-à-clef which, among other things, remembers late 1960s literary life and satirises its tendency to see individual freedom as a matter of male sexual liberation.

These writers are worth mentioning because of the temptation in surveys of this kind to notice only those whose work has made a continuing impres-sion over much, if not all, of the period. But any survey which ignored these writings would itself be the poorer, as would northern fiction. Not the least reason for this is these writers' common interest in working-class life and their sense that history can profitably be seen from below. The only other writers of the period whose work evinces this same sense are some of those memoirists and autobiographers whom we will consider later.

As against the now rather dated attitudes to sex and sexuality of the 1960s satirised by Foley, the novelists Benedict Kiely and Brian Moore have both explored catholicism in terms of sexual and other repressions and share the theme of loss and dispossession which leads to an interest in the relationship of the individual to communal and traditional structures. Both have produced work in which sexual liberation figures as an emblem of rebellion against puritanical Irish attitudes. Kiely represents an earlier, largely catholic,

Brian Moore

generation for whom Dublin, rather than Belfast, London or elsewhere, was the magnet. His work has moved from an early realism into a more expansive style in which fantasy and elements of traditional storytelling are used, most recently in anecdotal, digressive and somewhat folksy memoirs. Where Kiely's work turns nostalgically inward, Moore's work becomes increasingly internationalist whether as a way of dealing with exile from Northern Ireland, contextualising it in the modern world, or finding interests beyond it.

There can be little doubt that Moore, who died in January 1999, is deservedly the best-known and most important novelist from Northern Ireland over the last fifty years. By the start of our survey he had already left the north, as both setting and subject matter, behind. Moore's work and career may be taken as in many ways paradigmatic of the northern writer. Where

Maurice Leitch

Bell's fiction starts in a rural townland and moves to Belfast, Moore, starting from the urban with the justly acclaimed *Judith Hearne*, in which the stultifying atmosphere of 1950s Belfast was mercilessly delineated in a tersely realist style, moved through various Belfast lives in *The Feast of Lupercal* (1958) and *The Emperor of Ice-Cream* (1965) before moving to North America – *The Luck of Ginger Coffey* (1960), *An Answer from Limbo* (1963), or *I Am Mary Dunne* (1968) – and beyond. While precise and detailed observation supplies the basic texture of his work, Moore could play explicitly with the constraints of realism as in *Fergus* (1970), *Catholics* (1972), *The Great Victorian Collection* (1975) and *Cold Heaven* (1983) as part of his exploration of the issue of faith in a faithless world, his work's unifying theme. This work is influenced by such American contemporaries as Thomas Pynchon in its pursuit of meaning amidst meaninglessness. It also reveals that both in these novels and even in his earlier work, he is constantly testing the limits of realism and allowing for the possibility of something immeasurable lying just beyond the realist world of sense and substance. The last phase of his career situates questions of faith in

Bernard MacLaverty

political contexts in novels such as *The Colour of Blood* (1987), *No Other Life* (1993), *The Statement* (1995) and even his disappointing return to a Northern Irish setting, *Lies of Silence* (1990). True to unpredictable form, however, his last work – *The Magician's Wife* (1997) – was, like *Black Robe* (1985), an historical novel. The international range of his writing was matched by a deservedly international reputation based on both popular and critical acclaim.

Maurice Leitch – a protestant counterpart to Brian Moore? – details, in novels of great variety of style and setting, the experiences of Northern Irish protestant life. His early novels set in south Antrim are naturalist in their sense of the determinism of setting and environment; his Northern Ireland is a dark world of frequently sexualised violence (see *The Liberty Lad* [1963]; *Poor Lazarus*, [1969]; *Stamping Ground* [1975]). However, he has been breaking away from this ever since in the now familiar pattern of movement from the country to the city and beyond. *Silver's City* (1981), in some ways a Troubles novel, retains the sense of the sinister and corrupt aspects of life in Northern Ireland while also being a study of a character, Silver Steele, who is trying to break free of the social, ideological and emotional constraints of his background; it establishes a preoccupation with gangsterism which continues into *The Eggman's Apprentice* (2001). *Burning Bridges* (1989) follows Leitch's own move to England in the story of Sonny and Hazel on their pilgrimage through a deracinated England of an ersatz tourist-oriented culture. *Gilchrist* (1994) takes this further both geographically in its mostly Spanish setting, and by moving into the realm of psychology more fully and presenting a narrative which might or might not be explained by the existence of a dop-pelgänger for the central character, a corrupt evangelist whose alleged certainties are therefore undercut. *The Smoke King* (1998) returns to issues of rural Northern Irish identity and bigotry but by doing so through the presence of black American GIs during World War Two it once again shows Leitch taking an oblique approach to familiar subjects.

Bernard MacLaverty is unusual in being one of the few writers under discussion still to write extensively in the short story form. Only Benedict Kiely has written as much in this once dominant form. The most recent of MacLaverty's four collections, *Walking the Dog* (1994) interleaves more conventional stories with wittily meta-fictional and epigrammatic short stories featuring 'Your Man' as their central figure. Its title story is an exemplary Troubles tale. 'Walking the Dog' concerns a man kidnapped and quizzed in the usual catechetical manner by terrorists. His refusal to play the game saves him and, released by the terrorists, he begins to reflect on this cataclysmic eruption of near violence into his life before realising that the whole episode has taken ten minutes – about as long as it takes to read the story. The story's wit lies in its absolute intense concentration on a facet of the Troubles being juxtaposed to the deliberately anti-climatic revelation of just how small scale it is. MacLaverty has then moved from the rather earnest quality of *Cal* (1983), an early and famous version of the love-across-the-barricades story, though in the light of his other work *Cal* begins to seem to be concerned primarily with relationships. MacLaverty's triumph to date is his most recent novel *Grace Notes* (1997). Where *Cal* fails in subordinating the lives of its characters to the Troubles, *Grace Notes* succeeds in allowing its central character,

Catherine McKenna, to establish her own identity as both woman and composer from all of the components – family, education, travel, motherhood and the Troubles – which make up her existence. Her triumph, a performance of her orchestral work 'Vernicle', is itself then emblematic in that it uses the Lambeg drums which as a child she had learnt to see as symbols of oppression and sectarianism. She has therefore confronted the ascribed meanings of such elements in her past life, subordinated them to her own purposes and made use of them as one element in her own work, just as MacLaverty has done within the pages of the novel by allowing the reader to enter the fully-formed world of this character.

MacLaverty's depiction of a female central character, like Bell and Moore before him, prompts a turn to women's writing which deserves special mention not because it requires the shelter of its own section but because it has been another phenomenon of the past thirty years which was not previously noticeable – or at least noticed. In the previous two surveys in 1951 and 1971, although a number of women writers were mentioned, only Helen Waddell, Anne Crone and Janet McNeill were discussed therein. Therefore some mention must be made of Mary Beckett and Briege Duffaud here. Beckett, like Evelyn Conlon, Anne Devlin, Frances Molloy and indeed Duffaud, has gone some way to suggesting that the short story in Northern Ireland in recent years has been largely a female form.

Beckett's novel *Give Them Stones* (1987) registers the impact of the Troubles on a deliberately domestic scale. The central character, Martha Murtagh, frequently expresses her grievances and sense of alienation in terms of a nationalist rhetoric but they are even more frequently connected to her status as a woman. Like Beckett's other female characters, Martha's struggle for an independent identity within the family setting over sixty years, though often in parallel with the broader struggle about identity during that period, is also a critique of the shortcomings of that broader struggle in regard to women's identity. Duffaud's major work to date, *A Wreath Upon the Dead* (1993), is very different from Beckett's work. Where Beckett tends to rely on a single narrative voice of limited articulacy, her characters frequently being working-class and ill-educated, Duffaud's novel is told in a variety of voices, styles and forms including conventional narrative, stream of consciousness, journals, letters and pastiches of nineteenth century documents. Its central

Novelist and playwright Jennifer Johnston

character, Maureen Murphy, having escaped her Northern Irish background in Claghan, sets out to write a romance novel, a bodice-ripper, which will be a historical version of love-across-the-barricades. The novel is to be based on a local folk tale about a Robin Hood figure who elopes with the landlord's beautiful daughter but her researches uncover a messier, more ambiguous and ultimately unromantic story. Powerfully anti-nostalgic, the novel, despite its circular structure, works against the idea of the inevitability of history; the working out of history and its repetitions are to be seen more as contingent than necessary.

Jennifer Johnston, though originally from Dublin, must now be considered as the leading northern novelist, though too often and too glibly dismissed for what has been seen as her early novels' smallness of scale and use of conventional structures. Such remarks tend to forget that women writers in Northern Ireland, as elsewhere, have used the domestic as both a microcosm of society and as a challenge to the sense that the public sphere is automatically more important than the private. Those early works such as *The Gates* (1973) and *How Many Miles to Babylon?* (1974) dealt subtly with often destructive friendships across barriers of religion, class, gender and age. More recent novels have turned to female protagonists and more contemporary settings as in *The Illusionist* (1995) in which Stella, freed from an unhappy marriage by the accidental death of her sinister and controlling husband Martyn in an IRA car bomb, is turning herself into a writer, a theme continued in *The Gingerbread Woman* (2000).

One might say that Johnston's work is like Beckett's in detailing the struggle for independence of women, albeit in a different social class, but this is not to disparage either writer. Their shared critique of the traditional family as necessarily dysfunctional and imprisoning of women, hence Johnston's concern with unconventional relationships as an alternative, speaks directly to imperative contemporary social issues. The urgency of Johnston's voice, as represented in her economical style, is very much bound up with her consistent dwelling on the necessity of finding forms of satisfying individuality which can break with the deadening conformities of society.

The first of Deirdre Madden's five novels – *Hidden Symptoms* (1986) – is a Troubles novel but one which is, despite certain flaws to do with the nature of its rather self-obsessed characters, interesting in that it does not simply set the Troubles in front of the reader as a set of inexplicable events separate from, but impinging on, its characters' lives. Instead, and in this it is rare, it allows for the culpability not simply of a few but of society as a whole. In later novels such as *One by One in the Darkness* (1996) she is interested in the Troubles as simply one aspect of the socio-cultural context within which her characters move. This is a tale of three sisters who between them represent different attitudes to the idea of home: Sally has stayed in their homeplace on the northern shore of Lough Neagh, while the others have moved out, Helen as a solicitor to Belfast, and Kate – or Cate, as she re-names herself – as a fashion journalist to London. The novel covers a week in which Cate has returned home to announce her pregnancy, which is both a shock to the family and a kind of recompense for the death of their father who was murdered in mistake for his brother Brian. The novel is concerned with the nature of home and the ways in which home both changes and abides in response to various factors, among them the beginnings of the Troubles.

Eoin McNamee's early fiction in the form of two novellas *The Last of Deeds* (1989) and *Love in History* (1992) has been overshadowed by *Resurrection Man* (1994). Controversially based on the Shankill Butchers, the novel is an attempt to find a language appropriate to the horrors of sectarian butchery. It has been accused of aestheticising violence, though this is not a judgement with which I would agree. Even here though, or perhaps especially here, we might want to note that the Troubles are not all-consuming in accounting for the themes and power of the novel. Its depiction of the psychopathology of Victor Kelly can be read as an account of a particular form of masculinity, an extreme example of that form of masculinity which has long been valorised within Irish society both north and south and therefore one which might be said to have specifically Irish bearings. The novel can also be read in the light of international fictional concern with the figure of the serial killer, a modern day instance of the bogeyman and/or scapegoat figure onto whom societies in the West have recently projected many of their fears and ethical quandaries.

It would be difficult to find work more different from this novel than Colin Bateman's comedy thrillers, except that here again is a northern writer influenced by international trends. Bateman's work, starting with *Divorcing Jack* (1995), may take its lead from John Morrow in its blackly farcical version of Northern Ireland, but the influence of writers such as Carl Hiassen is also evident. Often featuring Dan Starkey, a drunken and rather shambolic journalist as their hero, Bateman's novels are accessible to a non-Northern Irish audience in terms of both their linguistic texture and their sense that the facts of Northern Irish life will always be stranger than any fiction.

Although Ronan Bennett has been vociferous as a critic in his call for engagement on the part of the northern writer, of his three novels – *The Second Prison* (1991), *Overthrown by Strangers* (1992) and *The Catastrophist* (1998) – only the first has been set in Northern Ireland and then only partially and in flashback. *The Second Prison* is concerned with Northern Ireland as set of determinants which exist outside the literal prison in which we find Augustine Kane. The novel charts Kane's efforts to free himself from both the physical prison and this broader socio-political prison. A powerful first

Jill Jennings, Christopher Hill Photographic

Novelist Glenn Patterson

part in which tightly intermeshed flashbacks reveal Kane's story gives way to a much weaker second half in which an English policeman, Henry Tempest is revealed as the balefully controlling force in Kane's life. As his name suggests Tempest has all of the power and mystery of a force of nature and the improbable account of his influence on Kane's life implies that the problems of the north are explicable only in such terms. Far from engagement, this seems to evade the facts of Northern life in favour of an overly neat explanation.

Glenn Patterson and Robert MacLiam Wilson are very much urban novelists for whom the Troubles are, again, only one part of the backdrop. Patterson has written about Belfast in 1969 in *Burning Your Own* (1988) while *Fat Lad* (1992) traces the return to Belfast of Drew Linden and gives an account of his family history. Patterson's concern with the urban features strongly in his novel about EuroDisney as a fantastical European city in *Black Night at Big Thunder Mountain* (1995). After the invective directed against Belfast in his first novel, *Ripley Bogle* (1989), in which it is clear that the central figure prefers the privations of homelessness and poverty in London to his native city, Wilson's *Eureka Street* (1996) sets the bomb-blasted Belfast of stereotype – which he brilliantly describes in one chapter – against a more luminous version of it as a paradisal place in a novel of a Dickensian scope and richness.

The Belfast that Wilson and Patterson represent, then, is not the provincial city of a Brian Moore in which snobbish professional middle-class catholicism turns its back on the protestant mercantile origins of the city, nor is it

Seamus Deane

the dowdily vicious city of a Maurice Leitch. Instead, Belfast in their work is a place of contemporary urban experience. The novel of Belfast, so significant in recent years, has been much influenced by the work of Ciaran Carson, primarily a poet, but one who has for long included prose pieces in his collections and who in recent years has also turned increasingly to prose writing in uncategorisable works such as *Fishing for Amber* (1999), *Shamrock Tea* (2001) and *The Star Factory* (1997) which is in part a memoir and in part an urban narrative labyrinth. His treatment of Belfast as both the place of the Troubles and as an archetypal city – shape-shifting, restless, alienating – in a celebratory writing whose improvisatory and digressive style is a formal analogue of urban life is thus linked to the memoir, itself another important phenomenon of Northern Irish writing of recent years.

A work such as Seamus Deane's beautifully written and engrossing *Reading in the Dark* (1996) is playfully and knowledgeably concerned with the relationship of fiction and autobiography, not least because of the influence of James Joyce. Insofar as *Reading in the Dark* is memoir it functions, like say John Boyd's marvellous *Out of My Class* (1985), to provide a continuity between the period before the Troubles and the conflict itself, disallowing a too easy sense of the Troubles as catastrophic shift in society. Where the Troubles thriller centres, wittingly or not, on questions of socio-political definition, memoir and autobiography can be seen as a form of writing which explores how such questions are addressed at the personal level, the level of individual identity.

The variety of individual narratives and perspectives provided by autobiography includes areas overlooked by fiction. The absence of the political novel is balanced by the range of political memoirs. From Bernadette Devlin's *The Price of my Soul* (1969) and Terence O'Neill's *Autobiography* (1972) through to Paddy Devlin's *Straight Left* (1993) and Gerry Adams's *Before the Dawn* (1996), politics is well served by autobiographers, especially if we were to include the work of civil servants such as Patrick Shea (*Voices and the Sound of Drums* [1981]) and Maurice Hayes (*Sweet Killough, Let Go Your Anchor* [1994]; *Minority Verdict: Experiences of a Catholic Public Servant* [1995]; *Black Puddings with Slim: A Downpatrick Boyhood* [1996]) in our reckoning. While there are writers who take pains to produce narratives in which they are to be seen as typical or representative figures – Eamonn McCann's *War and an Irish Town* (rev. ed. 1980) and Mary Costello's *Titanic Town* (1992) for example – the real value of this form of writing lies in the exceptional nature of many of these narratives. So Denis Donoghue's *Warrenpoint* (1991) tells of how he became, improbable though it may seem from such a starting point, an internationally renowned literary critic. Even odder is Max Wright's account of an upbringing among the 'peculiar people', the Plymouth Brethren, in the witty and disciplined *Told in Gath* (1990). What all such narratives reveal is the need not just to remain within the safe and predictable confines of a communal identity, but also to find an identity for oneself as an individual.

This can, I think, be linked to something that becomes evident the closer we come to the contemporary moment. Chance and coincidence, far from being flaws in fiction, are actually being used as a way of countering a previous reliance on fate and inevitability. The origins of fiction are conventionally seen to lie in the emergence of the bourgeoisie, an instance of social mobility which leads to political turmoil. Conservative fictional forms, such as the thriller, are often narratives which try to stabilise society in the wake of some kind of turmoil, narratives that is to say which cannot, on the surface, allow for chance and the random. In the face of the political violence of the north such novels respond by turning to fatedness and inevitability as explanatory patterns preferable to the idea of instability.

Many writers in the north now, however, proffer instability and randomness as precisely the characteristics of a society such as the north. Jennifer Johnston's use of an IRA car bomb to dispatch Martyn in *The Illusionist* may seem too coincidental to be true but it offers an instance of the operations of chance. The arbitrary gathering of guests in a hotel in Patterson's *The International* (1999) and the random intersecting of narratives in *Eureka Street* are two further powerful instances of this. Even Deirdre Madden's apparently more conservative *One by One in the Darkness* – more conservative because still rooted strongly in family – shows the diverging and individualised paths away from tragedy in one family. This intersection of the individual and the contingent suggests that society, even in the north with its deadeningly familiar communal identities and apparently inevitable and equally familiar conflicts, and the fictions in which it is represented can be beneficially unfamiliar. Fiction, like society, is a place where we meet strangers.

The Visual Arts

MARTYN ANGLESEA

During the last thirty years progress in the visual arts in Northern Ireland, and in Ireland as a whole, has been phenomenal. This includes both the creative side of art and the descriptive or historical side, which has blossomed into an industry. The period practically coincides with my own residence in Belfast, but I claim no credit for it. I accepted a research assistant's post in the Ulster Museum in November 1971 and took it up in January 1972. Two weeks after my arrival occurred Bloody Sunday in Derry, and six months later, in July, I remember watching from the gallery at the top of the Museum twenty-two palls of smoke rising all over the city on Bloody Friday. The first exhibition I saw in the Ulster Museum, *Concrete Poetry* (December 1971–January 1972), included work by such artists as Ian Hamilton Finlay. There was a local section at the end in which the most memorable object was an enormous inflated plastic tomato, created, I believe, by John Gilbert and Marcus Patton, both then architectural students in Queen's. But the most telling item was a plain white screen on which members of the public were invited to write their own concrete poetry with felt pens. In a short time it was covered with offensive sectarian graffiti and had to be removed. Such was the atmosphere of the time.

The Keeper of Art in the Ulster Museum, James Ford Smith, had shortly before become incurably blind because of diabetic retinitis. He had, in August 1971, publicised the museum's distinguished contemporary art collection in a supplement to the *Burlington Magazine*. In the previous year, 1970, there was a Belfast showing of the exhibition *Irish Portraits 1660–1860*, a landmark of Irish art history, organised by Anne Crookshank and the Knight of Glin. During Anne Crookshank's period as Keeper of Art in Belfast (1958–66) she instigated the policy of collecting international contemporary art, to the consternation of her own predecessor, John Hewitt, who believed in supporting local artists. Anne Crookshank culminated her career by setting up the History of Art Department in Trinity College, Dublin, and training a new generation of researchers in Irish art.

Re-evaluation of earlier Ulster-born artists, particularly Sir John Lavery (1856–1941) has been undertaken largely through the efforts of a Belfast-born art-historian, Kenneth McConkey, trained at Hornsey College of Art and the Courtauld Institute, who has taught for many years in Newcastle-upon-Tyne. McConkey did the research for the *Sir John Lavery* exhibition in 1984, and subsequently has organised many travelling exhibitions of Francophile painters of the late nineteenth century. These painters are now salvaged from unfashionable obscurity. It is instructive to recall that in 1949 the Lady Mabel Annesley, a prolific wood-engraver, wrote to her granddaughter: 'The Laverys certainly are AWFUL – and a whole roomful too!' In the last two decades the Ulster Museum has mounted important retrospectives of established Ulster artists – *William Scott* (1975 and 1986), *F.E. McWilliam* (1978 and 1981), *Cherith McKinstry* (1980), *Colin Middleton* (1985), *T.P. Flanagan* (1996) and *David Crone* (2000). John Kindness's *Belfast Frescoes* were bought by the museum in 1996.

Reflection of Ulster's political disorders in the visual arts has been surprisingly sparse. Many artists went on painting Donegal and Antrim landscapes

Artist T.P. Flanagan

as if there were no Troubles at all. However, Enniskillen-born T.P. Flanagan has touched on the Troubles. In the late 1960s Flanagan (who is also a poet) worked closely with Seamus Heaney on a series of sombre landscapes in north Donegal, patricularly near Gortahork where he painted some almost monochrome high-horizon landscapes which parallel Heaney's poems about the rich content of bogs and their preservative properties. Stress is placed on the sinister pagan practice of throwing the bodies of sacrificed victims into bogs. In 1974 Flanagan responded to the terrorist murder of his friend, a lawyer, Martin McBirney, with his painting *The Victim*. This is a life-size prone figure, shrouded in white, based on Poussin's figure of the dead Narcissus in *Echo and Narcissus*, in the Louvre. When Flanagan saw McBirney's body carried away on a stretcher, one bare foot was protruding from under the blanket, which immediately recalled Poussin. Thus Flanagan's *Victim* is ennobled as a symbol of all such people who have suffered in conflict.

Jack Pakenham, head of English in a Belfast school, and self-taught as a painter, was in the early 1970s one of the first artists to react to the Northern Ireland Troubles. In his personal way, Pakenham expresses horror of all para-military forces, often using a red-haired ventriloquist's dummy as symbol of the universal victim. Similarly, Joseph McWilliams has, since his student days,

Ulster Circus by Jack Pakenham (1986)

Jack Pakenham

reflected the current disturbances in a political, but not propagandist way. Sometimes his work can be highly comic, such as his series of *Peeing Orangemen*. F.E. McWilliam, born in Banbridge in 1909 and who died in London in 1992, created between 1972 and 1974, a long series of bronze sculptures called *Women of Belfast*, depicting women caught up in bomb-blasts.

Artists from outside Northern Ireland have occasionally paid visits resulting in impressive work. Ken Howard R.A. came here as an official War Artist with the British Army in the mid 1970s. In 1978 he expressed his experiences in a triptych with predella, *Ulster Crucifixion*, inspired by a west Belfast image of a small boy climbing up a lamp-post in a devastated street, and hanging from the crossbar as if crucified. Howard paid the boy to go up again while he took photographs. The altarpiece-like triptych was purchased by the Ulster Museum with the aid of a grant from the National Art Collections Fund in 1995. The English painter John Keane, who has a fascination for trouble-spots throughout the world, came to Belfast in 1989 and painted *The Other Cheek?* – a large combination of oil and mixed media, which the

Nuptial Grooming by Rita Duffy (1994)

museum purchased in 1998 from a Keane retrospective held that year.

A Californian photographer, Ed Kashi, first visited Northern Ireland in November 1988 as a journalist from the *San Francisco Examiner*. Between then and 1991 he paid five more visits which totalled over six months in the province, examining sympathetically and in detail the life and feelings of the protestant/loyalist communities, both urban and rural, whose confidence he managed to win despite initial suspicion. Rita Duffy is an artist with a wry sense of humour, always with a topical feminist cutting edge, such as in her *Metamorphosis* series of 1999, which makes a sewing machine turn into a revolver, and vice versa. She has also painted many autobiographical pictures featuring herself, her husband and children.

Victor Sloan, who lives in Portadown, is now one of Ireland's major artists. He has evolved a unique, original style incorporating elements of drawing and photography. Much of Sloan's subject matter is taken from the imagery of the Orange Order. The photographer Paul Seawright has used the trappings of Orangeism to produce unexpectedly exquisite cibacrome prints, from the standpoint and height of a small child, which is how he remembers them. Micky Donnelly, a graduate of Queen's University and of the Ulster College of Art and Design, concentrates on tribal symbols and their historical background. A fluent writer, he has published many thought-provoking articles, for instance in *Circa* magazine, and while Seawright is now living in Wales where he teaches, Donnelly lives and works in Dublin. The subject of tribal or sectarian symbolism is taken to surrealistic effect in terms of landscape by Dermot Seymour and the twin brothers, Diarmuid and Fergus Delargy. David Crone, a major painter by any standards, who has had to wait too long for full recognition, takes a gentler approach. Crone's impasted canvases never lose their representational qualities. He has taught for many years in the Belfast College of Art, and his street scenes with figures evoke the tense atmosphere of the time when there were pedestrian barriers and checkpoints in the city centre. Noel Murphy, born in London in 1970, studied at the University of Ulster in Belfast and the National College of Art and Design in Dublin. His soft-focus paintings are traditionalist and realist with a literary slant. He quotes from earlier art, and often sites esoteric subjects such as alchemy, astronomy and the mystical pursuits of his hero, W.B. Yeats.

The relationship between the Ulster Museum and the Royal Ulster Academy has fluctuated at times. What had once been the Belfast Art Society – one of the main agitating groups for a public art gallery in Belfast – changed its name in 1930 to the Ulster Academy of Arts, and obtained the Royal prefix in 1950. In 1958 Anne Crookshank, critical of the standard of work, antagonised many people by drastically pruning the RUA's annual exhibition to only thirty-seven items. William Conor, perhaps Ulster's most popular painter, served as President from 1957 to 1964, and his death in 1968 marked the end of an era. By 1970 the Academy had become moribund, its quality at its nadir. Certainly, no avant-garde art students would have wanted anything to do with it. The Academy might have faded had it not been for the lonely efforts of Patric Stevenson, President from 1970 to 1976. He stabilised its finances and preserved its records.

After the brief Presidency of Mercy Hunter, 1976–7, T.P. Flanagan took over as President, and standards gradually began to improve. In 1981, to mark its centenary, the Academy commissioned me to write its official history, which I found a more fascinating task than I had anticipated. As well as with T.P. Flanagan and the now elderly Patric Stevenson, I worked closely with painters like Raymond Piper, Lawson Burch and Neil Shawcross, who were making considerable efforts to attract younger, more exciting artists to contribute. Shawcross's position as a teacher at the Art College was advantageous in enabling him to persuade students to submit work. Later, Joseph McWilliams and Bob Sloan, the sculptor, were to do the same.

During the Presidency (1983–93) of David Evans, the Academy for some years did not hold its exhibitions in the Museum. Through Evans's offices as lecturer in architecture in Queen's University, the Academy was enabled to use the two-storey space of the new School of Architecture in Chlorine Gardens. There grew a tradition at the School of Architecture of serving Guinness and oysters at the openings, a practice which has since sadly been discontinued. The caricaturist and artist Rowel Friers assumed the Presidency in 1993, and the Academy returned to the Ulster Museum. The efforts of Harry Reid as Honorary Secretary have led to the annual exhibition –

The Barn (Blue II) by Basil Blackshaw (1991–2)

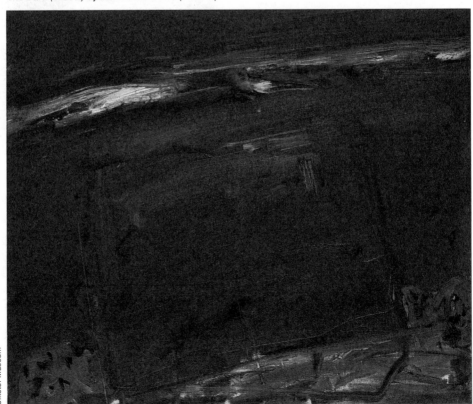

Ulkster Museum

although running for only three weeks each autumn – becoming the Museum's most popular and well-attended event.

Regular contributors to the RUA include T.P. Flanagan and his fellow student at the Belfast School of Art in the late 1940s, Basil Blackshaw, who works in the deep countryside near Antrim, and takes his imagery from the world of horse and dog fanciers and breeders. Despite his apparent affinity with the natural world, he has also painted formal portraits. Raymond Piper (born 1923), while distinguished as a portrait painter, is also internationally respected as a botanical illustrator and an authority on Irish orchids. Brian Ferran, now retired as Chief Executive of the Arts Council of Northern Ireland and currently concentrating on painting full-time in his Donegal studio along with his wife Denise, currently Head of Education in the Ulster Museum, have both exhibited work with the RUA.

Hector McDonnell, the younger brother of the present Earl of Antrim, is a truly international artist, having studied in Munich and Vienna and worked

Light Falls Within by Carol Graham (1978)

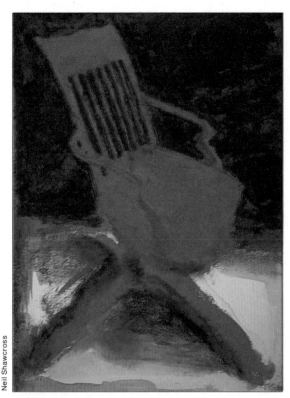

Red chair, Neil Shawcross (1999)

and exhibited extensively in Africa, Asia and the United States, as well as locally. Carol Graham, a graduate of Belfast College of Art, made her reputation in the 1970s with photo-realist paintings showing sunlight filtering through translucent materials like skirt fabrics. She went on to be a successful painter of formal portraits, much in demand. She has recently escaped this pigeon-hole and has concentrated on sombre Mourne landscapes and symbolic figure subjects. Graham Gingles, who teaches in Ballyclare has for some years constructed intriguing compartmented boxes with surrealistic juxtapositions of images. Veronica Wallace, a member of the Belfast Print Workshop, makes sensitive monotypes of animals such as hares and pigs. Lancashire-born Neil Shawcross has taught in Belfast College of Art since 1962, and is active in teaching art to children. A fast worker who finishes his painting at one go, Shawcross has painted many portraits including *Francis Stuart* (commissioned by the Ulster Museum in 1978) and *Alderman David Cook* (commissioned by Belfast City Hall in 1979).

Among the emerging young artists worth noting are Mark Shields (born 1963), whose detailed portrait studies have won wide acclaim, while Paul

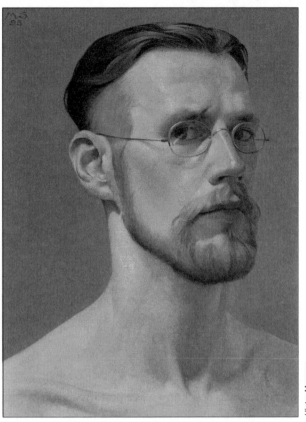

Self-Portrait: The Troubled Look by Mark Shields (1995)

Walls (born 1965) paints thickly-impasted landscapes. Likewise Simon McWilliams (born 1971), son of Joseph and Catherine McWilliams, is now receiving deserved acclaim for his gesturally-painted landscapes and interiors.

In the field of Applied Art at the Ulster Museum, two exhibitions organised by the curator, Michael Robinson, had an inestimable influence on current work in Ireland. These were *Contemporary Studio Glass* (January–March 1973), and *Contemporary Ceramics* (January–March 1974). Up to that time, Irish glass meant traditional Waterford crystal, and Irish ceramics the work turned out by craft potters. Studio glass rather than factory glass was pioneered in the 1970s in Finland and later in Czechoslovakia, and this was now shown in Ireland for the first time. Perhaps even more so, the *Contemporary Ceramics* exhibition transformed the standards of Irish studio ceramics, and gave rise to a generation of potters including Cormac Boydell, Jill Crowley, Christopher Keeney and Alex Scott, to name just a few.

Terrorist incendiary bombs at Malone House, a late Georgian villa on the southern outskirts of Belfast, in November 1976, destroyed practically the whole of the Ulster Museum's collections of costume and textiles stored there. But this disaster bore unexpected fruit when compensation money enabled the curator, Elizabeth McCrum, to build up a new collection, and to concentrate on contemporary material. She set up a policy of each season buying an *haute-couture* dress and a high street chain store outfit, thus creating a valuable chronology of contemporary fashion. Important exhibitions in this field have included *Jean Muir* (January–March 1980), *David Shilling Hats* (September–December 1981), culminating with *Fabric and Form: Irish Fashion since 1950* (October 1996–February 1997).

The outstanding fine art event in Belfast in the early 1970s was the visit of the charismatic German, Joseph Beuys (1921–86), who had been brought to the Edinburgh Festival Fringe by the former gallery owner and now impresario Richard Demarco, a frequent visitor to Belfast. Beuys's large exhibition of drawings, *A Secret Block for a Secret Person in Ireland*, was shown at the Ulster Museum in November 1974. While regarding himself primarily as a sculptor, Beuys was best known as a performance artist, and as part of this exhibition he put on a three-and-a-half hour performance. A founder of the Green Party, Beuys was passionately concerned with environmental issues, as well as an idealistic form of socialism. Dressed in his invariable trilby hat and combat waistcoat with a rabbit's paw pinned to it, he spoke for over three hours on politics, economics and social matters, during which time he covered four blackboards with symbolic diagrams and notes, starting with the eternity spirals from the megalithic tomb at New Grange. John Hewitt the poet and Francis Stuart the novelist sat side by side in the front row, politically poles apart and seemingly unimpressed. These blackboards were afterwards sprayed with fixative varnish, framed, and are now part of the museum collection. Ironically, when comparable Beuys blackboards now come on the market, they can fetch prices of between twenty-five thousand pounds and fifty thousand pounds each. Beuys would have been appalled, as he wished to sabotage the art market. In contrast, the following night Beuys gave a similar performance in the Belfast College of Art, after which the boards he used there were scrubbed clean.

A memorable event of a different sort occurred at the museum in December 1978, the touring exhibition *Art for Society: Contemporary British Art with a*

Social Purpose. This had been organised in London by the Whitechapel Art Gallery, which is situated in a deprived part of the East End of London and runs an important community outreach programme. The exhibits, mildly left-wing in nature, had occasioned no controversy at the venues they had been shown in the United Kingdom. Not, however, in Belfast. While working on its installation in the gallery, we sensed murmurs of disapproval from a certain section of the warder staff, who eventually decided to black it out. Apparently it contravened all they had been brought up to believe in, was anti-British and pro-terrorist. One work – a feminist anti-rape painting – they took to be supportive of rapists and therefore obscene. Particular objection was taken to an anti-racist poster inscribed *Silence the National Front*. Some days of delicate negotiation ensued, and some staff received threatening letters. At last, the Arts Council succeeded in defusing the crisis by identifying the half dozen works the warders found objectionable, and removing them for exhibition at the Arts Council Gallery in Bedford Street. The matter blew over, but not without leaving a nasty taste in the mouth, which took years to abate.

Ted Hickey at the Ulster Museum instigated a practice of occasionally commissioning portraits of people concerned with the creative arts in Northern Ireland, beginning in 1974 with the iconic but puppet-like *Seamus Heaney* – known irreverently as 'look, no chair!' – by the austere Dublin painter Edward McGuire (1932–86). There ensued a remarkable series: Clifford Rainey's detailed pencil drawings of *William Scott* and *F.E. McWilliam* (both 1976); Neil Shawcross's *Francis Stuart* and *Paul Muldoon* (both 1978); *John Montague* (1983) by Edward McGuire; Ross Wilson's large charcoal drawings of *John Carson* (1980), *Anthony C. West* (1982) and *Brian Moore* (1985); *Brian Friel* (1986–7) by Jack Crabtree; *Dr D.B. McNeill* (past Chairman of Trustees, 1987) by Rita Duffy; *James Galway* (1988) by Carol Graham; *Michael Longley* (1989–90) by Peter Edwards; Philip Flanagan's bronze head of the boxer *Dave 'Boy' McAuley* (1991); *Barry Douglas* (1990) by Tom Phillips; *Dr Liam McCormick* (1992) by Robert Ballagh; and *Anne Crookshank* (1994) by Laurence Coulter, her American neighbour in Ramelton, Donegal.

The Ulster Museum series is rounded off by Rodney Dickson's full-length of *'The Hurricane'* (Alex Higgins, 1992) painted from drawings made in

Salford Snooker Club while Higgins was practicing for the World Championship, wearing a matador's cape draped round his shoulders. This was not commissioned by the museum, but was generously donated by the artist, who is now working mostly in New York. Dickson featured in a two-man show at the Engine Room Gallery on the Newtownards Road in 2000, along with the sculptor Tom Bevan, another artist who seems better known in the United States than in his native Ulster. From 1972 Bevan started working in potteries in the Channel Islands and in Morocco, and has worked as artist-in-residence at a mid-western American ceramic factory which specialises in sanitary ware. He used the factory's techniques to create a major work in relief sculpture, consisting of about one hundred and fifty glazed ceramic panels. When not in America, Bevan lives and works in a remote farmhouse near Ballynahinch, County Down, without electricity, running water or a telephone.

In May 1981 the Art and Research Exchange, a charity based in Lombard Street in central Belfast, providing photographic, screenprinting and exhibition services for artists and community groups, circulated a poster inscribed 'DO YOU REALLY HAVE A FUTURE IN ART?' There followed a list of demands which the Exchange believed were not being fulfilled:

> 'Do you feel enough new ideas in art are encouraged in
>   Northern Ireland?
> Do you have access to studio and workshop facilities outside of
>   college, school or university?
> Is there a regular art magazine produced in Northern Ireland?
> Do you have wide-ranging opportunities to externalise your
>   work?
> Are there sufficient facilities to transport your work to events
>   outside Northern Ireland?
> Do you have regular contacts with other artists?
> Have you received any grant aid for your work?
> Do you feel you have any control over financial and
>   policy decisions which affect the development of art
>   in Northern Ireland?'

A meeting was called at the Exchange on Thursday 28 May 1981, to which response was immediate and numerous. The result was the formation of the Artists' Collective of Northern Ireland, to act as a debating forum for artists, a provider of artistic resources, and as a lobbying body to approach institutions and funding authorities. They found common ground with British societies such as Artlaw and the Artists' Union in creating solidarity, co-operation and the elimination of isolation, rivalries and waste – in fact, the long-overdue unionisation of art. The third question on the above list was quickly addressed, and a publications committee was set up to produce a new Northern Ireland art journal, *Circa*. There had been an earlier attempt to publish a journal, *Art About Ireland*, which received support from the Arts Council of Northern Ireland, but did not last long. *Circa*, however, did survive and is now Ireland's leading contemporary art magazine, issued quarterly. Early editions were somewhat spartan. The magazine was printed in black and white throughout and did not aim to express a corporate opinion, but rather attempted to strike a balance between articles with inter-views about particular artists, and wider analyses of the social and political position of art.

By 1992, under the editorship of Mark Robinson and Tanya Kiang, *Circa* had become a truly international glossy magazine with editorial offices in Belfast and Dublin, and supported by the Arts Councils of both Northern Ireland and the Republic of Ireland. Now, with Peter Fitzgerald as editor, *Circa* has its editorial office in the Temple Bar area of Dublin, and its admin-istrative office in Ormeau Avenue, Belfast. The editorial board changes reg-ularly with membership by invitation, and a panel of contributing editors based in Dublin, Belfast, Cork, England and New York emphasises the international ambitions the magazine has long retained.

One other significant publication for the arts in Ulster is the *Irish Arts Review* which first appeared as a quarterly journal in 1984 but which four years later became a yearbook, going on sale just before Christmas. Its glossy format and wealth of colour illustration makes it an attractive outlet for articles and reviews on all forms of Irish art, and there is always a substantial contribution from the north.

In the early 1970s the Arts Council set up the Belfast Print Workshop in its premises at Riddell Hall, off Stranmillis Road, with the Lurgan born artist James Allen in charge. His wife Sophie Aghajanian, of Armenian descent, is also a printmaker and pastellist, and their daughter Neesha, who discovered an original approach to ceramic sculpture, now lives in Bologna, Italy. Since the 1990s the Print Workshop has been independent but is still at Riddell Hall. The Arts Council moved to MacNeice Hall on Stranmillis Road, leaving the Print Workshop in Riddell Hall, which is still open to the public, and provides facilities for etching, aquatint, lithography and screen printing. Since the 1970s it has appointed a series of printmakers-in-residence, mostly from outside Northern Ireland, many of whom settled in Belfast for long periods after their residency expired. They have included Alfonso Monreal (from Mexico), the late Mary Farl Powers (from America), the late Steve Barraclough (from England), Ibrahim Ehrari (Iranian, based in Berlin) and Terry Gravett (from England). Gravett also served a period as artist-in-residence at the Ulster Museum, where he worked empathetically with school parties. He has developed the mixed techniques of screen printing and woodblock printing to unprecedented levels both in size and colour. In 2000 the Arts Council cut its revenue grant to the Belfast Print Workshop by nearly one third, from seventy thousand pounds to fifty thousand pounds while Ulster's other public print studio, the Seacourt Print Workshop in Bangor, is less well funded again, having an Arts Council grant of twenty thousand pounds.

Apart from Leonard Kaitcer who was murdered, the Belfast dealer who suffered most during the early years of the Troubles was George McClelland. Bombed out of his art and antiques gallery in May Street in December 1971, McClelland opened a new gallery on the lower Lisburn Road the following year. Here he mounted important shows of work by Colin Middleton, Tom Carr, William Scott, Louis le Brocquy and F.E. McWilliam, while commuting from Dublin where he had moved his wife and family. As a result of prolonged intimidation, in 1974 McClelland decided to close his Lisburn Road establishment and move permanently to Dublin, where he still lives. The building was destroyed in a bomb-blast soon after. In Dublin, McClelland took the opportunity to enrol as a mature student at the National College of Art and Design, taking up sculpture. For a time he acted as agent for the distinguished Irish artist Tony O'Malley, who worked mainly in St Ives. More recently, McClelland has generously placed his collection of over four hundred contemporary Irish artworks on long-term loan to the Irish Museum of Modern Art.

The situation of commercial galleries in Belfast has developed greatly in the past two decades. The Bell Gallery, opened in Alfred Street in 1964, has moved its location twice and is now run by Nelson Bell from his home in Adelaide Park. Bell's stable of artists include the late Tom Carr and his grandson James McKeown, the late Lawson Burch, Richard Croft, Hector McDonnell, James MacIntyre and the sculptor Carolyn Mulholland, who is now working in Dublin. The Tom Caldwell Gallery in Bradbury Place, opened in 1969, specialises principally in interior design, but has put on a regular programme of one man and group exhibitions since its opening.

In the 1980s the Fenderesky Gallery was set up by Jamshid Mirfenderesky, an Iranian who had come to Belfast to study philosophy at Queen's. Now established in the same building as the Crescent Arts Centre, the Fenderesky Gallery has put on important shows by such distinguished artists as David Crone, Jack Pakenham, Micky Donnelly, Rita Duffy, Alfonso Monreal and many others both local and from further afield.

Joseph and Catherine McWilliams, both painters, opened the Cavehill Gallery in their home on Old Cavehill Road in north Belfast, thus adjusting the geographical balance away from the University quarter. Their annual Christmas mixed show has become a prestigious social event, and is usually sold out during the private view. Joseph McWilliams has more recently diversified into journalism, his outspoken Thursday column in the *Irish News* having marked him as Ulster's answer to Brian Sewell of the London *Evening Standard*. The Senior Common Room of Queen's University has mounted a series of commercial exhibitions in the bar area since the building was opened in the early 1970s. These are at present organised by Ted Hickey, formerly Keeper of Art in the Ulster Museum. The Kerlin Gallery, started in Belfast in the calmer 1980s, moved eventually to Dublin. Very recently, Roderick Duncan, formerly Chief Schools Inspector for Art in Northern Ireland, has set up the New Kerlin Gallery in University Street.

In Derry, the Orchard Gallery on Orchard Street was set up in the 1970s, quickly establishing itself as a lively venue for contemporary art under its energetic first Director, Declan McGonagle. McGonagle's international reputation earned him a subsequent position in the Institute of Contemporary Arts in London, and later the post of first Director of the Irish Museum of Modern Art (IMMA) in the Royal Hospital, Kilmainham,

Catherine and Joseph McWilliams

Dublin. Besides Armagh County Museum, which is part of the Ulster Museum organisation, local authorities have set up museums with art exhibiting facilities in Derry, Enniskillen (Fermanagh County Museum), Downpatrick (Down Museum) and Lisburn (The Irish Linen Centre and Lisburn Museum). Throughout Northern Ireland, arts centres and studios have been established liberally over the past two decades. As well as organising exhibitions, some of these centres have a varied programme of activities – lectures, practical instruction, performance and dance.

Belfast alone has the Old Museum Arts Centre in College Square, the Crescent Arts Centre – which houses the Fenderesky Gallery – and several former linen warehouses converted into studio space, most notably the Queen Street Studios. Catalyst Arts in Exchange Place was founded in 1983 as an artist-run gallery and studios, emphasising cross-disciplinary and inter-disciplinary approaches to the making of art. It now has an international membership of over three hundred. Similarly, the Proposition Gallery in North Street Arcade promotes the production and awareness of high quality non-commercial art. Carol Graham has her studio in Harmony Hill Arts Centre at Lambeg.

Further afield, the Ards Art Centre occupies part of Newtownards' elegant classical town hall. Portadown has Craigavon Arts and the Peacock Gallery. The North Down Heritage Centre is in Bangor town hall; the Newry and Mourne Arts Centre is in Bank Parade, Newry. Clotworthy House Arts Centre is in Antrim and the Flowerfield Arts Centre is in Portstewart. In Hillsborough, T.P. Flanagan's wife Sheila and their sculptor son Philip have for years mounted exhibitions in the summer months in the quaint Shambles Gallery, which they own. Philip Flanagan has his studio here. As well as doing large-scale sculpture, Philip has built himself a reputation as a portrait sculptor in bronze. At one stage he was working on a bizarre combination of commissions at the same time – *The Reverend Ian Paisley*, for Martyrs Memorial Church, for which the sittings were held in the Shambles, and *Cahal, Cardinal Daly, Archbishop of Armagh*, for which the sculptor had to travel to Ara Coeli, the Primate's palace in Armagh.

Mention must be made of some of Ulster's exported artists: Roy Johnston, born in Pomeroy in 1936 was, from 1974 principal lecturer in painting in the Belfast College of Art, and Ulster's foremost minimalist or systemic painter. He later left Belfast for the University of New York at Syracuse and turned to art history, becoming an authority on the Irish post-impressionist Roderic O'Conor. John Aiken, born in Belfast in 1950, has achieved the highest status in the world of sculpture. Trained at Chelsea College of Art and the British School at Rome, he has taught in many art schools throughout the world. As Professor of Sculpture at the Slade School in London, Aiken re-organised the sculpture studios and in 2000 became Slade Professor of Fine Art at University College, London.

Felim Egan, born in Strabane in 1952, who was a postgraduate at the Slade in 1975–7 and a Rome Scholar in 1979, is now possibly the most internationally recognised painter of the 'younger' generation in Ireland. He has taught at the National College of Art and Design in Dublin since 1981, but frequently returns to the north, where he is a member of the Art Committee of the Ulster Museum. Egan plays Irish traditional music, and finds visual equivalents of its rhythms in his own abstract painting. A limited edition book *Squarings*, in which Egan collaborated with the poet Seamus Heaney, was published in Dublin in 1991. Another County Tyrone painter, Clement McAleer, born in Coalisland in 1949, left Belfast College of Art for

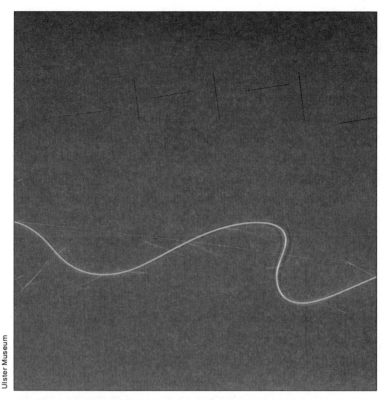

Score by Felim Egan (1981)

Canterbury College of Art in 1972, and studied at the Royal College of Art in 1975–8. He now works mainly in Liverpool, having a studio in the Bluecoat Chambers there.

The most prominent female artist currently working outside Northern Ireland is the Lurgan-born sculptor, Carolyn Mulholland, who moved to Dublin in 1991. As well as large-scale commissions for churches in County Antrim and the Cavehill Road, Belfast, she has made portrait sculptures of *Séamus Heaney* (1969), *Mercy Hunter* (1972), *Betty Lowry* (1975), *Stanley Worrall* (1982) and *Joseph Tomelty* (1991). In the early 1970s she made a full-length bronze statue of the athlete *Mary Peters*.

The printmaker and illustrator Stephen Conlin, from Armagh, studied classics at Trinity College, Dublin, before entering Belfast College of Art. His work consists of astonishingly meticulous architectural fantasies. In collaboration with the Dublin-born historian Jonathan Bardon, who lives in Belfast, Conlin illustrated two architectural histories published by Blackstaff Press, *Dublin: One Thousand Years of Wood Quay* (1984) and *Belfast: 1000 Years* (1985). He later moved to London for a period, and is now settled in Bath.

Another classics graduate of Trinity, but not a practising artist, Seán McCrum, left the staff of the Ulster Museum in the mid 1970s to become the first curator of the newly established Douglas Hyde Gallery, a temporary exhibition space in the arts building in Trinity College.

Artists of the older generation who died in this period include the major modernist painter William Scott (1913–89) and the sculptor F.E. McWilliam (1909–92). Frank McKelvey (1895–1974), Ulster's primary anti-modernist painter, who lived from 1967 in My Lady's Mile, Holywood, died in 1974. Possessed of considerable hand-skills in landscape, seascape and portraiture, McKelvey tended to accept rather too many potboiler commissions. Colin Middleton (1910–83), Ulster's sole surrealist painter, and one of the generation who began their careers as linen damask designers, lived for the last twelve years of his life in Bangor, where he died. From 1961 to 1970 he had been head of the art department at Friends' School, Lisburn. He was awarded an MBE in 1969, elected RHA in 1970, and given an honorary MA by Queen's

Self-Portrait with Veneer Jug by Tom Carr (c.1980)

Ulster Museum

University in 1972. Tom Carr (1909–99), who was painting up to the end, spent his last years living with his eldest daughter and her husband, who run a National Trust property in Norfolk. Their son James McKeown is a painter now living in Normandy. Derek Hill, born in 1916, high society portrait painter and founder of the Glebe Gallery, County Donegal, died in August 2000. His painting activities on Tory Island inspired a whole school of local primitive painters. Hill was the main instigator of the Alice Berger Hammerschlag memorial trust, which since 1969, has provided financial support for young Irish artists.

A volatile political situation, such as Northern Ireland's, is bound to generate satire and caricature. Caricature flatters politicians' egos, and many politicians are avid collectors of original drawings of cartoons of themselves. Regular cartoonists in Ireland are few in number. Rowel Friers (1920–98), one of the old generation of Belfast artists who, like Conor, served lithographic apprenticeships in the poster firm of David Allen, for many years drew cartoons for the *Belfast Telegraph*, and also contributed cartoons to the *Irish Times, Dublin Opinion, London Opinion* and *Punch*. Friers was elected an academician of the Royal Ulster Academy in 1953, and forty years later, in 1993, became its President. Martyn Turner, a working-class boy from Croydon who had the misfortune to win an open scholarship to an English public school, which he claims scarred him for life, came to Belfast in the late 1960s to study geography at Queen's. He became involved in the foundation of the current affairs and cultural magazine *Fortnight,* contributed many cartoons to student magazines, and after graduating moved to Dublin where he is still resident cartoonist of the *Irish Times*.

Ian Knox, the regular cartoonist for the *Irish News*, is a disillusioned architect who forsook that profession for something more rewarding. After qualifying in Edinburgh, Knox worked briefly in London but now lives in a remote part of County Down with his German wife and many animals. He also draws the graphics for BBC Northern Ireland's current affairs programme *Hearts and Minds*.

In June 1995 the Ormeau Baths Gallery in Belfast was officially opened by Michael Ancram MP, before a crowd of over nine hundred people from all over the world. Occupying the east wing of the Victorian baths building, the gallery provides four bright exhibition spaces with 10,000 square feet of

Culture Vultures by Ian Knox

hanging space. It carries on the tradition of temporary exhibitions formerly fulfilled by the Arts Council with its gallery in Bedford Street, but is completely separate from the Arts Council, having its own Board of Trustees and Director. In March 1996 the gallery won second place in the prestigious National Art Collections Fund Prize competition, in recognition of its contribution to the increase of public enjoyment and awareness of the visual arts. Important retrospective exhibitions held there have included: *Jack Pakenham* (October 1995); *Basil Blackshaw* (November–December 1995, later touring Ireland and the United States); *Jack B. Yeats* and *Bruce McLean* (June–July 1996); *Mary Farl Powers* and the *Weltkunst Collection* of works on paper (August–September 1996), *Brian McCallion* and *Bill Woodrow* (October–November 1996); *Brian Kennedy* (January–February 1997); *Patrick O'Reilly* (June–July 1997); Micky Donnelly's *Reflex Series* (August 1997); Rita Duffy's *'Banquet'* (August–September 1997); *Martin Wedge* (October–November 1997); *Humphrey Ocean and Jock McFadyen* (November–December 1997); Bill Viola's *The Messenger* (November 1997), and his *Nantes Triptych* (November 1998); *Alastair McLennan* (December 1997); *Yoko Ono* (November–December 1998; and *Gilbert and George's Recent Works* (October 1999–January 2000). The private view of this last exhibition was a memorable occasion. Over eight hundred people must have attended, but to enter, all had to run the gauntlet of a hymn-singing picket from the Free

Presbyterian Church, who regarded the exhibits as obscene. Gilbert and George, in their identical suits, were courteously signing catalogues in the centre of the gallery. The next morning Gilbert and George were on local radio debating with a free presbyterian minister. The pair are highly argumentative and articulate: 'You control religion, do you want to control art? We wouldn't dream of picketing your church!'

Following the establishment of a new Department of Culture, Arts and Leisure, the Northern Ireland Visual Arts Forum was set up in 2000 with the intention of acting as a liaison group for the visual arts, particularly for lobbying the Department in their interests. Eileen Bell was elected Chairperson, Shelagh Boucher as Secretary and Patricia Macintosh as Treasurer. Its first Annual General Meeting was held on 27 September that year. The first of a series of monthly *Spotlight on Art* programmes was held on 21 November 2000 in the McCausland Hotel, Belfast. Hugh Mulholland of the Ormeau Baths Gallery, Carol Graham, Anne Hailes and myself gave presentations.

Prospects for the immediate future of the visual arts in Northern Ieland could be very exciting if events happen for the best. Belfast aspires to be European City of Culture in 2008, a designation previously held in these islands by Glasgow and Dublin. The opening of the Waterfront Hall and the adjacent Belfast Hilton hotel has revitalised a neglected part of town. Deborah Brown's bronze *Shepherd and Sheep* and John Kindness' *Big Shark*, both formerly on open-air display at the Arts Council's sculpture park at Riddell Hall, have been relocated to the riverside area. Another remarkable recent public sculpture is the bronze monument by Ross Wilson to Belfast's most famous literary scholar and Christian apologist C.S. Lewis (1898–1963), erected in the forecourt of Holywood Arches Public Library in 1998. This depicts a life-size figure – not a portrait of Lewis – opening a wardrobe, the entrance to the imaginary kingdom of Narnia.

Currently the Ulster Museum, Armagh County Museum, the Ulster Folk and Transport Museum and the Ulster American Folk Park are undergoing a merger as the Museums and Galleries of Northern Ireland (MAGNI), with one Board of Trustees and one Executive Officer, Michael Houlihan. MAGNI's first major publication was the illustrated concise *Catalogue of Drawings, Paintings and Sculptures* held on all four sites, a monumental undertaking edited by

Dr Eileen Black and involving new colour photography of all items. In early 2002, the Ulster Museum is to be the third and final venue for the large *Stanley Spencer* exhibition, which starts at Tate Britain in London and goes on to the Art Gallery of Ontario in Toronto. As a blockbuster exhibition, this is an important coup. It is appropriate for Belfast as Stanley Spencer frequently came to visit his musician brother Harold, who lived here.

The next decade should hopefully see the creation of a separate national museum of art for Northern Ireland, so that the Ulster Museum's collections can be properly displayed to the public. At present, about ninety per cent of the collections are kept in store, as the museum is seriously short of gallery space. There are three alternatives for the erection of an art museum currently being considered. First, extension to the present Botanic Gardens site, which is possible, as the strip of land between the museum and the Tropical Ravine belongs to the museum and not to Belfast Parks Department. Second, a city centre location, either an adapted existing building or a completely new site, which is the choice favoured by most of the staff. The third alternative is a location outside Belfast, which is unlikely, but which has to be considered as part of the scheme.

In any case, the building should be designed by a major architect and should act as a landmark and an attraction for both professional and casual visitors, thereby encouraging potential donors and benefactors to increase the quality of the national collections. In 1999 the Ulster Museum refurbished its large temporary exhibitions gallery, which had the effect of making the remaining nine look very shabby. The bold decision was then made to refurbish all the art galleries at Stranmillis, and to fill them with contemporary work from the permanent collections. These displays were formally opened on 31 May 2001, as a *Countdown* to work towards the intended new art museum, and though negotiations for the museum itself are still at a sensitive stage, details about an architectural competition for the project will emerge in due course. This event coincided with the opening of a selection of contemporary Irish art from the collection of the Allied Irish Bank. The guest on the occasion was the veteran jazz singer and art pundit George Melly, no stranger to Belfast, who after singing with a jazz band in the gallery, made a perspicacious speech on the content of the displays and the possibilities for the future. The countdown to that future has surely begun.

Film

MIKE CATTO

Film. It's a very short word, but it covers an enormous number of related areas and questions. Even calling it by a fashionable title – Film Culture – still implies a homogeneity of subject which is inaccurate and misleading. To discuss film in Northern Ireland between 1971 and the start of the new century is to be forced to draw into the debate topics such as: the production, distribution and broadcast diffusion of locally made features and shorts; the cinema distribution and broadcast diffusion in Ulster of film from around the globe; the idea of a definable industry in this region; the teaching of film theory and practice in higher education here; the impact of changing technologies and markets on making, distributing and watching; the role of the regulatory and funding bodies, and finally who makes what. And all of that – what we might call form – is bound up in the frequently contentious issues surrounding the content of film and video, including representations of our troubled times in the province, throughout the island of Ireland and beyond.

It was so much easier for Sam Hanna Bell in 1951 and the *Causeway* team in 1971. They ignored film completely. Admittedly, low budget features had been made on the Antrim coast by Richard Hayward in the 1930s and big budget feature films were made on location in the Republic from the 1950s onwards. However most of the latter, from *Moby Dick* (John Huston, 1956) through *The Blue Max* (John Guillermin, 1966) to *Zardoz* (John Boorman, 1973) were set in times and places which had nothing to do with their Irish locations. They did, nevertheless, contribute to the idea that the offer of an Irish film-making facility, backed by government tax concessions, could in time assist the formation of an indigenous film industry built up around the local technical and creative crews who worked on these films.

None of this was of direct help to those who wished to work in film in Northern Ireland. Anyone in the 1970s who wanted to act in a film, work as a member of crew or be a member of a film support company – providing locations, art direction or catering – had to make a sporadic foray south, when there was news of a feature being made, or elect to go elsewhere, particularly to Britain. The problem was not simply the lack of a suitable film base or superstructure – for the same was true of both Scotland and Wales in the early 1970s. In fact the Troubles in Ulster made it almost impossible for most people to envisage any new media industry being set up here.

At the same time the Troubles compounded the problem of already rapidly falling local cinema attendances. When in 1985 Michael Open wrote his book *Fading Lights; Silver Screens* about the history and physical architecture of Belfast cinemas, it seemed like an epitaph for the dying social phenomenon of going to the pictures. Television had caused sharp declines in cinema audiences everywhere in the UK and here, both the threat of violence and the reality of bombed and empty town centres, led to even more rapid closures of cinemas than in Great Britain. At one point in the 1970s there were only four cinema screens still lit in Belfast.

One of these was the Queen's Film Theatre, opened at the very end of the 1960s as the local equivalent of the regional film theatres which the British Film Institute – the BFI – part-funded throughout the UK to further the Art of the Film, as it was then called. Curiously, at the time, BFI support for the

QFT was not financial, thanks to an omission in the BFI's original charter in the 1930s, which failed to include Northern Ireland. The financial position of the QFT has always been precarious but its continued existence was and is due to funding from Queen's University and, until recently, the Arts Council of Northern Ireland. No such funding was available to commercial cinemas across the rest of Northern Ireland. The QFT, for all its problems, demonstrated that there was a select audience for good new foreign and repertory classic films. Many in that dedicated audience were the same people who attended plays at the Lyric or concerts at the Ulster Hall. In short, QFT was and is a legitimate part of the wider arts scene. In 2001 its funding was drawn from a wider range of sources including the Northern Ireland Film Commission – NIFC – Belfast City Council, Europa Cinemas and from the BFI. The need for such diverse local, national and European support further demonstrates that some aspects of the film culture, and its need for external financing, will resemble more the position of opera than that of the competitive, commercial circuits.

QFT's former relationship with the Arts Council of Northern Ireland also provided an opportunity for film to be added to the roster of artistic practice eligible for support from that source. By 1980 the Arts Council had incorporated film into the title of a sub-committee it called 'Film, Photography and Video'. Its budget was modest in the extreme but, working with its counterpart in the Arts Council in the Republic, it did represent an opportunity for seed money for short film projects. It also offered sponsorship of film documentaries about established figures of the Ulster arts scene such as John Hewitt. The notion of support for film from the Arts Council of Northern Ireland was greater than the funds given out to film-makers, and this eventually led, albeit circuitously, to the current position of National Lottery money being made available linked to funding from the NIFC.

It would be wrong to give the impression that the Troubles meant that little film was being made here. The contrary was in fact true, but much of the film or videotape that went through cameras in the 1970s and 1980s was in the form of global media coverage of politics and paramilitary violence. From being almost unknown in image or sound to its neighbours in Great Britain in the 1960s, thirty years of broadcast images of death, damage, misery and tub-thumping meant that images of Ulster were being sent round the world on film and on videotape. They were not, of course, the images people living here might have wished for.

Despite that – and notwithstanding the fact that TV companies from around the world sent their own reporters and crews to cover the events in Ulster – locally based cameramen and sound recordists did work for the UK companies, and indeed several of them worked in a freelance capacity for European, US and even Far Eastern networks. This provided important experience for individuals and small companies in the 1980s and is, to some extent, one of the ways in which a trained workforce became available locally.

In addition to news and current affairs film coverage of the Troubles, the social consequences of civil unrest made their effects felt on drama output, particularly that produced by BBC Northern Ireland. The filmed and video-taped plays, dramas and films – the distinction between a play and a film blurred in the 1980s and most TV drama is today considered to be cinematic – offered a strong fare of harsh accents and routine working-class violence which became an unwelcome reminder to audiences in Great Britain of the conflict not so very far away. The ostensible format of these TV offerings could and did use humour, such as the 1991 *Arise and Go Now* (written by Owen O'Neill and directed by Danny Boyle) which used broad comedic conventions to look at republican politics in a small rural community. Equally, it could be the harrowing, hypnotically repetitive violence of *Elephant*. Collectively such films established images of Ulster as a site of human-sized conflicts, tragedies and failings when they were aired beyond the island of Ireland.

From a long list of controversial dramas, *Elephant* (Bill Morrison and Alan Clarke, 1989), is mentioned because it demonstrates that point at which the traditional concept of the well-made play could not encompass what the pro-duction team wanted to portray. In essence, it is a word-free reconstruction of a series of sectarian murders which works by showing the viewer the brief, almost casual way in which people from both sides of the community had been killed. While the silent protagonists – killers and victims alike – are played by actors, this is a *film*. It stands or falls by its use of the medium and techniques of cinema. *Elephant* is also important in that it was never given a second showing by the BBC having been condemned by local and national politicians, several of whom indicated their preference for the domestic dramas of the *Billy* trilogy of plays. Written by Graham Reid and starring the young Kenneth Branagh and Brid Brennan, they were first screened between 1982 and 1984 and re-broadcast in 1987.

Not to give a film a second showing may or may not count as censorship, but that important issue has long been a source of debate regarding media coverage of this province. As in the rest of the UK, theatrical releases of feature films were subject both to national censorship through the British Board of Film Censors – later, and significantly renamed, the British Board of Film *Classification* – and to local censorship through councils and council sub-committees. There were various examples where the local authorities felt that Ulster audiences should not see films screened elsewhere. These included the risible Rod Steiger revenge movie *Hennessy* (Don Sharp, 1975) in which a mild-mannered Belfast catholic plotted to assassinate the Queen after his

James Ellis as Norman and Kenneth Branagh as Billy in the acclaimed BBC drama
Too Late to Talk to Billy

BBC Northern Ireland

family had been accidentally killed by British troops, as well as Bertolucci's *Last Tango in Paris* (1972) or Scorsese's *The Last Temptation of Christ* (1988). *Last Tango in Paris* is interesting in that while Belfast City Council held that it should not be shown in commercial cinemas it was able to be screened under its original Italian title as an Associates Only film at QFT. Others were able to go to cinemas outside Belfast to see the film there. One of the many effects of the video revolution of the 1980s was that feature films and documentaries which might not get screenings in cinemas could be hired easily from neighbourhood video libraries and watched at home.

Censorship does not just mean stopping people seeing something which has already been made; indirect censorship can also mean not giving partisan practitioners access to the processes of making and transmitting work reflecting their particular points of view. In the early 1970s a number of European film-makers such as Chris Marker realised that it was not enough for professionals to make films about social or political subjects and then to vanish to another project. Those directly involved in the issue could and should be empowered to use the technology of film-making to voice their own experience. This shift in the thinking behind social film-making began to percolate into Ireland in the late 1970s, especially when video equipment began to become as standard as, and easier to use than, 16mm or 35mm film equipment.

When Channel Four was set up at the start of the 1980s it promised both to produce new work and to transmit existing work which continued and developed a long alternative cinematic tradition of, as the company put it, 'films which passionately argue a particular case or maybe simply utter a scream of protest or pain at injustice'. This meant not having to adhere to the notion of the balanced, dispassionate documentary. In its first few years such polemical Channel Four series as *Ireland: The Silent Voices* and *Women on Film,* screened as part of the umbrella series *The Eleventh Hour,* combined fiction, documentary and community film and video-making to present images and voices which had not been aired on BBC or ITV before. The conflict in the north took its place alongside other issue-based subjects such as colonialism, gender, the Third World and sexuality.

Some of the output of *The Eleventh Hour* and *People to People* was the transmission of film already made, such as the bizarre but original *Writing on the*

Maeve (Mary Jackson) at the Giant's Causeway in Pat Murphy
and John Davies' *Maeve* (1981)

Wall (1981) directed and conceived by the European film-maker Armand
Gatti and shot in Derry. The film developed out of improvisational commu-
nity-based workshops and in the final version – which also includes comic
strips and graffiti – the young loyalists were played by catholics and the
young republicans by protestants.

Another significant purchase was *Maeve* (1981) by Pat Murphy and John
Davies, first shown on TV in March 1983. *Maeve,* made by the BFI Production
Board, told the story of a young woman's return to Belfast and her encoun-
ters with family and friends. Through these meetings, which tended to take
the form of longish dialogues, Maeve herself began to examine issues of
personal and 'national' culture, of identity and tradition which placed the
individual story in relation to the wider and much more public conflict. The
film is significant not only for being shot on location here – including a
crucial sequence at the Giant's Causeway which brought together past and
present, place and person – but also because it demonstrated that there were
intelligent and alternative ways of using cinema to explore life beyond the
dramatic immediacy of violence.

However the real importance of these Channel Four slots was the commissioning of new films. Commissioning editors such as Rod Stoneman felt that
the channel needed to be pro-active in creating environments in which film
and video development and production could be assisted rather than simply

relying on existing film-makers. Franchised workshops were set up through-out the UK with two based in Northern Ireland. The first product of this new scheme was *Acceptable Levels* (John Davies, 1984) made by Frontroom Productions in conjunction with Belfast Film Workshop. *Acceptable Levels* is a complex work of fiction which revolves around an English TV crew making a documentary about the effects of civil insurgence on the people and, in particular, on the children in one area of Belfast. This dramatic con-struction permits the film both to tell a narrative story about the police, the military and civilians and to show its audience how points of view were created and mediated through the ostensibly real conventions of the TV documentary. It is also significant that this feature film was made using a high percentage of locally skilled technicians on locations in Belfast ranging from the ubiquitous Europa Hotel to Divis Flats. The previous norm for shooting Ulster located dramas was to dress parts of Dublin or housing estates in English industrial cities to resemble the more depressing housing estates of Belfast. Of course there were very sound reasons for not filming in Ulster, but each time local professional and semi-professional actors were shipped out to the likes of Bradford, it was another lost chance for aspiring film technicians and support crews to hone and demonstrate their skills.

Another important local development for Northern Ireland film-makers to present their case came from the Derry Film and Video Collective – later Workshop – set up in 1984. From 1987 to 1990 it was one of the biggest of the Channel Four franchised workshops anywhere in the UK. *Hush-a-bye Baby* (Margo Harkin, 1989) is often remembered for featuring the young Sinéad O'Connor among the professional and amateur cast members. However the film's true significance lies in the way in which its subject – the pregnancy of a young Derry girl – is shown as being both grounded in the culture of nation-alist Derry at a precisely delineated time of violence, unemployment and hopelessness while at the same time, raising themes and issues which had, and continue to have, much wider cultural connotations. *Hush-a-bye-Baby* is a mature film in its resonances: it and its high viewing figures fully vindicated Channel Four support. The film's director, Margo Harkin, continues to play an important part in the burgeoning film industry of the province with her production company, the insightfully named Besom Productions – besom being both the name for a broom and a forceful woman.

Michael Liebmann and Emer McCourt in *Hush-A-Bye-Baby* directed by Margo Harkin

Lest this essay be seen to present the Channel Four contribution in nothing but a glowing light, it was another Derry Film and Video Workshop production for that station which became the centre of a *cause célebre* involving censorship. Early in 1988 Anne Crilly completed a documentary entitled *Mother Ireland* which looked at ancient and modern personifications of Ireland as female. The controversy stemmed from the fact that the film's words, images and music were openly nationalist and in its complex argument – which drew in cultural traditions, politics and religion – it celebrated in particular the role of women in what is often called 'the armed struggle'. The film was dropped. Crassly, Channel Four tried at first to claim it was 'not of a *technical* quality compatible with broadcast television', but the real reason was that in both the UK and in the Republic, it fell foul of broadcasting restrictions on material which openly supported Sinn Féin and the IRA. There is a certain irony here in that much of the criticism leveled at television programmes and films about the Troubles has come from establishment figures who believe coverage has mainly demonstrated a sympathy towards nationalist communities and their plight. Some have gone further and claimed that film and TV have at best marginalised protestant culture and unionist traditions and at worst, demonised them.

Independent film-makers and broadcast television companies have consistently denied this claim of nationalist or republican bias. Nevertheless, it is an accusation still heard today. Recent examples include the BBC/RTÉ co-production *Rebel Heart*, first screened in January 2001 and internationally acclaimed historical features such as Neil Jordan's *Michael Collins* (1996), Jim Sheridan's *In The Name of The Father* (1993), Ken Loach's *Hidden Agenda* (1990) which gave voice to allegations of a shoot-to-kill policy amongst sections of the security forces, and Terry George's fictive take on the hunger strikes *Some*

Brian Cox and Frances McDormand in *Hidden Agenda* (1990)
directed by Ken Loach.

Mother's Son (1996). The truth is that if films and videos continue to be made which address the issues behind the divisions in our community – and when those issues are clothed in narrative fictions – accusations of partisanship will continue. One of the simple reasons for these attacks on film or TV drama content is because films and television dramas do reach such large audiences and they often come under the category of entertainment. Without claiming that the average filmgoer in Birmingham, Berlin or Boston is chronically uneducated, it is nonetheless true that he or she is likely to be unfamiliar with the historical details and political interpretations behind dramatised scenes relating to events in 1916 or 1976. Merely to decry the absence of protestant voices in a film like *Acceptable Levels* is negative criticism, and a few film-makers did attempt to show positive images from the traditions of protestantism and unionism. Chief among these was Desmond Bell, a sociologist who attempted to redress the balance through video productions such as *We'll Fight and No Surrender* (1990) and *Facing The Future* (1991).

Just as the actual events in Northern Ireland since 1968 have been the focus of intensive scrutiny and debate among commentators and academics from around the world, so too the films made in or about this region have been pored over by film critics and academics. But where the public and politicians tend to judge and criticise films for their *content* – politics, violence and sex – and for the putative effects of that content, educationalists involved in film and TV studies reflect upon and tease out the construction, the *form* of the cinematic image. Film education or film studies must not be thought of simply as university undergraduates discussing films dealing with Ulster and Ireland. Aspects of film and media studies education were, and continue to be, found in secondary education as well as in further and higher education. In the 1970s the BFI and SEFT – the Society for Education in Film and Television – held workshops and conferences in Northern Ireland, as in other regions of the UK, to assist those teachers who wished to see film studies either as a distinct curriculum subject or as complementing other critical studies subjects.

Sometimes called Media or Communications Studies, the loose confederation of critical subjects grew throughout the 1970s and 1980s. Admittedly, the Thatcher administration tried to marginalise such studies in schools when it was shown that teachers and students had been highly critical of media coverage and government policy of events such as the miners' strike, the Falklands War and, inevitably, the Troubles in Northern Ireland. Nevertheless, thanks to general introductions in the classroom and to populist UK film magazines such as *Empire*, most secondary schoolchildren are now much more aware of basic issues such as film genres, gender representation and the star system than they were in 1971.

While the focus of Film Studies may have moved away from the European masters such as Bergman or Godard, today's pupils have had greater exposure to filmic examples and exemplars than ever before. At a basic level this can take the form of familiarity with innovative music videos. Local Ulster pop bands can, and do, get their music videos made here and audiences of the so-called MTV generation can see experimental, promotional film and animation twenty-four hours a day, in a way that would have been unthinkable thirty years ago. In 1999 an Irish pop music paper – and it is significant that pop music and film are thought of together – polled its readership about bought and recorded videos. Over half of respondents claimed to have personal video collections of more than one hundred feature films. However unreliable the statistics, it would have been difficult in 1970 or even in 1980 to have predicted that individuals would be able build up highly personalised film collections in the same way that people did with cheap paperback books in the 1930s and 1940s.

Against this background of general interest in film and television, Northern Ireland's two universities have contributed to scholarship and educational understanding of film culture. The University of Ulster at Coleraine – formerly the New University of Ulster – has highly successful undergraduate and postgraduate courses in media studies with huge application numbers each year. The academics who teach on these courses, such as Martin McLoone and John Hill, have national and international reputations and have been instrumental in the production of many books, articles and papers which have examined with clarity and erudition a wide range of film topics, including that of the growth in films and programmes made in or about the north. In 1999 the Queen's University of Belfast created a chair in film studies, and the decision to appoint Sam Rhoddie to this position, along with Queen's continued support for the QFT, continues to demonstrate that film culture is part of the educational framework of a modern university.

The End of the World Man on location in Belfast

Graduates of both universities who left with theoretical or practical skills in film and video have gone on to hold jobs in film and television production here, but the position in the 1980s and early 1990s was such that the development and delivery of what might be called actual *product* was still sporadic. The Blair government has championed the use of the term 'the creative industries' but for most of the period under review, film in Northern Ireland was little more than a cottage industry. That is not to decry it in the slightest. Individuals and very small companies persevered and films *were* made, but there was almost no sense of consistency and continuity. For example, there was much praise for the children's feature film *The End of the World Man* directed in 1985 by the late Bill Miskelly and written by Marie Jackson. It was a charming and well-made comedy, but it was chiefly reviewed at the time in relation to the fact that while it was shot in Northern Ireland with local actors, it made no mention of the Troubles. More significantly still, it was funded by the *Irish* Film Board. There were those who saw that as a positive pointer to a future when not every film had to tackle the issues raised by the Troubles and where funding could come from any source, including south of the border. But there was also contemporary criticism that the very absence of any references to the Troubles – other than a few shots of RUC vehicles – somehow trivialised the reality of children living in and growing up in a divided Ulster. Finally, though the film won first prizes at film festivals in Chicago, Los Angeles, Vienna and Berlin and can rightly be deemed to have been a success, it did not immediately lead Bill Miskelly's company, Aisling Films, towards making other features.

While some individual film-makers in the Republic such as Thaddeus O'Sullivan, Joe Comerford and Pat O'Connor appeared to be carving out names for themselves in the 1980s with one successful project after another, the position in the north seemed much more hesitating and sporadic. If there was one film-maker from Northern Ireland, though, who was looked upon as a genuine *auteur* with a distinctive and consistent personal style it was John T. Davis. The middle initial T is important, in order to distinguish him from the John Davies who made *Maeve* and *Acceptable Levels*. Davis, a graduate of the College of Art in Belfast, first came to public attention in 1978 with *Shellshock Rock*, a documentary on the then punk phenomenon, Belfast style. What was liberating about the film was not simply the music by local punk legends such as Stiff Little Fingers and The Undertones but the fact that John T. Davis showed with a certain subversive irony that the fans of Ulster punk

'Just another drifter on the Highway of Dreams',
John T. Davis directing *Route 66* in 1984

came from both sides of the community divide. This short documentary was the right film at the right time and when it was banned from the Cork Film Festival that somehow heightened the feeling that it was a raw and impolite look at an alternative Ulster – to quote the Stiff Little Fingers song-as-manifesto. Viewed from 2001, *Shellshock Rock* offers us a remarkable archival and nostalgic snapshot of the punk era and clearly shows the beginnings of a thesis that Davis was to develop through his later films, *Power In The Blood* and *Dust On The Bible*. In brief that thesis was that an examination of the role of music within specific communities would shed light on the wider cultural traditions and beliefs of those communities. As an example, *Power In The Blood* (1989), a documentary screened by BBC's Arena series, charts the journey of the American old-time country gospel singer Vernon Oxford from Nashville to Northern Ireland and in particular to protestant mission halls. Juxtaposing this with images of Ulster's home-grown evangelicals and religio-political fundamentals, Davis begins with Oxford in his home territory, the protestant and evangelical southern states of the USA, and ends with him singing for Northern Ireland prison officers dressed as dude cowboys, some of whom even proudly demonstrate their dummy six-gun twirling skills. This last sequence is all the more remarkable because Oxford sings both sentimental country songs and straight-up old-time revivalist gospel songs to men who were members of the Prison Officers Country Music Society – sitting in their bar inside the Maze Prison. Davis did not seek to ridicule any of the people who appear in the film – although that memorable Maze scene is hugely comic to some viewers and hugely scary to others. Where Davis' films succeeds best is in forcing the audience to see the common bonds of religious and social faith which unite many Ulster men and women with like believers elsewhere.

These films and others like David Hammond's *Steel Chest, Nail in the Boot and the Barking Dog* (1986), about Ulster working men as local characters, reflected upon the traditions within the two communities which had directly and indirectly led to the Troubles. But more than that, many of the best personal documentaries made by small local independent companies were extremely cinematic, sometimes in a poetic way, and that raised them above the idea of documentary as some kind of grim didactic reality. But these films were singular, handcrafted subjects and behind each was a story of the difficulty of obtaining development and production money and problems with distribution and broadcast. The film-makers were rivals for a smallish pot of money, but collectively they knew that there had to be a coherent collective body to speak on their behalf and to demonstrate the existence of a media industry in Northern Ireland. There was an oft-quoted remark in the 1980s which ran along the lines of: 'Industry? There is an industry – it's called the BBC!'

Mention has already been made of the courageous role of the BBC, both nationally and regionally in Northern Ireland itself, in making local, issue-based films throughout the 1970s and 1980s. These were not just shown on national television: some were also screened at film festivals, conferences and symposia around the world and in the 1990s, spurred on by the commercial success in cinemas of Channel Four's Film On Four productions, the BBC developed its distribution arm in addition to its proven strengths as a film-maker. Some of the most remunerative films – such as John Madden's *Mrs Brown* (1997) from BBC Scotland – indicate how a supposedly ailing British film industry could be revitalised through the direct funding of feature film projects which might have a cinema release in addition to a few airings on television. Without this bulwark of assistance from television companies such as the BBC and Channel Four it is unlikely that a film like *Divorcing Jack* (1999), based on the popular novel by Colin Bateman, would ever have been made.

Inadvertently too, BBC Northern Ireland has helped create a large pool of freelance and trained film-makers and technicians. Formerly the television companies such as the BBC and Ulster Television provided training and job security for their staff members, but those staff could not work openly on productions which were independent. Changes in technologies linked to corporate restructuring and new roles for film and broadcast unions meant that many staff – from cameramen to set designers; from producers to make-up artists – left the big companies and set up as freelance creative and technical talent in the independent sector. Risky at the best of times, it would have been foolhardy in the 1980s, but in 1990s with the creation of the Northern Ireland Film Council – now Commission – it became feasible.

The impetus for the creation of the NIFC came from the growing number of local film-makers and is outlined in the report entitled *Fast Forward*, commissioned by the Independent Film, Video and Photography Association and published in 1988. The report condemned the lack of support – both financial and in terms of training – from the public sector and, crucially, it demonstrated that such support, when applied in other countries, had done much to provide direct and indirect employment, never mind creating intrinsically worthwhile films.

The Northern Ireland Film Council in its 1989 manifestation was a voluntary organisation with no funding other than the twenty pounds which each of the original 120 signatories contributed. However, it used its collective resource to lobby on behalf of a single agency representing a nascent film and television industry. It received practical support, but no funding, from the BFI which, in 1991, finally recognised Northern Ireland as a UK film region. A year later the NIFC obtained real government funding through the Department of Education Northern Ireland, which in the first few years went mainly on setting up and running the now internationally recognised children's film festival, Cinemagic. After considerable changes and restructuring, however, it developed a stronger funding base including taking over the ACNI's role and film/video budget and in the late 1990s it evolved into the present Northern Ireland Film Commission.

The former self-nominated board was replaced by a new panel of eleven members, five of whom came as statutory nominees from key organisations such as the Arts Council, the film producers' association PACT, the Department of Education and more significantly still the Department of Economic Development. Other board members include the chief executives of the government-backed UK champion of film development, British Screen, and Skillset, the official training body for the media industries. It is worth detailing the NIFC composition because it demonstrates that by the late 1990s there was a properly constituted, official body working with equivalent national and regional bodies in what the EU calls the 'audio-visual industries', to promote investment in film, to assist the production of film and to market locally made film to the world. As Ronnie Kells, NIFC chairman said in 1998, 'we are only in the first phase of the council's work but its initial task is simple to state: to go out and market Northern Ireland as a good place to make films and to demonstrate that we can make it easy for film-makers to come here and make their films'.

Direct funding from government agencies and the National Lottery has helped the NIFC to compete nationally and internationally, but it also needs indirect funding for specific projects. To achieve that it has had to reassure the bond companies which put up venture capital for films, that there is the stability and the pool of talent needed to make competitive commercial films in Northern Ireland. When one considers that even a five minute short film can cost thirty thousand pounds and the most modest feature may cost three million pounds, this is now an area where only a single agency working closely with many partners and investors can hope to bring in large sums of money on a regular basis. There is no room in today's market for the occasional windfall or commission. Furthermore, the range of activities with which the commission is involved is immense, covering as it does location scouting for companies, careers days and schemes for practitioners and an educational outreach which links with the domestic film festivals which are now a feature of the Ulster film calendar.

Indeed festivals warrant a special mention. At one time the nearest thing to a local film festival was special programming at QFT during the Belfast Festival at Queen's. In 2001, in addition to Cinemagic, which itself has events and workshops in various places around the province complementing its main Belfast venues, there is the long running and successful Foyle Film Festival. Equally, in 2000, the former West Belfast Film Festival broadened and enlarged to become the inaugural Belfast Film Festival. Such events not only bring in examples of current international film and video making and makers/critics/actors, they also act as a showcase for locally made product and practitioners to show their wares. The same is true of the seemingly endless number of film festivals around the world: they exist to show off their local talent but they also give a much needed opportunity for our makers to exhibit their work to foreign audiences. This is especially important for short films. Cinemas rarely show shorts these days and TV channels tend to put shorts on, if at all, as fillers at ungodly hours.

Festivals and film markets are important showcases and in effect modern day hiring fairs. The productions act as portfolios for their makers who hope to secure the opportunity to make something bigger and longer. Although *Dance Lexie Dance* (1997, director Tim Loane for Raw Nerve/BBC-NI and NIFC) did not win an Oscar in 1998 there is no doubt that its being shown at

Kimberley McConkey and B.J. Hogg in the Oscar-nominated
Dance Lexie Dance (1997) directed by Tim Loane

festivals across the world led to the singular honour of receiving an Academy Award nomination. The publicity generated by the nomination has had important long-lasting direct and indirect consequences for Tim Loane and for the individuals and companies involved in its making. NIFC is involved in an annual scheme called Premiere which funds and markets locally made shorts. The reason why such shorts can cost thirty thousand and pounds as previously mentioned is that they now employ fully professional writers, directors, technicians, designers and caterers – all of whom get a credit in lists which sometimes seem as long as some of the films themselves. The overall quality of the work may be variable, but some pieces are very original. Not all shorts cost so much, especially if they are the product of a labour of love, and that aspect of film-making still exists in the province as is proved by Enda and Michael Hughes' feature length spoof horror film *The Eliminator* (1996) which was completed for less than eight thousand pounds.

The pool of talent for the production and post-production of so many projects needs constant refreshing, and existing makers need to be acquainted with the new technologies. At the end of 2000 there were several schemes and organisations which offered a combination of training and education. Of these the Nerve Centre in Derry best encapsulates the holistic approach to media and technologies. Participants ranging from schoolchildren to professionals had access to, and training in, a wide variety of programmes including digital video, animation, sound design, cinema management and the technologies and business of music. The Nerve Centre is linked to the NIFC, to Cinemagic, to the Foyle Film Festival and to outreach centres elsewhere including Belfast. The audio-visual web continues to expand at a remarkable rate. A significant example of this is the NIFC supported new multi-million pound technical facility and studio complex recently opened in the now revitalised dock and riverside area of Belfast. This offers state of the art resources to a wide range of media practitioners.

The historian Brian Winston contends that the actual form of innovative technologies determines the form and content of what is made with them. Today the speed of technological progress is frightening and the creative possibilities boundless. In 1971 most local film-makers still shot on celluloid and spliced film mechanically. Today, the *film*-maker may shoot using digital means and edit on a computer. Indeed the i-MAC computer on which this essay is written has, as a standard part of the package, a movie-making and editing facility more powerful than that of the professional AVID machines of just five years ago. Anyone reading this in thirty years time will be as amused at how primitive that reads in the way that someone today smiles at the mechanical devices with which we made films in 1971.

In 1971 the few remaining cinemas in Northern Ireland were of the single screen, single auditorium kind and most films played for only one week – if even that. Then came the splitting of existing cinemas into two or three screens and today we take for granted the multi-screen cineplex and leisure centre, and some of those are gearing up for digital projection to replace the scratchy business of running fragile celluloid in front of a beam of light. Even digital projection may go if the need for cinema itself goes. At present it is claimed that there are more cineplex cinema seats per thousand of the population here in Northern Ireland than anywhere else in the EU. But if we soon can swiftly download entire feature length films from the internet with the ease that we can create MP3 files for music to replace the CD, who knows what is just around the corner?

A real pointer to the future came with the launch in late 2000 of the Digital Film Archive for Northern Ireland. There are many archives around the world but normally only scholars can access the delicate celluloid or video-tapes held there. This new archive, the first of its kind in the UK, was developed by the NIFC in conjunction with the BFI, and it transfers film and tape to a digital format. The films can then be accessed by anyone through ordinary PC terminals in six educational centres around the province. Footage from Castle Place, Belfast, in 1897 through to some of the productions mentioned in this essay can be watched time and again with no loss of picture quality and no risk to the safety of the original. Already, in this digital era, some local makers of live films, promos and animations are posting their work on the internet for all to see, and the BFI has upwards of twenty shorts available to view in that format. Whatever the short or long-term changes, there is now in Northern Ireland a degree of modest confidence that we have the means, the will and the creativity to continue to redefine what we still call film – but what may well come to be known by another name in the years ahead.

Classical Music

JOE McKEE

Considering its size, Northern Ireland does very well for itself in terms of the performing arts generally, and reasonably well in the specific area of classical music. The province has never been better off when it comes to venues, and promoters will tell you it is increasingly difficult to schedule events in a regional calendar full of local and touring attractions. Thirty years ago there were fewer professional music events, most were centred on Belfast and the Belfast Festival at Queen's was popularly perceived as an oasis in an otherwise cultural desert. So what else has changed? Almost everything: a growing musical sophistication, greatly encouraged over recent years by a proliferation of moderately priced classical recordings of the highest standard and swept forward by the compact disc revolution; the consolidated position of music within the school curriculum; National Lottery funding, greater cross-border co-operation in touring and programming and, of course, a greatly improved security situation. But there is here too a stubborn, almost genetic conservatism.

The Ulster gourmet of the 1970s who sought out nothing more exotic than his prawn cocktail, followed by the well-done sirloin and the obligatory sherry trifle à la maison, now has an eye for Parma ham, poached halibut and crème brûlée. So too his musical tastes have been similarly broadened. Both the restoration of Belfast's Grand Opera House, which now attracts a succession of West End music shows, and the development of the Waterfront Hall with its international orchestras and soloists, have opened up unprecedented opportunities for those who wish to avail of this rich fare. And here, of course, is where we discover the paradox. In times of adversity, when options are limited, the Ulster person is perhaps at his or her stoical best, but present a surfeit of choice and things begin to go awry. In 2001 it has been possible to hear good classical music all year round in Northern Ireland, and in venues that equal those in the rest of the British Isles, but there is a lack of buzz and excitement that is sometimes disconcerting. The choice of venues might be wider but there are also far more empty seats at too many concerts and recitals. The local audience is very hard to satisfy and in opera, for example, very few can be coaxed out to see anything beyond *Carmen, Madame Butterfly* or *The Marriage of Figaro*. At the same time we are a community of critics, ever quick to write off what we do not like or understand. We seem to be as resistant to new music – even 'new' music from the nineteenth and twentieth centuries – as we are conservative in our attitudes to new political thought. The past thirty years have witnessed some dramatic transformations to the musical landscape, while other aspects have carried on with hardly a whiff of change. Central to so much else in this area, is the provision of professional orchestral music and opera.

In the 1950s and early 1960s Belfast had two orchestras. The BBC NI Orchestra recorded studio programmes and provided incidental music for plays. It also came together regularly with other professional instrumentalists, with the official blessing of the local BBC management, to create the much larger City of Belfast Orchestra directed by Maurice Miles. This symphony orchestra received public funding from CEMA – the Council for the Encouragement of Music and the Arts, the forerunner to the Arts Council – and played programmes, often of big romantic works, to sizeable audiences in the Ulster Hall. The arrangement worked well, but then the BBC decided to augment its local orchestra and employ the players on full-time contracts. At the same time, the Arts Council of Northern Ireland – ACNI – began to look at ways of creating an orchestra which could give regular series of concerts, accompany local opera performances and carry out educational work in schools. It was, in effect, writing the job description for the Ulster Orchestra as we know it today. A new orchestra was launched in 1966 with thirty-five full-time professional players and Maurice Miles as its first conductor.

It soon became clear, however, that all was not well. The audience that had grown up with Maurice Miles' big orchestra in the Ulster Hall now felt under-nourished on this new diet of leaner fare – mostly Haydn and Mozart – in the modern architectural ambience of the RUAS Members' Rooms at Balmoral in south Belfast. There was something dispiriting too, for supporters and players alike, in exchanging audiences of eight hundred or one thousand enjoying Elgar and Tchaikovsky for three hundred or fewer listening to Viennese classics. Quite apart from anything else, the sums simply did not add up when it came to paying the bills. Initially, the Arts Council exerted direct control on the management of the Ulster Orchestra, but in 1970, this was ceded to Malcolm Ruthven, who became its first general manager. Ruthven later went on to follow a career in broadcasting with BBC Radio Three and was followed as general manager of the Ulster Orchestra by Beattie Cromie, Roger Lloyd, Michael Henson and David Fisk.

It was not until 1981 that an amalgamation of the BBC NI and Ulster Orchestras was finally resolved. BBC senior management in Belfast and London, as well as the ACNI, felt that the national broadcaster was best placed to take over responsibility for a newly amalgamated orchestra and even considered calling the group 'The BBC Ulster Orchestra'. But things did not follow that course. The BBC in London decided to commission a comprehensive review of its entire orchestral output. The review provoked a widespread public debate even prompting industrial action by leading members of the music profession. At the end of the process, the BBC made fundamental organisational changes to its orchestral provision in England, Scotland and Wales. It decided to abolish its orchestra in Northern Ireland, paving the way for an augmented Ulster Orchestra, which eventually became the fully independent Ulster Orchestra Society Limited. An important link was retained in that the BBC, conscious of its long-standing commitment to 'live' classical music in Northern Ireland and to a number of its former employees, undertook to become one of the orchestra's principal funding partners, a relationship which survives to this day.

The list of the Ulster Orchestra's Principal Conductors makes for interesting reading: Maurice Miles (1966), Sergiu Commissiona (1969), Alun Francis (1974), Bryden [Jack] Thomson (1977), Vernon [Todd] Handley (1985), Yan Pascal Tortelier (1989), En Shao (1993) and Dmitry Sitkovetsky (1996). Thierry Fischer took up the position in September 2001 and Takuo Yuasa was appointed first Principal Guest Conductor in 1996. Any appraisal of the work of the orchestra's principal conductors is bound to be highly subjective and will be closely tied in with the personality and public face of each man. Audiences recall the vigour and self-assurance of Francis, the no-frills but always rewarding work of Thomson, the cool elegance and authority of Handley, Tortelier's amazing mix of raw excitement coupled with his sophisticated Gallic charm, but little of En Shao other than his subsequently splendid work with the Ulster Youth Orchestra. Sitkovetsky struggled to win anything like the popular following of a number of his predecessors, but during his time he did introduce some wonderful new soloists – personal friends from the international solo circuit in which he himself moves as a violinist.

Today the orchestra itself is in good shape and the 1999/2000 season in particular had an unprecedented number of large-scale concerts, thanks largely to additional funding from the National Lottery. Not since the glory days of Tortelier, with his regular concerts of Ravel and Debussy, had Belfast audiences heard anything quite like this. Instead of lavish French scores, we were treated to Mahler (*Symphonies No. 7 & 8*), Bruckner (*Symphony No. 8*), Bernstein (*Symphony No. 2*), Shostakovich (*Symphony No. 15*) and Berg (*Three Orchestral Pieces*). There are still those who yearn for a bigger string section, something which is most unlikely to happen in the current climate of arts funding and unnecessary, perhaps, when additional players can readily be contracted as and when they are required.

Perhaps the greatest strength of the Ulster Orchestra is its versatility. One week it might be playing Mahler's *Symphony No. 8*, the next, accompanying the Belfast Philharmonic Choir in Tippett's *A Child of Our Time*. Another week the orchestra might be playing a programme of Viennese music, followed by a week of studio recordings for BBC Radio Three. On top of this, the players will be expected to play as a pit orchestra for opera and visiting ballet companies. In addition to a full schedule of rehearsals and concerts, individual members of the Ulster Orchestra make an often-overlooked contribution to instrumental tuition in the greater Belfast area. Down the years hundreds of young musicians have benefited from their tutelage. The orchestra itself has a busy education department which places individual players or groups in schools, either in its 'Adopt a Player' scheme or in other specific projects. Less visible is the work of individual players such as Steve Barnett (trombone) who work to encourage local brass bands, either by coaching them or by providing first-class arrangements for them to play.

The orchestra, naturally, has its faults. From time to time, the players exude a dispirited weariness which occasionally comes across in their playing. This is an orchestra that knows who and what it likes and, more to the point, who and what it does not. It does not relish prolonged exposure to new music nor to conductors who, in the opinion of the players, make unreasonable rehearsal demands. In fairness to the players, they do seem to get their fair share of uninspiring conductors, although this should never be allowed to come across to the members of the public who have paid good money to hear as decent a performance as is possible. Finally, the orchestra has had to struggle since its inception against an ill-informed notion, in some quarters, that it somehow represents an imported clique of English musicians. The players are all there on merit, whether they be of local, English, Scottish, Welsh or Australian extraction. The idea that the Ulster Orchestra is a band of middle-England toffs, imposed on the good folk of Ulster by some politically motivated and manipulative arts quango, is not worthy of serious consideration.

Barry Douglas, the Belfast-born international concert pianist, returns home regularly to play with the orchestra. Douglas first came to national attention in 1978 when he was a piano finalist in the BBC Young Musician of the Year, the same year in which he went to London to study at the Royal College of Music. Since his 1986 triumph as Gold Medallist at the

Barry Douglas takes the applause with the Ulster Orchestra at the Waterfront Hall

Tchaikovsky International Piano Competition, Douglas has played with many of the world's most distinguished orchestras including the Berlin Philharmonic, the Leipzig Gewandhaus Orchestra, the Philadelphia Orchestra, the Cleveland Orchestra and all of the major London orchestras. Increasingly, however, he is investing his time in the affairs of Camerata Ireland, a chamber orchestra made up of professional Irish musicians living in Europe, along with some players from the Ulster Orchestra, the National Symphony Orchestra of Ireland, the RTÉ Concert Orchestra and the Irish Chamber Orchestra. Douglas founded Camerata Ireland which he conducts, invariably incorporating a piano concerto, often by Mozart, in their programmes. Although only launched in April 1999, the chamber orchestra has already provoked great critical interest, not least in the Americas.

Also happy to return home to his roots is that virtuoso performer, styled 'the man with the golden flute', Sir James Galway. Born in Belfast in 1939, Galway is one of the most famous musicians of his generation, highly

Sir James Galway

regarded for both his musical interpretation and for his mass audience appeal. Galway began his career at Sadlers Wells Opera and the Royal Opera Covent Garden. He subsequently held flute positions with the BBC Symphony Orchestra, the London Symphony Orchestra and the Royal Philharmonic Orchestra. He was appointed Principal Flute of the Berlin Philharmonic in 1969 and six years later began his career as a soloist. Over the past two and a half decades Galway has travelled the globe giving recitals, performing with the world's leading orchestras and, more recently, turning his attention to conducting.

If the past thirty years have witnessed the evolution and development of a single regional orchestra from the merger of two quite separate groups, the same unfortunately cannot be said of opera. As is so often the case in specific arts forms, one crucial individual was at the heart of all the activity, creating a unique dynamic energy both in the inspiration of others and, in his case, directing performances. This individual was Dr Havelock Nelson, Northern

Conductor, Havelock Nelson, in action

Ireland's undisputed 'Mr Music'. Rarely has there been a better example of the right man in the right place at the right time. The Cork-born, Dublin-educated Nelson (1917–96), possessed impressive natural skills. An excellent all-round musician and one of the country's most accomplished pianists, he could readily cope with the most awkward orchestral transcriptions for piano. As the BBC staff accompanist in Belfast, Nelson became a household name through his work on radio and later as the regular local conductor on *Songs of Praise*. He was a born impresario and showman. Most important of all perhaps in the specific field of opera, he had the uncanny knack of getting others round him to do a great deal of the dull but essential background work, freeing him to look after the most important aspect – the music.

Nelson outlined the growth of his Studio Opera Group in his 1993 autobiography, *A Bank of Violets*, where the reader can readily detect the author's passion for chamber opera in a remarkable period of artistic enterprise that lasted from 1950 through to 1985. The largely amateur Studio Opera Group (SOG), incorporating its Studio Orchestra, had by 1970 established an enviable track record in providing good quality opera, both in Belfast and, more importantly, in its regular tours throughout Northern Ireland and occasionally in the Republic. Nelson demonstrated that SOG could present Mozart, Rossini, Humperdinck, Purcell and Haydn, and in the 1970s the group secured an even stronger reputation for itself by presenting a successful sequence of Britten's stage works that included *Let's Make an Opera, Noye's Fludde, The Rape of Lucretia, Albert Herring,* and *The Turn of the Screw.*

In 1970, on the other hand, the local 'senior' opera company, The Grand Opera Society of Northern Ireland (GOSNI), found itself dealing with increasingly difficult financial problems. In fairness, things were not at all easy when it came to mounting grand opera as opposed to SOG's touring chamber productions. Venues in Belfast especially were problematic: the Grand Opera House had been allowed to deteriorate physically and was used for all kinds of variety shows. A number of small bombs in the early stages of the Troubles added to its general dilapidation. GOSNI found itself staging concert performances in venues such as the Whitla Hall at Queen's, the ABC Cinema and the Ulster Hall where the company even mounted a concert version of Wagner's *The Flying Dutchman!* The Arts Council was faced with a dilemma. Nelson and his Studio Opera Group were going from strength to strength while GOSNI was finding it harder and harder to make ends meet. Clearly there was not a sustainable audience for two competing companies.

The proposed solution was to attempt a merger, administrative at first, with the formation of the Northern Ireland Opera Trust (NIOT). Alison Taggart became the administrator and was charged with sorting out GOSNI's declining fortunes while simultaneously bringing a greater degree of good management practice to what had been the largely amateur set-up at SOG. At the time there was hope that the two might even come together artistically. In practice this was always going to be nigh on impossible because the two companies were such completely different creatures. Nelson saw the development of local singers and a commitment to touring as his raison d'être, whereas GOSNI and its successor NIOT saw themselves wedded, in the Carl Rosa tradition, to bringing in professional singers from outside, albeit complemented by a local amateur chorus. In terms of music theatre, however, SOG scored with the public when it came to actual performance because Nelson's hand-picked singers knew each other's strengths and weaknesses and tended to produce performances that were cohesive and strong in terms of ensemble. The company also had a policy of always singing in English, something that helped when performing to town-hall audiences across the province.

Nineteen eighty-five was a crunch year. Havelock Nelson had decided to retire from SOG, chiefly to enable himself to spend more time in the West Indies with a company he had helped establish there. Studio Opera Group at the same time, and with serious misgivings, reluctantly agreed to look at the Arts Council's suggested merger with NIOT to form a new company, Opera Northern Ireland (ONI). James Shaw was the SOG representative on the ONI Board and one of the attractions of the new company was that local singers, like Shaw and others, would be offered worthwhile roles in productions. Although it was publicly stated at the time that ONI was the logical union of NIOT and SOG, the latter staged its final production of Mozart's *Marriage of Figaro* coupled with Offenbach's *Robinson Crusoe*. Almost immediately the company re-formed under Ian Urwin and Jack Smith's leadership, two of SOG's leading men, as Castleward Opera. The subsequent reluctance by ONI to use local soloists, as we shall see, proved to be a major hurdle.

So yet again there were two opera companies performing in close proximity, two poachers working the same small stretch of river. In the beginning, their relative David and Goliath funding positions created a situation where each went about marketing and delivering two quite different products. ONI administrator Alison Taggart – and then subsequently Randall Shannon – and artistic director Kenneth Montgomery, all made a good job of staging full-scale productions in the appropriate setting of Belfast's Grand Opera House. The critics were full of praise for the 1986 productions of *Falstaff* and *Ariadne auf Naxos* and the 1990 version of *The Magic Flute*. At the same time Urwin, Smith and their team were developing a uniquely distinctive product for music-lovers in the courtyard theatre of one of the National Trust's outstanding buildings in Northern Ireland, Castleward. Quite apart from the obvious delights of a rural setting, the high quality of the food available during the hour and a half Glyndebourne-style intervals and the apparent attraction of rubbing shoulders with the great and good, Castleward Festival Opera consistently turned in productions which were often very satisfying and occasionally excellent. There were shortcomings too, not least the cramped conditions for audience and performers alike and an acoustic that was less than ideal. But there was a sense of genuine music theatre that was immediately compelling and an ambience that drew the audience into the performances. Perhaps too, part of the lure of the earliest days of Castleward was the impression that here was a team of people battling against almost impossible financial odds to produce something really worthwhile.

During the 1980s and 1990s the two companies co-existed. ONI received the greater part of the Arts Council's opera grant and Castleward survived for the most part on box office and commercial sponsorship. Latent unease surfaced slowly. ONI was perceived to be receiving large sums of public funding, yet there were often far too many empty seats. The commitment to touring was somehow not shown to be as important as perhaps it ought to have been, and fewer and fewer local singers were given any significant solo roles. Meanwhile Castleward was bridging the quality gap so that the perceived artistic distance between the work of the two companies was appearing to shrink. Each season ONI attempted to pair a popular piece with a less well-known work. In its latter seasons, this resulted in decent productions of *The Cunning Little Vixen, Fidelio, Idomeneo* and *Hansel and Gretel,* but these played to disappointing audiences which inevitably led to lost revenue that the company could ill afford to sustain. As the deficit grew, so too did the undercurrent of criticism that the ONI chorus was musically below par and certainly not equal to the more committed singing, albeit in a much smaller theatre, of the ladies and gentlemen of Castleward. Most damaging of all in terms of arts politics, it was often claimed that ONI had overlooked the importance of a strong public profile, that it had somehow failed to create a loyal constituency. Aspects of this were demonstrably at the core of its modest rival's success. The Castleward management was astute in being seen to work hard at audience development, taking events out of its theatre to venues such as Campbell College and Stormont. In the millennium season the company even staged a well-publicised recital of light opera classics in a Belfast fish and chip shop, making the point that popular opera can be enjoyed every bit as much with a fish supper as with smoked salmon and champagne.

The final demise of ONI in September 1998 was undignified and messy. The Arts Council pulled the financial plug from under the company, as it launched its autumn season of *The Magic Flute*, in an atmosphere of deep recrimination. ONI countered with press releases detailing a catalogue of past triumphs that were fair and to the point, but too late. The horse had bolted. In its place, opera enthusiasts would see enhanced public funding go to Castleward, enabling the company to continue to bring its productions to the Grand Opera House, which would also play host to visiting large-scale shows from Welsh National Opera. There would be occasional visits to the Waterfront Hall by visiting foreign companies, mainly from Romania and other eastern European countries. From the south, the Dublin-based Opera Theatre Company, a shining example of an arts organisation with a genuine commitment to all-Ireland performances and one enjoying funding from the two Arts Councils on this island, would tour more extensively in Northern Ireland.

Opera Northern Ireland's Stephen Barlow (left) and Kenneth Montgomery in the opulent surroundings of the Grand Opera House

Opera in Ulster seems to have covered a great deal of ground since 1971 without necessarily getting anywhere. The long-term future for Castleward seems no more assured than the future was for GOSNI in 1971. The company may well find that having a substantially increased grant from the public purse can bring fatal consequences. As the natural heir to the Studio Opera Group, it would do well to reflect on those pioneering productions of the 1960s and 1970s. The two Arts Councils have made no secret of their mutual interest in developing an all-Ireland opera company. In the years ahead this may well prove to be the critical dynamic for this particular art form.

Before leaving opera it should be noted that there is great popular support for the amateur light operatic movement, an art form which survives with very slight public funding. Companies such as St Agnes' Choral Society, Belfast Operatic, Ulster Operatic, New Lyric, Fortwilliam, Lisnagarvey, Newry, Bangor, Londonderry and others, regularly produce excellent shows involving large casts of singers and, provide unique performance opportunities for talented solo singers. There is a strong emphasis on the dramatic element – an aspect that the 'serious' opera companies sometimes neglect in favour of the purely musical content – and choreography too is taken seriously in many productions.

Chamber music is similarly enjoyed by a large number of aficionados. This is surprising perhaps in a culture with an apparent preference for music of the country and gospel styles, and which draws criticism for being conservative in its taste and outspoken in its disdain for 'high-falutin' music. The Belfast Music Society (BMS), the Classical Music Society in Derry, as well as established series in Armagh, Portstewart, Enniskillen, Downpatrick and Whiteabbey, provide invaluable opportunities for lovers of chamber music and song recitals. The two Arts Councils have adopted a sensible all-Ireland strategy to chamber music. Leading artists who want to tour in Ireland can now easily co-ordinate their visits, enabling them to plan cost-effective itineraries and offer concert promoters a product they can afford in a way that would be impossible if the same promoters were bringing over big names for single events. On top of this basic provision there has been a steady increase in chamber programming from the two universities, the Belfast Festival at Queen's and the music department of the BBC.

Chamber music has also been one beneficiary of the new venues which have emerged in Belfast in the last decade. Many of those attending chamber music recitals have confessed to preferring the somewhat drab surroundings of the Elmwood Hall rather than the glitzy but impersonal ambience of the Waterfront's Studio. The same is true of the Ulster Orchestra's regular patrons who seem to prefer the Ulster Hall, with all its obvious current draw-backs, to the counter-attractions of the Waterfront. The main reason, apart from affection for an old friend, seems to be the conviction that the Ulster Hall has a superior natural acoustic for orchestral music. Orchestral music, in particular, loses much of its impact in the Waterfront, even in the case of large touring orchestras. The same music in the Ulster Hall invariably sounds fuller and has a richer 'bloom'. Some time ago Belfast City Council outlined its intention, in principle, to refurbish the Ulster Hall. It is to be hoped that this can be achieved soon and the present gradual decline in the hall's appearance can be reversed. The Ulster Hall, and its Mulholland Grand Organ, are assets too valuable to be allowed to fall, as before, into a state of disrepair.

Over the past thirty years there has also been a very considerable increase in the number of indigenous composers. Few can earn a living on composition alone, but by balancing some general freelance work with perhaps a little teaching, this growing number of musicians have found they can devote more time to composition than others have been able to do in the past. For much of the 1970s and 1980s Queen's University, in collaboration with ACNI, ran a very productive composer-in-residence scheme where the university provided a base and some income from teaching while the Arts Council pro-vided additional money and occasional composition projects. The scheme certainly raised the profile of composers generally and introduced generations of QUB students to living, breathing composers. Piers Hellawell, who was to adopt Belfast as his home and stay on as a lecturer at Queen's, and other young composers, broke down many of the false barriers that surrounded composers and demystified many aspects of the art for their students. During his time in Belfast, Kevin Volans in particular was composing fresh and accessible new work which was achieving international acclaim, not least because of his interest in African music and the availability of his music on commercial CDs.

There is now a vibrant community of composers spread throughout Ireland. Alongside the big names of Gerald Barry, Seóirse Bodley, Jerome de Bromhead, John Buckley, Raymond Deane, Eric Sweeney and others in the Republic, Northern Ireland can readily produce an impressive list of composers whose work is acknowledged as being of high quality. David Byers, Philip Hammond, Kevin O'Connell, Michael Alcorn and Eibhlis Farrell all represent the very best of the homegrown writers. Others such as Adrian Thomas, Piers Hellawell and David Morris were drawn to Northern Ireland by work in the universities; while Elaine Agnew, Deirdre Gribbin, Brian Irvine, Deirdre McKay and Ian Wilson represent the generation following on from Byers and Hammond. Of these, Wilson is by far the most ambitious and his music is regularly performed outside Northern Ireland.

David Byers has a large and impressive catalogue to his credit. He deserves particular credit for his vision and courage in consistently promoting a great deal of high-quality, new music, throughout his thirty years as a music producer with the BBC. The composer and arts administrator Philip Hammond finds himself in an awkward position. As Director of Performing Arts at the Arts Council, his work cannot attract the sort of financial support it would undoubtedly otherwise merit, either through ACNI project grants or from lottery funding which operates through ACNI. From his early works for piano and voice, often for the mezzo-soprano Daphne Arlow, Hammond now writes on a bigger canvas. His *Die Ersten Blumen* (1996) was toured by the Ulster Orchestra and his *Psalms and Songs from the Hebrew* (2000), was scored for four separate choirs, two vocal soloists, organ and orchestra. This was Hammond's largest work to date and was premiered at the Belfast Festival at Queen's in November 2000. *Psalms and Songs* embodies many important elements of Hammond's mature output. He avoids parochial concerns in favour of a profound interest in international poetry and themes and has a deeply subjective view of human spirituality and the essential emotions surrounding love and death.

The Belfast-born, Dublin-based composer Shaun Davey, has regularly used Irish history as the source for his work. Three of his compositions, which have combined conventional orchestral instruments with elements from traditional Irish music, have been widely accepted and, a rare distinction for a local composer, have been incorporated into the Northern Ireland music curriculum for schools. Davey's *Granuaile Suite, The Relief of Derry Symphony* and *The Brendan Voyage*, seem likely to retain their unique position and continue to be played, from time to time, by the Ulster Orchestra. While Davey has drawn on episodes from distant Irish history in his work, no other Ulster composer of the past thirty years has appeared to draw any significant inspiration from the all-pervading political situation. In many other art forms, especially poetry, prose, theatre and television drama, the Troubles have been there, either as a backdrop or as a major theme. Perhaps the concerns of a constitutional struggle, based on national identity, are language-based and therefore more suited to literature.

Whatever the reason, the apparent reluctance of local composers to confront any of the issues relating to Ulster's unfolding tragedy – throughout the entire period – seems strange to say the very least. If individual composers have been working away at such themes, they have managed to keep their work well hidden. There have been occasional choral and vocal pieces, sometimes linked to particular events, such as an anthem inspired by the Enniskillen Remembrance Day bomb which was subsequently sung by the local cathedral choir at the British Legion Festival in the Royal Albert Hall. Generally, however, there has been no major professional composition and certainly nothing that has caught the public imagination. A time capsule of the period used to illustrate the arts in the years under review might well contain a recording of Phil Coulter's *The Town I Love So Well*, with its vivid lyrics referring to street violence in Derry, but what other music reflects the turmoil of Northern Ireland from 1971 to 2001?

Finally, the period saw the death, at advanced years, of two local-born and highly influential composers. Joan Trimble (1915–2000), from Enniskillen, was a music graduate of Trinity College, Dublin, who later studied composition with Herbert Howells in London in the 1930s, as well as with Vaughan Williams and Arthur Benjamin. She took a practical view of composition, avoiding anything that smacked of pretension in her work and although popularly remembered for her piano-duo concerts with her sister Valerie, deserves to be revered principally as a composer of songs, piano pieces and the television opera, *Blind Raftery* (1957). A year before Joan Trimble died, Howard Ferguson, regarded as Ulster's most distinguished native composer and one of its finest musicologists, died in London at the age of ninety-one. Most of his adult life was spent in England after his studies at the Royal College of Music and, while he wrote relatively little, what he did produce was always well regarded.

So much for the biographical details of the companies and individuals that tell one part of the story. How is classical music faring in the wider context, thirty years since the publication of *Causeway*? In some aspects little has changed. As Edgar Boucher pointed out in relation to professional singers in 1971, 'our musical life has not yet reached the stage where performers of this class [Heather Harper and Jean Allister] can make a living at home in Northern Ireland.' Much the same could be said today. A group of young female singers appeared in the 1980s and 1990s – Mary Nelson, Maureen Murphy, Catherine Harper, Rachel Fisher, Victoria McLaughlin – but they nearly all left to train in London and Manchester. Today they return home only for occasional engagements, to sing for one or other of the provincial choral societies and music clubs.

From a generation earlier, singers like Norma Burrowes (soprano), Pascal Allen (bass), Uel Deane (tenor), Mervyn Collins (tenor) and Alan Ewing (baritone), rarely return. Thirty years ago there were many more training and performance opportunities for singers. Havelock Nelson, as we have seen, gathered round him a group of immensely talented local singers, kept busy singing opera or on the concert platform as soloists in oratorio. Irene Sandford, Florence Innis, Jack Smith, Ian Urwin, Daphne Arlow, Janette Simpson, Mary Gilmore and others, were able to sing at this level thanks to the training they received from local teachers such as Sam and Carys Denton, Donald Cairns, Frank Capper, John Patterson and, in Derry, James McCafferty. Many also benefited from the work of the outstanding local répétiteur Michael McGuffin. The brothers Eric and Henry Hinds, fine bass/ baritones, were exceptionally busy on the concert and recital scene, although their interests did not extend to opera.

Today there is a feeling that we are less well off in terms of singing teachers – although pupils of Irene Sandford, Linda Snell, Margaret McAusland, Nuala Anthony, Margaret Smith, Aubrey McClintock and Judith Sheridan might disagree. Nonetheless, at competitive musical festivals, especially in some of the bigger vocal classes, the standard of performance demonstrated by young singers from Dublin is often significantly ahead of local voices. Those with longer memories assure me this is a sea change; thirty and forty years ago, Belfast singers at the Dublin

Feis Ceil, regularly carried away the major trophies.

To make matters worse for singers, there are also fewer opportunities for well-equipped semi-professionals to perform than there were thirty years ago. Concert opportunities across the province are much reduced and the BBC records fewer singers for its radio schedules. Throughout the 1950s and 1960s the BBC Northern Ireland Home Service filled the airwaves with local singers, from school children through to accomplished adults such as George Beggs, in a number of programme strands such as its *Ballad Concerts*, *Ulster Airs* and *Ulster Serenade*. Times were different then: musical tastes and public perceptions were far removed from those of today and it is perhaps a pointless exercise to wonder how things might be if Radio Ulster were to find space for a weekly song recital in the year 2001. I imagine there would be calls, not entirely without justification, to take such a programme off on the grounds of its perceived lack of quality. But why does that not seem to happen in the context of local sport, where there is similar relentless exposure without any apparent regard to significant success or achievement?

Success has been found at the two Schools of Music in our universities. Thirty years ago there was an established university in Belfast and a vigorous young polytechnic at Jordanstown where Dr Donald Cullington was appointed to establish, what immediately became, a thriving new department with a strong emphasis on performance. At various times over the years there have been rumours of an amalgamation, but such speculation appears to be in decline, not least because each department has so successfully created a distinctive identity of its own. At Queen's, the pioneering work of the late Professor John Blacking in the field of ethnomusicology was being carried out, not in the School of Music, but within the School of Anthropological Studies. Blacking attracted an almost cult following in the 1970s and 1980s on account of the quality of his research, the strength of his personality and the calibre of his teaching. An important aspect of Blacking's work was in encouraging postgraduate students from across the British Isles to study various regional aspects of music in a social context. In 2000 Queen's refurbished the Harty Room, and the School of Music as part of a ten million pounds investment in music, confirming in a very public manner, the university's commitment to the performing arts.

Formal education at the universities and in schools has been supplemented by the creation of the Ulster Youth Orchestra and the Ulster Youth Choir, both supported by Philip Hammond with significant funding from the Arts Council. These developments have created enhanced expectations and have provided opportunities for high-quality performances for young people in their teens and twenties. The UYO in particular has provided a logical progression beyond the excellent work of the symphony orchestras of the various education boards. It might well claim to be the regional equivalent of the Irish Youth Orchestra or the National Youth Orchestra of Great Britain. Choral singing in Ulster's schools, once in the doldrums, has been given a new competitive edge with remarkable successes in the Sainsbury's Choir of the Year competition for Grosvenor High School, the Boys' Choir from St Eugene's Cathedral in Derry and the Girls Choir of Methodist College Belfast in recent years.

One perplexing aspect of schools' music is that very few young people seem to continue to play orchestral instruments after the age of eighteen. There are precious few amateur orchestras and these have a high percentage of older players, many of whom pre-date even the large investment in instrumental tuition which began in the 1960s. The Studio Symphony Orchestra (SSO), directed by David Openshaw in direct line of succession from Havelock Nelson and Alan Tongue, continues to do excellent work, both in adventurous orchestral repertoire and as accompanist to various amateur choral societies. In its earliest days the SSO was able to attract exceptional players of the calibre of James Galway and Derek Bell, as well as giving Barry Douglas his first concerto experience. More recently, the orchestra has become involved in a number of ambitious cross-border choral and orchestral projects.

No survey of amateur music in Northern Ireland could omit reference to bands and choirs. Conductors of both complain about the increasing difficulties faced by individuals when asked to commit to regular rehearsals. Despite this, many local bands continue to produce performances that are impressive, not only in terms of technique but also in terms of repertoire. The Field Marshal Montgomery Pipe Band, under the direction of Richard Parkes, has achieved extraordinary international success, especially in the past ten years. Northern Ireland pipers and drummers are regularly in the top places at the World Championships and the various prestigious Scottish competitions.

Regrettably, there are now fewer military brass and reed bands and the long established and much respected Grosvenor Hall Military Band folded due to insufficient players.

It is a matter for regret, too, that the civil disturbances of the past thirty years, with the subsequent rise in sectarianism and the growth of street politics, have created a false perception of the nature of flute bands. The type of melody flute band that exists to accompany Orange and republican marchers should not be confused with that unique provincial ensemble, the Ulster Flute Band. All across the province there is a network of amateur flautists who find great satisfaction in exploring a repertoire embracing folk melodies, brass band transcriptions, songs from the shows and film music. In the generations immediately before this, hundreds of men and women, many of them working-class, got their first exposure to orchestral music through arrangements which had been carefully commissioned for flute bands. The story of James Galway's early training by the late Billy Dunwoody and others is undoubtedly exceptional, but Colin Fleming, principal flute for many years with the Ulster Orchestra, followed a similar path. His father, Arthur Fleming, did outstanding work as conductor with the Ballyclare Victoria Flute Band, of which the young Colin was a member. He in turn studied with Galway in Berlin before embarking on his own career.

Whereas choral music in schools is probably as good as it has ever been, the same cannot be said of the adult sector. Changes in public worship and in attitudes to church attendance have resulted in a radical reappraisal of the place of church choirs and this has had a deleterious effect on secular choral groups. By the end of the 1960s there was still a relatively strong choral tradition across the country. The bigger provincial towns often had good four-part choirs, directed by competent organists, while Armagh, Belfast, Derry and Newry all supported cathedral choirs capable of performing impressive music. For catholics, the Second Vatican Council had already begun to dilute the impact of classical church music so that the tradition of Latin masses and motets was overtaken by music which called for rather more modest attainments. Perhaps the biggest change in choral music since then has been the decline in the pre-eminence of the cathedral choirs and the rise of small, specialist choral groups. Here one must record the sterling work of Ronnie Lee (1929–92), both with his school choir at Grosvenor High and with the adult group Renaissance. Both choirs – but especially Renaissance – created a new standard by which other Ulster choirs could measure themselves in the 1970s and 1980s. Following Harry Grindle's time at St Anne's Cathedral in Belfast, which ended in 1975, Jonathan Gregory went on to inspire a generation of singers and instrumentalists to do great things, both at St Anne's and subsequently at St George's Church. Gregory had the energy and vision to create the St George's Singers and Orchestra, groups which still perform today, although many will look back to their earliest years as the time when they produced their best work. Harry Grindle found a new outlet for his undoubted gifts as a choral conductor over a number of years in the 1980s and 1990s with the Priory Singers. The same attention to detail and characteristic clean sound has recently been reborn with a further Grindle ensemble, The Minster Singers, the title of this and the earlier choir pointing to Dr Grindle's love of liturgical music. In the 1970s, following his return from the Royal Academy, David Byers produced exciting and interesting programmes with his New Belmont Consort, and Bill Lloyd, a colleague of Byers in the BBC, briefly created very fine sounds and challenging programmes with a group called Singet. Both of these groups no longer exist. Donal McCrisken and his chamber choir, Cappella Caeciliana, which he formed in 1995 to sing the great polyphonic repertory of the catholic tradition, produce a refreshingly full and vibrant sound with only fourteen voices.

There has been a regrettable decline in the number of local choral societies capable of tackling large-scale choral works. The Belfast Philharmonic Choir is the largest of these and appears regularly in the Ulster Orchestra's season of concerts in the Waterfront and Ulster halls. The choir is aware of the importance of high standards and has lately insisted on re-auditions for its members, although the recruitment of new, younger voices, remains a priority. The Philharmonic, with its long and distinguished history, is to be congratulated for bringing over to its weekly rehearsals a professional musician from England, Marion Wood, as its chorus master. There are choral societies in the cathedral cities of Armagh and Derry, the latter based around the Two Cathedrals Festival where the Derry chorus has achieved a number of very fine performances in a relatively short time. There is some concern, however, at the time of writing that the future of the Two Cathedral Festivals is less than certain.

This chapter began by looking back to the middle of the last century. At the start of this new millennium, the School of Music at Queen's University in Belfast, has recently announced major capital funding to create a Sonic Arts Research Centre (SARC). This new facility, the first purpose-built research centre for music and technology in the United Kingdom, will be directed by Dr Michael Alcorn and will stimulate and co-ordinate collaborative work in the fields of music, computer science and electronic engineering. This is the country's most exciting new music-related project for many years and will provide a £4.5 million facility that is likely to be, for a long time, the envy of university departments throughout the United Kingdom if not across the world. The project is impressive both for its cutting-edge nature and its sheer scale. Elsewhere in this survey there have been suggestions of a regional propensity for artistic conservatism, not least in the field of music. Northern Ireland now has the musicians and the infrastructure to look to the future with confidence. One can only hope that out of this confidence will grow a new era of exceptional creativity.

Traditional Music and Song

TONY McAULEY

Traditional music and song in Ulster are both rich and varied, indeed argu-ably more so than in the rest of the country. In addition to the native tradition, they have absorbed much of the richness of the Scottish tradition, in terms of both melody and lyric. An indication of how traditional music and song used to be perceived by the cultural élite of the north can be gained from the 1951 edition of the *Arts In Ulster*. They were pretty well ignored. Not a single living exponent of folk song, balladry or traditional music is mentioned. The author of the chapter on music in Ulster observed that, 'by far the greater part of the old folk music is still unknown to the general pub-lic. So much of it is still tucked away in journals or published in a form which does not make it readily available for anyone but students.' This was written at a time when there were numerous traditional singers and musicians in every county with plenty of local songs and tunes. They were out there, practically on the doorstep, but those who ought to have known better did not acknowledge their existence and as a result, a great deal of traditional folk culture was irrevocably lost.

The late 1950s and 1960s saw a massive growth in both public awareness of, and support for, traditional music and song. It diminished in the 1970s and 1980s, and in these days of comparative political stability in the north, it is once again on the increase. Regrettably, traditional music and folk song are perceived in some quarters as being cultural appendages of nationalist and republican politics, despite a centuries old process of cross-fertilisation with the Scottish tradition. The term 'Fenian music' is not uncommon. Yet prior to the 1970s, people from both communities supported traditional music and song – they went to the clubs and they were regular attenders at the various county fleadhs. However, as the Troubles worsened, so too did the perception of traditional music in protestant areas. The catholic community had always seen music and song as an extension of its cultural and political identity, and in some staunchly nationalist areas traditional music inevitably came to be seen as part of the ideological struggle. The protestant community was alienated, and members of that community who wanted to play traditional music for its own sake, were faced with a dilemma.

Ironically, the situation was made much worse by a decision arrived at by Comhaltas Ceolteórí Éireann, the governing body in traditional Irish music, whose function it is to promote the welfare of music and song both in Ireland and abroad. In 1971 it decided to cancel the All Ireland Fléadh Cheoil as a protest against the introduction of internment in Northern Ireland. Once that happened, traditional music was dragged unwillingly into the political turmoil of the Troubles. That decision effectively undermined whatever cross-community support traditional music had up to then enjoyed. Supporters of traditional music within the protestant unionist community felt betrayed, and each new political crisis saw a further dwindling in support within that community. Political divisions were reinforced by an ever-widening cultural chasm that even music's most ardent supporters within the protestant community could not cross. The longer this sense of alienation lasted, the deeper it became. In August 1993 in north Down, the loyalist terror group the Red Hand Commando did what many musicians had

Performer, broadcaster and writer Tony McAuley

always feared might happen – it threatened to blow-up any hotel or pub in the Newtownards area that played host to traditional music. The threat was ridiculous and unjustifiable, but it was deadly nonetheless. It was made in the belief that traditional music was part of the ethos of what those responsible for issuing it termed the 'pan nationalist front'. There was an immediate outcry from several quarters and the threat was withdrawn, but traditional musicians and their followers were left in no doubt as to how they were perceived in the eyes of some. The threat was an indication of the way in which a unique and important cultural resource had been manipulated and misunderstood.

In recent years, meanwhile, there has been an apparent reluctance on the part of the local television stations to make programmes featuring traditional music. For almost a decade, there has been little on either of the local stations that does justice to the vast amount of talent within the world of traditional and folk music in Ulster. This was not the case in the 1970s and 1980s, when BBC television in particular, broadcast a great variety of series featuring traditional and contemporary folk music. These programmes were timely, popular, and of cultural importance and they included *Folk Weave, One Night*

Stand, The Gig in the Round, As I Roved Out, In Performance, and *The Corner House.* The long-running television series *As I Roved Out* was of particular significance. Produced annually from 1976 until 1988, it provided a sorely needed platform for much of the emerging talent that nowadays is part of the iconography of Irish music: Planxty, the Bothy Band, Dé Danann, Mary Black, Maura O'Connell, Arty McGlynn, Paul Brady, Andy Irvine, Davy Spillane, Kieran Goss, Frances Black, and Enya all featured on the series, many of them making their television debuts. The series was studio-based; it was under-funded in relation to other music-based programmes at the time yet it was synonymous with quality. Other guests included Makem and Clancy, the Chieftains, the Dubliners, Ralph McTell, Clannad, and Christy Moore. One of the programme's last, and finest, achievements was to present the Chieftains and Van Morrison in concert.

The series that followed was quite different. It moved from featuring the major talents in a live studio audience format, to the intimate and more familiar surroundings of the pub. *The Corner House,* a joint BBC/RTÉ production, featured local players in their own immediate locality, playing before a small local audience. It aimed to reveal the breadth and the wealth of traditional music in each northern county. The programmes had no presenter – the music and the songs spoke for themselves. When the doors of *The Corner House* closed after two years in 1993, they were to remain closed. Ironically, this was at a time when the popularity of traditional music was on the increase both here and abroad. Traditional musicians and singers were performing in unprecedented numbers throughout the world. The international success of *Riverdance* placed Irish music on the world stage and further enhanced its already increasing popularity.

The music has come a long way from its humble and inauspicious origins without shedding entirely the attendant imagery of the crossroads, the turf fire and the small cottage. Most tourists who visit Ireland actively seek out at least one session of traditional music and song. That most certainly is the case in the Republic where it is seen as a key cultural resource and the vibrancy of the traditional music scene today contrasts sharply with the situation that existed throughout Ireland up to the late 1950s. Until then, the playing of reels, jigs and hornpipes was seldom heard outside the parochial confines of the local céilí, and céilí dancing was in decline. It was perceived by the younger generation of the time as being old fashioned. The show-bands were the craze, and across Ireland the showband sound was all the rage. Instruments like fiddle, accordion, flute, piano, banjo and basic drum kit were displaced by trumpet, saxophone, trombone, and electric guitar. Venues which had promoted the céilí turned to the showbands for their dance music. It was either that or shut down, and in some cases, that is exactly what happened to the halls which persisted in promoting regular céilí functions.

There had been some renowned céilí bands in the north where musicians had practised their skills, but céilí dancing with its little or no bodily contact, and its increasingly coy rural image, went into rapid decline in the early 1960s and was never able to recover. Those men and women whose skills in traditional playing had been honed and given a social function with the céilí bands, found themselves redundant. For a young person to be seen with a fiddle was almost a guarantee to invite mockery and banter. If céilí dancing was not in vogue, neither was the music.

The same kind of paralysis was happening to traditional song. Indeed it was even less frequently heard in public. Stirring songs of patriotic fervour were heard from time to time, but the real tradition of balladry was stagnant. It was regarded as second-rate and if a song did not have a regular beat – waltz time being the most favoured – then it was seldom sung. The roots of the revival were nourished by radio in the 1950s and by what was known as the roving microphone. Following the example set by Radio Éireann, which had taken the microphone into areas of rural Ireland in search of local music and song, the BBC in Belfast produced a number of distinguished and popular radio programmes, notably *Music on the Hearth*. Such programmes introduced singers like Sarah Makem, her son Tommy, Brigid Tunney, Paddy Tunney, Peter Kelly, David Hammond and the McPeakes to the local public. The men producing the programmes knew and fully appreciated the available material. Often the recordings were spontaneous and not always of studio quality, but they were nevertheless important and effective.

Later, Sam Hanna Bell devised a monthly series for BBC Northern Ireland called *Listen Here Awhile*, where Maurice Leitch, who inherited the production of the programmes, set about bringing the microphone into places where the music was happening. Broadcast until 1968, *Listen Here Awhile* featured the talents of singers and players from every county in Ulster who continued to make an important contribution, and to demonstrate that, in those days at least, the BBC was committed to the fostering of local music.

In fact the broadcasters were responding to what was happening all over Ireland and further afield. The folk revival which had begun in America had made traditional song popular. People were looking for music that was 'rooted' and performers like Pete Seeger, Joan Baez and Bob Dylan were fashionable. The Clancy Brothers and Tommy Makem were at the forefront of what was known as the ballad boom in Ireland, and dozens of groups who cloned their style and line-up of four singers accompanied by guitar and banjo, soon appeared. Ballad singers in a variety of line-ups followed them. Individual singers with an array of repertoires and styles entertained audiences in pubs, clubs and concert halls. The majority played guitar, but there were a few unaccompanied singers as well.

A variety of folk clubs sprang up in towns like Portadown, Lurgan, Bally-mena, Derry, Armagh and Enniskillen while in Belfast, there was a thriving club at Queen's University. One city club in particular was more robust and popular than any other. The Old House, at the junction of Albert Street and the Lower Falls, was always crowded for the regular Thursday and Saturday night sessions. These venues, which were frequented by people of all ages and from both communities, were a guarantee of great entertainment and they continued to attract a following despite the increasing political unrest of the times. But nothing by way of entertainment could survive the cataclysmic events of August 1969. Venues promoting traditional music and song were particularly vulnerable. The Old House was demolished, the city centre became a kind of no man's land and out in the countryside, venue after venue, stopped promoting indigenous music. Many of them turned to 'country and Irish' instead.

By the time the 1970s dawned, traditional music and song throughout the north were confined within a cultural ghetto from which they are only now starting to emerge. Regrettably, the quality of this emerging music has not been acknowledged in areas where recognition can be of most use. Many local councils appear to have no interest in supporting or promoting what in most other countries would be seen as an important tourist attraction. Some, indeed, are actively opposed to it. Were it not for the annual Folk

Club concerts held at Queen's University as part of the Belfast Festival, the Belfast Folk Festival and the ongoing support of the Arts Council, traditional music in the north would have had to go it entirely alone. The efforts of Michael Longley and Ciaran Carson – who between them were responsible for the nurturing and promotion of the traditional arts over many years at the Arts Council – were determined and effective at a time when the obstacles seemed insurmountable.

Elsewhere in Ireland in the early 1970s the ballad boom, which had propelled various singers and groups into semi-stardom, was beginning to wane. The general public was growing tired of re-runs of ballads which were now becoming clichéd, sung in a style that only served to expose the musical limitations of the singers. Inside traditional music circles there were major changes taking place that would catalyse the whole musical scene. The changes were undoubtedly influenced and hastened by the Chieftains, who played and presented traditional music in a style that was radically different from the old céilí bands. Originally formed in the mid 1960s, the group

BBC Northern Ireland

Van Morrison and the Chieftains in concert for the BBC in Belfast

played ensemble, but each of the musicians was afforded an opportunity to display his individual skills. Moreover, the group did not confine its repertoire to reels and jigs. The Chieftains played slides, mazurkas, slow airs and planxties, and founder Seán Ó Riada explained things to their audiences. He told them something about the piece they were about to hear and the music was played before people who had paid and were prepared to sit down and listen. Songs and tunes fused together in performance. The Chieftains used traditional instruments like the fiddle, the flute and the uilleann pipes but they were open to experimentation and in years to come they would get together with musicians from other traditions and cultures as far apart as China and the Appalachian Mountains. The experiment, it must be said, did not always work, but it was indicative of the way in which the music was developing confidence and assurance. Moreover, its quality was being recognised throughout the world.

The Chieftains were the first stars of traditional music, the first of many groups who would become household names during the 1970s and 1980s. But all of these groups with real pulling power and popular appeal, groups capable of innovation and of change, came from outside Northern Ireland, where most musicians, with some notable exceptions, could only observe and copy. There was a major shift in the way Irish music was now perceived and it was observable throughout Ireland. Traditional music was rapidly becoming a product that could be packaged, presented and sold on a commercial basis. Traditional musicians and singers had, for generations, played and performed in kitchens and small halls. That would continue to happen, but many of the new generation took to the stage in theatres, halls, community centres and television studios. Some signed deals with international labels and some would earn more money in a few years than their predecessors would have earned in a lifetime.

Other younger groups followed the Chieftains. They continued to demonstrate to audiences at home and around the world, that Irish traditional music and song was perhaps the finest and most varied of its kind. The level of musicianship and skill climbed to hitherto undreamed of levels and with that ability there emerged new sounds, new methods of presentation, new line-ups and fresh interpretations of old material. Within the céilí band line-up there had been many gifted players on a variety of instruments, but they were rarely afforded the opportunity of demonstrating their abilities. Within the new line-ups, and before their seated audiences, the virtuosos could at last showcase their talents. That in turn motivated hundreds of younger musicians to learn how to play. Traditional music was now part of popular culture.

These younger musicians, weaned on rock and roll, blues, and a variety of popular music, were impatient with the style and image traditionally associated with Irish music and song. They wanted to break away from the stereotypical sound and image of the ballad groups and the céilí bands – images that were parodied as often as they were imitated. The days of the Aran sweater, the three-chord guitar thumper and the chorus of voices singing lustily, though often poorly, were over. These new groups pioneered sounds that were different, and instruments whose range and function had never been fully realised. They set about making further inroads into the once relatively still waters of traditional music. They utilised traditional instruments like the fiddle and the pipes, but they poached and soon mastered, instruments like the bouzouki which had been adopted from other cultures. They used mixing desks, quality sound systems, proper microphones, and they were backed up by agents and road managers. They played exciting music, they sang a variety of songs, and they didn't invite or require audience participation.

Nineteen seventy saw the emergence of a young group that was destined for greater things almost from the time it was formed. Clannad were well-accustomed to playing together. They came from the same part of Donegal, they played regularly in Leo's Bar near Crolly and they were all related – hence the name, derived from *Clann as Dobhair* – the family from Gweedore. They won the first prize at the prestigious Letterkenny International Folk Festival and although two members of the group were still young students, Clannad were already preparing to turn professional. They were the first group to adapt and arrange in a contemporary style the traditional Gaelic songs of north-west Donegal, using guitar, bass, flute, harp, synthesizer and close harmony vocals. Clannad were popular not only in Ireland but throughout Europe as well, and were the first group to bring songs in Irish to international attention. Their composition and performance of the signature tune for the television series *Harry's Game* in 1982, took them to the top of the British recording charts. By the time they had followed that success with the theme music for the series *Robin of Sherwood* in 1984, Clannad had a worldwide reputation for the 'Celtic twilight' quality of their music. The youngest member of the group, Enya, left to pursue a solo career in 1984 and when she recorded the music for yet another television series, *The Celts* in 1989, she achieved a celebrity status hitherto undreamed of by solo artists who employed Irish as a first language.

Where Clannad had gone, others would follow. Skara Brae, an acoustic group with strong north-west Donegal connections, released a hugely influential album of native songs. Produced and recorded in 1972 on a tiny budget, it was of poor sound quality, but it too went on to raise the profile and potential of the music and song of Donegal. The members of Skara Brae were both young and inventive, they sang traditional Irish songs but sang them in a contemporary style. They were among the first to put guitars and Beatles-style harmonies to old songs from the Gaeltacht. The group members, Maighread, Tríona and Mícheál Ó Dhomhnaill along with Derry man Dáithi Sproule, went on to pursue successful solo careers.

Altan, probably the best-known Irish group playing traditional music at present, continue to promote the musical culture of Donegal. Formed by Belfast man Frankie Kennedy and Mairéad Ní Mhaonaigh in the late 1980s, the group plays a variety of traditional Irish and Scottish tunes. Most of the songs are in Irish and the band has followed in the footsteps of Clannad to win international acclaim. Altan are one of the few groups to have taken a regional style with northern roots and played it internationally. Altan and Clannad are unique – no other groups with Ulster connections have come close to achieving similar success at an international level, and no other groups have displayed their individuality and originality in combining the 'sean-nos' or old style and the new age.

Four Men and a Dog, founded by the skilled Tyrone fiddle and banjo player Cathal Hayden, also remained close to the tradition. They showed great promise but, after various changes in line-up and several gruelling tours in Europe and America, they disbanded to go their individual ways. Their music was characterised by the high energy and speed of the playing, much of which was a result of Hayden's direct and driving style. That fast style is the one preferred by younger players and deplored by the old-time tradi-

Arty McGlynn

tional school, often suspicious and frequently resentful, of innovation. Four Men and a Dog's first CD, *Barking Mad*, is generally deemed to have been the band's best, with much of its success attributed to the presence of the Omagh-born guitar player and producer Arty McGlynn, one of the most influential musicians ever to emerge from Northern Ireland.

McGlynn, whose guitar skills had made him prominent in the showbands era, made his first public appearance as a player of traditional music in a television programme recorded before a large audience in the Students' Union at Queen's University. The programme, part of the *Folkweave* series, also featured Paul Brady, who was then pursuing a solo career. Brady was asked to select a guest to play along with him in some numbers. Without any hesitation, and with the vast array of individual talents available throughout Ireland, Scotland and England at the time, he chose the relatively unknown Arty McGlynn who went on to establish a reputation as probably one of the world's best interpreter of traditional Irish music on guitar. In 1980 he released his first solo album, *McGlynn's Fancy*, which must rank as one of the defining recordings of the last thirty years. Few other performers have had such an impact on music in Ireland.

Paul Brady, originally from Strabane, had been a guitar player and singer with the well-known Johnstons Folk Group. The group disbanded in the early seventies and Brady subsequently teamed up with Andy Irvine. Their joint album *Paul Brady and Andy Irvine*, recorded in 1976, was a milestone in the maturing of the folk tradition. It featured a collection of important songs which were hitherto unknown to the general public. Some of them were taken from the comprehensive collection of Ulster songs made by Coleraine man Sam Henry, and were arranged in a style that was radically different to anything that had gone before.

Brady's subsequent solo album, *Welcome Here Kind Stranger*, further demonstrated his ability to breathe new life into old material and inspire a host of singers and musicians into taking an equally radical approach to old

BBC Northern Ireland

Left to right: Andy Irvine, Christy Moore and Paul Brady recording for BBC television in Belfast in the 1970s

material. Brady is both an innovator and a preserver. He is certainly one of the most important and influential performers of recent decades and his interpretation of big songs like 'Arthur McBride', 'The Lakes Of Pontchartrain', 'The Homes of Donegal', and 'The Rocks of Bawn' has yet to be equalled for creativity and sheer energy. I doubt if it ever can be.

Paul Brady joined Planxty in 1974 and played with the group until it disbanded for the first time in 1975. The group was unique in its talent and in its choice of material – Irish, English, American and Balkan. It was by far and away the most influential group to appear in Ireland since the formation of the Chieftains, but, whereas the Chieftains specialised in played music, Planxty arranged and performed a heady mixture of melody and song that was both contemporary and traditional. Only one of the group members, uilleann piper Liam O'Flynn, came from a background of traditional music and so they were not at all restricted by traditional convention. Planxty's line-up also included mandolin, guitar and bouzouki, an instrument that wasn't introduced to Irish music until the seventies, but one which has been in regular use since then. There were several imitation groups but none equalled Planxty, who were, incidentally, one of the few groups willing to tour the north at that time.

Two other groups formed in the 1970s have had a major influence on the growth and interpretation of traditional music – Dé Danann and the Bothy Band. They both concentrated on music rather than song and indeed the 1970s saw a gradual drift away from the old Clancy Brothers and Dubliners style of ballad performance. These new groups were more selective, more cautious and more self-critical in their approach. They approached their music in a way that was often indifferent to what was popular. Their influence was immense and indeed still is. The Bothy Band was dynamic in its rhythm and careful blend of instruments. It was a powerful force for change and it had strong northern connections in players like Tommy Peoples, Tríona Ní Dhómhnaill, and her brother Mícheál. Donal Lunney, a musician and arranger with Donegal and Fermanagh connections guided them. Lunney, probably the single most important innovator in Irish music for thirty years, continues to have an immense influence today.

Most northern groups in these recent decades found it difficult to continue performing locally. The venues often weren't there and the ones that remained in business weren't large or popular enough to make performing on a regular basis a paying proposition. Moreover, the agencies that specialise in promoting traditional music are mostly based in Dublin. Northern groups who based themselves here, found it almost impossible to succeed at the highest level. Those which did remain could only perform on a part-time basis and at a limited number of venues, so missing out on the financial and artistic rewards which would have helped hold them together. It was, however, the amateur musicians who kept the music alive during the darkest days of the Troubles. Musicians who determined they would not let the existing political and social climate prohibit them from playing. Listeners at pub sessions were frequently sparse and audiences at public performances frequently even more so, but they persevered and young traditional musicians honed and developed their skills, even when living in the most difficult conditions. In Belfast where the Troubles were most evident, musicians met regularly in places like Tom Kelly's, the Rossa Club, Pat's Bar and the Rotterdam Bar. The Sunflower Club in Corporation Street operated at the very heart of the Troubles in surroundings that sometimes resembled post-war Berlin. The venue provided an invaluable platform for singers and musicians from all over Ulster and beyond. It is doubtful they would have been able to appear at all had it not been for the zeal and enthusiasm of people like Geoff Harden who has promoted and supported folk music in the north since he arrived from England to work here almost thirty years ago.

Francis McPeake, a member of the well-known McPeake family, ran popular weekly whistle playing classes for young people from all over Belfast, and in particular from the Falls Road area. Partly as a result of the large number of the young people playing tin whistle, the tradition of flute playing – an instrument rarely seen at local sessions before the 1960s – began to flourish. Rare too, in Belfast and across the north until recent decades, was the traditional flute. Apart from older men like James McMahon and Leo Ginley, both of whom played the silver and not the wooden flute, this was not an instrument associated with northern traditional music outside County Fermanagh. Today, the flute is one of the most common instruments at sessions throughout the north and, particularly in Belfast. There are various reasons for this, but some of the credit must be attributed to the fact that one of the finest makers of the wooden flute lives and works in Belfast. The quality of Sam Murray's craftsmanship is internationally recognised.

The story of the uilleann pipes is a similar one. Rarely heard in the north where the main exponents included old Francis McPeake from Belfast, Wilbur Garvin from County Antrim, Seán McAloon who had left Fermanagh to work in Belfast, and the young Finbar McLaughlin from Derry, today there are dozens of fine uilleann pipers throughout Ulster. The instrument has been saved from the near obscurity it seemed headed for. Trevor Stewart, who won an All-Ireland title in the early 1970s, is among the best known northern pipers as are Neil Martin and John McSherry from Belfast, Robbie Hannon from Holywood, as well as Killian Vallely from Armagh and Tiernan Dinkin from Monaghan, two pipers who learned much of their art at the Armagh Pipers Club. It was players like these who showed the rest of the country that the north could hold its own on an instrument not traditionally associated with music in Ulster.

Few organisations have put as much into traditional music as the Armagh Pipers Club, founded by Brian and Eithne Vallely in the 1960s, with a view to promoting and fostering traditional music within the immediate community. Classes were taught in Armagh and subsequently in Markethill, Monaghan and Coalisland. Instruction was given in the playing of the fiddle, the pipes, flute, accordion and the concertina. Regular concerts were held: young players were entered for various competitions where they did well, and today the Armagh Pipers Club runs eighteen classes for children and four for adults. In addition, it hosts the annual William Kennedy Piping Festival, which features piping from the Irish, Scots, English and European traditions. Several renowned musicians learned their art in the Armagh Pipers Club and traditional music in Armagh, Monaghan and Tyrone has been greatly enriched as a result. Something in the region of three thousand musicians have learned their music as a result of the commitment demonstrated by Brian and Eithne Vallely. Incidentally, their son Niall is one of the greatest living players of the concertina, an instrument not widely played in northern musical circles.

The fiddle continues to be the most popular instrument played in Ireland. The north has been well served by the quality of the playing but the whole notion of a regional style has largely gone. There are now outstanding fiddle players in every county and there is what might be loosely defined as a northern style of fiddle playing – tight, staccato, more direct in the bowing and less ornate than that of Sligo, Kerry and north Clare for example. The northern tradition, and that of Donegal in particular, has been greatly influenced by the Scottish tradition while still remaining essentially Irish. There are many excellent fiddle players throughout the north, but the most influential has been the legendary Seán Maguire from Belfast who continues to be the father figure.

The Ulster song tradition is still healthy but its exponents are not as numerous as they might be. As a result of the ever-growing popularity of the playing tradition, song seems to have taken a back seat and there does not appear to be the same enthusiasm for the folk song as there was even thirty years ago. The many ballads aired in those days were fresh and hadn't been sung before. A singer's repertoire would include songs and ballads of the English and Scots traditions, as well as the Irish, and it was inevitable perhaps that many good songs that once sounded fresh were soon done to death. Moreover, the folk club scene where good order could be guaranteed, naturally favoured the singer, but the folk clubs no longer exist to any significant extent. Traditional song requires an attentive audience, and such audiences can be increasingly hard to find. As a result, singers find themselves to be the exception in places when they were once the rule, and today the singer takes second place to the musician at sessions. There is an ongoing, though scarcely acknowledged, rivalry between the two. Musicians feel that once singers get going in a session they are hard to stop. Singers feel the same about musicians. It is interesting to observe that when musicians play at pub sessions, the surrounding noise level rarely abates. Singers get better attention, but only for a while. The music becomes part of what is happening and the players are immune to audience response. They no longer expect any, and consequently some older musicians will come to a session but they won't play. The singer is more exposed and therefore even more wary. This does not mean that the song tradition is in any way under threat. It is alive and it has been well served and supported by the people who cherish it, but the conditions that fostered the traditional folk songs and moved people to write them, belong to another era. The singer's art is severely challenged by the pub atmosphere in which traditional music apparently thrives. The majority of folk and traditional singers prefer the intimacy of the small and familiar setting of the parlour and the back room where the songs are not quite so divorced from their natural base.

The 1970s saw the maturing of several fine singers. One of the finest was Gemma Hasson from Park, near Feeney, in County Derry. She was exceptional in both her singing ability and in her songs, many of which were from the south Derry area. She recorded two excellent albums which featured some of them alongside songs from other parts of Ireland. Small and slender with an unusually strong voice and a natural empathy with audiences, Gemma Hasson was undoubtedly among the best in the country. She featured regularly as a folk singer on radio and television throughout the 1970s, but there were no venues in the north promoting that kind of live entertainment. She turned to singing country music without much success, for by that time country bands were in favour, and Gemma decided to retire while she was still in her early thirties.

The city of Derry produced some fine singers as well, notably Kevin Mitchell and Brian Mullen, both excellent unaccompanied singers with a large repertoire of songs. Mitchell, who now lives in Glasgow, sang in the open-air style of the ballad singer. His voice was strong, strident at times and he had a natural sense of how to ornament a song. Mullen has a more subdued and sweeter voice, though no less commanding, and he is equally at home in Irish as in English. Both Mullan and Mitchell have some unique songs from different areas of Ulster.

The late Geordie Hanna from Derrytresk near Coalisland in County Tyrone, became well known around the same time. His father was a singer as was his cousin, George, who lived nearby. His sister, Sarah Ann O'Neill, is well known in traditional singing circles too. She shares a similar style to her brother's – intense, powerful and well ornamented, with regular short pauses in the flow of the melody and the narration – a style that is sometimes referred to as 'stop gap'. Geordie Hanna had a remarkable store of traditional songs. Many were from the lough shore tradition – 'Old Ardboe', 'The Fishers Cot', 'Brockagh Brae', 'Erin's Lovely Home' and several others which had rarely been heard outside the immediate area before he became known to a wider public.

Geordie Hanna had a commanding presence as well as a unique voice. He was one of the few singers in the north at the time who chose to sing in public

A young David Hammond appearing in front of the camera

in the old unaccompanied style. The guitar was considered a desirable accompaniment and few considered themselves to be true balladeers without it. There were a few who took to using the five-string banjo in the style of Luke Kelly of Dubliners fame, but mercifully they remained in the minority. Geordie Hanna preferred the raw bar and, where he had gone, others would soon follow. There are probably as many singers today who prefer the unaccompanied style as there are who use the guitar.

Repertoires vary from singer to singer and some have an extensive song list collected over the years. In County Antrim two men almost single-handedly revived and helped preserve the tradition. Joe Holmes from Ballymoney and the younger enthusiast Len Graham uncovered and presented songs from all over the north. Graham continues to sing and to perform both here and abroad. He has guested with many excellent groups including Skylark in particular. He performs regularly with the north's finest storyteller, John Campbell from Mullaghbawn in County Armagh, and is married to another outstanding talent, the singer and songwriter Padraigin Ní h Ullachain. John Kennedy is another excellent traditional singer from north Antrim. David Hammond continues to represent and combine the urban and the rural traditions in his distinctive singing voice. His album, *The Singer's House*, is still among the best to have been released in the last three decades. His contribution to folk song in Ulster and throughout the wider island has been ongoing and exceptional. He has been the source of many songs and an inspiration to many aspiring singers.

Other singers from County Antrim also made themselves known to a wider public, among them Jeannie McGrath and Archie McKeegan. They helped to make known the wealth of the local song tradition, one that uniquely cross-fertilised with that of nearby Scotland. John Moulden, now living in Portrush, is one of the most respected collectors of traditional song and has been acquiring and researching material for nearly forty years. He has written and published extensively about the Ulster song tradition and about songs of emigration in particular. The same depth and richness of tradition however, does not appear to be quite so prevalent in County Down. Parts of the Ards Peninsula and the Killyleagh area, though, are an exception. There, where there is a strong Ulster-Scots tradition, music and song continue to thrive but the Mourne district, where one would expect a similar situation, is remarkably deficient in music and in performers. The Sands Family from Mayobridge were to the forefront of music in the south Down area from where they travelled extensively into Europe. Tommy, Ben and Colm Sands have each written some fine contemporary folk songs. The Sands Family are essentially a singing group, and that makes them something of a rarity nowadays, for most other groups make the music their speciality. Mention must also be made of the consistency and dedication shown by the Downpatrick Folk Society and by the late Pat Connolly in particular, a founder member and a regular performer, who helped promote and preserve traditional music in the area. On the other side of Strangford Lough the town of Portaferry hosts an annual festival which attracts many musicians and singers. It is also home to the gifted singer and songwriter Rosemary Woods, one of the best writers of song in Ireland and, a performer with a compelling presence.

Armagh is rich in both music and song. Sean O'Boyle – who wrote the chapters on traditional music and song in the two previous volumes of this series in 1951 and 1971 – lived and taught in the cathedral city itself. He is affectionately remembered by the numerous men and women he influenced, as is his fellow teacher and long-time colleague, the late Jerry Hicks. The town of Keady, is not surprisingly, proud of its connection with Sarah Makem and her son Tommy and today the south of the county is more fortunate than ever in both the quantity and the quality of its singers and musicians, particularly those living inside the renowned Ring of Gullion area. Briege Murphy from Forkhill is a fine writer of contemporary songs; the traditional world is well represented by Mick Quinn. Len Graham and Padraigin Ní hUllachain live nearby in Mullaghbawn and there are regular sessions of music and song throughout the area. Fermanagh, the county with the smallest population in Ulster, is more than well represented in traditional song by singers like Paddy Tunney, Rosie Stewart, Gabriel McArdle and Cathal McConnell, who are known wherever they sing.

It is worth noting that despite the continuing popularity of folk song, as well as the number of accomplished singers, no songs of lasting merit have appeared which have a direct bearing on the recent troubled history of the north. The Troubles have engaged the attention of the poets, the writers and the dramatists, but remarkably few songs of worth have been written. There are several accomplished singer/songwriters from the region, but if the songs have been written they have not been brought to public attention. There are of course exceptions. Phil Coulter's 'The Town I Love So Well', Mickey McConnell's 'Only Our Rivers Run Free' and Tommy Sands 'There Were Roses' are all well known, but little else of note has so far been recorded, apart from James Simmons, 'Claudy', which is also a poem. The recurring images we have seen of body bags, bombed streets, flags and funerals have exposed the grim realities of conflict and have effectively silenced the triumphalism of songs glorifying tribal loyalty and marching men.

The world of traditional music and song, in the words of the poet Michael Longley, 'is intimate and at the same time vast, a uniquely rich confluence of English, Irish and Scottish songs and tunes; and it is that very richness which produces social problems, social complexities'. The troubled history of the north of Ireland over the last thirty years has affected every aspect of our lives and, at a wider level, the perception of our traditional culture has been adversely affected. The practioners of traditional music have, all the same, remained united in their conviction that the music should survive. They continued to meet and to play with generosity and glad hearts despite the bad times.

There are those who lament the inevitable loss of what they see as cultural purity: those who declaim the speed at which reels and jigs are now played, those who moan about the commercialism of shows like *Riverdance* and *Lord of the Dance* in which music, song and dance are presented in an electrifying performance and where commercial interests are paramount. The popularity of those big stage shows will fade, but in city, town, village and townland the music and the songs will continue to flourish without a thought of box office or profit. A corner has been turned. A new millennium has come and with it an ever-growing awareness of the richness of the Scottish tradition as well as the Irish. In a session nowadays, the music will skip and move between the two cultures, to such an extent that they are regularly fused together as one. Traditional musicians, as always, value a good tune irrespective of its place of origin. It is thanks to them and to the people from both communities who remained constant in their support – the keepers and guardians of this priceless cultural resource – that the future of traditional music in Ulster is assured.

Popular Music

STUART BAILIE

Popular music in Northern Ireland has a history that's messy, maddening and just a bit remarkable. The practitioners have struggled to put their mark on a medium that is fickle by nature and ruthless in its business practices. But they have made a difference, indeed more so than artists from many other parts of the western world. Our musicians have excelled in the fields of pop, dance and rock and roll in defiance of the problems that geography and economics have thrown at them.

The arts hierarchy in Northern Ireland has been slow to credit the achievements of our rock and rollers, our sundry strummers, pickers and songwriters. Yet popular music has been a key medium here in the past thirty-five years. In its raw state the music may be outspoken, racy and visceral, but these days we reserve our favoured musicians for important civic events – to sing

Van Morrison and Bob Dylan

before presidents and suchlike – as the notion of cultural tourism emerges. Nowadays artists such as Van Morrison, Paul Brady, David Holmes and Neil Hannon figure internationally, giving our aspirations and nightmares a potent voice. They have taken advantage of pop's great democratic force by which a novice can create a fresh musical statement without academic training or heavy investment.

Popular music provides an easy entry into the arts and Van Morrison is a great example of this – the working-class boy from a secondary school who has penned some of the most sublime expressions in any discipline. His songs have weathered well. He is now regarded as a perennial, one of the few cultural totems we can be proud of. We tend to celebrate his gruff style as an element of the local character – Van after all wastes little time on the fripperies of the music industry. He often portrays himself as a workman, simply doing the gig. Yet special things still happen when this man gets into an artistic spin. Van is renowned for his ability to zoom out of the mundane and into the mystical. He may seize on a jazz motif, stretching the possibilities of the tune, scatting and experimenting. Alternatively, he may be deepening his music into the swirl of a twelve bar blues, or perhaps even roaring himself into a frenzy, name-checking writers as diverse as Seamus Heaney, Arthur Rimbaud and Jack Kerouac. In a few startling cases he may be finding his rapture in the Ulster diet, eulogising the pastie supper, the barnbracks, wagon wheels and snowballs of his childhood – his own particular variety of soul food.

Some of Van's best work may not always look great on a page, bereft of the author's phrasing and tone, but you can still sense the import of a lyric like, 'you may call my love Sophia, but I call my love Philosophy' or 'Sense Of Wonder' or the lilt of, 'I'm Tired Joey Boy', which self-consciously pays homage, to the style of the Glens of Antrim poets. Then there is 'Summertime In England', a wonderfully sustained meditation that considers the art of Coleridge, T.S. Eliot and Yeats, while cocking an ear to the brass band coming across the field as the author simultaneously hails the legend of Avalon. Many exciting moments later, the singer wails, with understandable awe, 'It ain't why, it just *is*'.

Van has been consistently passionate about the music that he grew up with. He was raised on his parents' rich record collection. He schooled himself on the most vital corners of American roots music, from the folk narratives of Leadbelly and the Carter Family, the raw country of Hank Williams plus Chicago blues, be-bop and primal rock and roll. On the track 'Wild Children' (from *Hard Nose The Highway,* 1973), Van tried to contextualise his generation of post-war baby boomers. He was born in 1945 and thus was old enough to appreciate the skiffle boom that was launched in the UK by Lonnie Donegan, who charted with 'Rock Island Line' in 1956. Van picked up the essentials of guitar and then saxophone, and worked his chops in a series of rock and roll bands. Just as the Beatles honed their act in Hamburg, Van featured in Cologne, Heidelberg and Frankfurt with the Monarchs showband, playing standards to US servicemen and evolving his own voice. His musical tastes anticipated the rhythm and blues boom of the mid 1960s, and thus he was well placed to take the initiative in Belfast. As frontman with the act Them, he became a regular, rowdy draw at the Maritime Hotel in Belfast in 1964. Them charted in 1965 with a version of 'Baby Please Don't Go' and were nurtured, according to record company fashions, as a gang of dangerous malcontents. Van was displeased at such tactics and his mistrust of the music industry has been a constant since then.

There were other notables on the home scene. The likes of the Wheels, the Mad Lads, the Luvin' Kind, the Aztecs, the Bats, the People, the Interns and the Just Five, also served. Unfortunately, the likes of singer Sam Mahood rarely graduated beyond the status of local heroes. Sometimes the bands lacked songwriting skills; others were unable to outlast a particular musical fashion. A routine problem with the music scene in Northern Ireland has been a lack of astute businessmen. The blossoming of the Maritime era owed something to the acumen of Mervyn and Phil Solomon, who echoed the activities of Brian Epstein in Liverpool, presenting regional talent to the London-based record labels. Sadly, there have been few other such facilitators.

Whatever, Van came out of the experience with his creativity intact. Some of the songs that he had written for Them were already marked with a peculiar vision. For example, there was 'Mystic Eyes', a shuddering blues experience with a lyric that envisaged a young girl by a graveyard, juxtaposing beauty with a deeply morbid sensibility. He was already writing like a metaphysical poet, albeit a scowling, amplified version. And with 'Gloria', Them made their most durable statement, a stormy assignation at the midnight hour, clanging around a primitive three-chord guitar pattern. The song is now regarded as a classic of its time, revisited by garage bands of successive generations. Them had a limited impact in America – their stay at the Whiskey A-Go-Go in Los Angeles is the stuff of enduring legend – and that gave rise to a solo career for Morrison and a hit in 1967 with the single 'Brown-Eyed Girl'. Van had signed to the Bang label, headed by the pop-minded Bert Berns, who had previously worked with the Drifters and Ben E. King. The singer grew to dislike his boss and he was unhappier still when a cache of uneven New York sessions was released as an album, *Blowin' Your Mind*. When Van finally freed himself from the contract, though, he delivered his masterpiece.

Released in America in late 1968 and in Britain the following year, *Astral Weeks* is a regular feature in music critics' 'Best Ever' polls – up there alongside the Beach Boys' *Pet Sounds*, Marvin Gaye's *What's Goin' On*, the Beatles' *Revolver* and Bob Dylan's *Blonde On Blonde*. The record is of its time in that it blows through the limits of the three minute pop song, a generation aiming for adventure. Several tracks on *Astral Weeks* are lengthy and improvised in the studio. The form owes something to the soul-jazz hybrid – an NME review of the album compared Morrison to the contemporary troubadour José Feliciano – and certainly there seems to be some appreciation of John Coltrane's rhythmic verve. This was a period when the Byrds and the Beatles were looking east to the mesmeric possibilities of Indian raga, and again, *Astral Weeks* has some of that quality, matched to the incantatory blues of John Lee Hooker. In its original vinyl format, the album was divided into two parts, titled 'In The Beginning' and 'Afterwards'. This gave the impression that there was some kind of thematic plan to the record, perhaps akin to William Blake's *Songs of Innocence And Experience*. The lyrical setting moves from Belfast to America to London, building up a great deal of homesickness. We meet Madame George, a character who apparently dresses in drag. There's an unnamed girl on 'Cyprus Avenue', a spacious tree-lined street near Van's own east Belfast home, and there's a fragile female, possibly a heroin user in London, plus a ballerina on the east coast of America.

Beyond that, nothing is sure, as Van weaves dreams, memories and chronologies together. On 'Beside You', he seems to be hyperventilating, inducing himself into a trance state. On 'Madame George', he unleashes a semantic whirl of ideas that is almost Joycean: 'And the love that loves the love that loves love that loves. The love that loves to love the love the loves to love the love that loves.' Absolutely. *Astral Weeks* sold modestly at first. It was then taken up by psychedelic seekers, bedroom dreamers and folks on the hippy trail, and became a cult item. And in time, it came to define Van as an otherworldly Celt, who like W.B. Yeats, was deeply fascinated by the potential of epiphanies and visions, what the latter termed 'the trembling of the veil'. On several occasions, Van has compared the crackle of a transistor radio, picking up the faint tones of Radio Luxembourg in his youth, to the psychic signals that he also apparently receives.

Van, of course, has produced exceptional music since then. He followed *Astral Weeks* with *Moondance*, a collection of catchy, beautiful songs. Every Van aficionado has a favourite album, but a sure highlight is *St Dominic's Preview*, which appeared in 1972. Aside from the title track, in which Van recalls his days as a window cleaner in Belfast, there's a delirious passage called 'Listen To the Lion', which finds the singer moaning and proselytising, thinking about his art and ancestry, trying to get to the raw meaning beneath mere words. Still, there's a special poignancy in *Astral Weeks* that Northern Irish listeners are most sensitive to. As well as being the first great Irish pop album, it is also the last to document a period of relative peace here. Thereafter, the Troubles would be writ large over all of the arts, and over music in particular.

The Miami Showband, a bunch of unpretentious young entertainers, was stopped on the road from Banbridge to Newry in the early hours of 31 July, 1975. What the band members had assumed to be a UDR checkpoint was in fact a UVF team who had decided to plant a bomb in their van. The bomb exploded prematurely, and several band members – Fran O'Toole, Brian McCoy and Tony Geraghty – were shot at point blank range in the fracas that followed. The music industry in Northern Ireland had been severely depressed at this stage. In many of the major towns, the centres were deserted at nights. Sure, there were a few events to be welcomed, like Led Zeppelin's 1971 show in Belfast. Rory Gallagher was a regular visitor, even in the worst moments, doubtless remembering the good times that he'd experienced at the Maritime. Some of the old heads from the 1960s were still at large. Jim Armstrong who fronted Light had a residency at the Pound, one of the venues that still made an effort, while Kenny McDowell was at large with Sk'boo. But the interest and the infrastructure were largely gone. The Miami Showband killings ensured that few international acts came visiting. It was also a severe blow to the faltering showband scene.

Some of the best musicians had migrated to Dublin. In the 1970s, Thin Lizzy were regarded as the city's proudest sons, even though the original line-up had included two Belfast players, guitarist Eric Bell and keyboard player Eric Wrixon, who had both played in different incarnations of Them. The latter moved away fairly quickly, but Eric Bell was a key feature for the first three albums. His greatest contributions were on 'The Rocker', a Hendrix-inspired romp and on Thin Lizzy's famous adaptation of 'Whisky In The Jar'. Bell's guitar solo on this record was lyrical and blue, a priceless moment in the island's rock history. Another Ulster player, Gary Moore, replaced Bell. He was the son of a ballroom manager in Holywood who had nurtured the boy's prodigious skills. As a teenager Gary had cut two albums with Skid Row, the Dublin act headed by Brush Shiels. Moore had been hailed by Peter Green of Fleetwood Mac and had supported Frank Zappa at the Filmore West, San Francisco. Gary's first tenure with Thin Lizzy had been brief, recording a single, 'Little Darlin', before taking up jazz-fusion with Colliseum II. But he rejoined Thin Lizzy on a few occasions and made a dextrous imprint on the *Black Rose* album in 1979. Simultaneously, he was plugging a solo album, *Back On The Streets*, which sold well. He later returned to the blues, making a series of records that reaffirmed his standing.

Another guitarist with an impressive CV was Henry McCullough from Portstewart. He made his name with the People, a psychedelic act rebranded as Éire Apparent, which was guided by Hendrix manager Chas Chandler. The band toured with Jimi in 1968 before McCullough left. For a time he played with Sweeney's Men, one of the most creative acts working in the folk idiom. He had a tenure with Joe Cocker's Grease Band, appearing at Woodstock, before joining Paul McCartney in Wings, 1972–3, taking a fine solo on the single 'My Love'. He has subsequently worked with the likes of Roy Harper and Marianne Faithful.

David McWilliams from Ballymena scored a hit with 'The Days Of Pearly Spencer', making a series of albums which are highly collectable. Dana, a schoolgirl from Derry, was the surprise discovery of the Eurovision Song Contest, when 'All Kinds Of Everything' was the winner in 1970, setting her up with a career in light entertainment and latterly politics. Another Eurovision contender was Newry-born Clodagh Rodgers, who represented the UK in 1971 with 'Jack In The Box'. Specific reference is made to female singers only to point out that aside from Clodagh, Dana, and Ruby Murray from an earlier era, Northern Ireland has been severely under-represented by female singers and musicians. The only other act that comes to mind is Brianna Corrigan who guested on several records by the Beautiful South in the early 1990s.

The most successful figure from these parts during the 1970s was Phil Coulter. Born in Derry, he was a student at Queen's University when one of his songs, 'Foolin' Time', was recorded by the Capitol showband in 1964. He began working with Phil Solomon, assisting on sessions with Them and even the Bachelors. Since then he has touched the careers of everyone from Sinead O'Connor to Ken Dodd. He played a key role in highlighting

BBC Northern Ireland

Composer and performer Phil Coulter

Planxty, an act which brought traditional Irish music to new levels of popularity. At the same time Coulter, often partnered by Bill Martin, delivered Eurovision hits, such as, 'Puppet On A String', and 'Congratulations' and bolstered the career of the Bay City Rollers with a series of cute anthems. Some of Coulter's material is undeniably strong. 'The Town I Loved So Well' is a restrained but powerful reaction to the plight of his hometown during the hardest of times while 'My Boy' documents the end of a marriage and the ensuing complications. Elvis Presley empathised with the words and recorded a suitably trembling version. Later, Coulter made a series of *Tranquillity* albums which combined soothing strings with fey melodies. They were massively successful in Ireland as were the subsequent tours, and later albums, classified as 'new-age' music, would see Coulter nominated for a Grammy award in 2001.

Barry Devlin, from Omagh, played bass with Horslips, one of Ireland's most colourful acts. From 1970 to 1980 the group combined traditional influences with florid rock and roll. Horslips made a virtue out of playing outside the normal rock circuit, engaging with rural audiences and mining the themes of Irish mythology. *The Tain* (1973) and *The Book of Invasions*

Ronnie Matthews of Rudi on stage at the Pound, 1978

(1977) were high points in this process. Devlin later produced an early U2 session and worked on some of the band's most famous videos. He still features in the film and television industry, and rumours of a Horslips revival are increasingly loud.

The late 1970s, however, were characterised by another sound. Punk rock was launched in London in 1976, putting an emphasis on attitude, musical economy and street credibility. The roots of punk are complex and highly contested by the original participants, but they were partly a reaction to the increasingly vapid music which was being produced by maturing, millionaire rock musicians from the previous decade. The garage band aesthetic was rediscovered – and Them's 'Gloria' featured in many ferocious set-lists of the day. Some of the punk agitators also preached all-out revolution, citing the student riots of Paris 1968 as an ideal. Perhaps the most fundamental definition of punk rock comes from the American critic Greil Marcus who

Terri Hooley

Cliff Mason, Avalon Photography, courtesy of Immortel Records

compressed the notion into two words: 'question everything'. And if there was any place that was ready for a new, questioning attitude, it was Northern Ireland. Punk gave a generation of music fans the chance to participate. Also, punk bands from abroad were not frightened by the reputation of Northern Ireland, and so the live scene picked up. It was a highly dramatic time when Belfast, Derry, Portadown, Omagh and many smaller towns, were unleashing creativity and passionate sentiments through their teenagers.

At first, the punk bands adopted a do-it-yourself style, and booked hotel function rooms and youth clubs to hold their gigs in. A few sympathetic venues like the Harp Bar and the Pound in Belfast, the Casbah in Derry and the Trident in Bangor, were also adopted. The first wave of acts such as Rudi and Victim wore their David Bowie and glam influences without shame. The former band had a mission statement called 'Time To Be Proud' which was shared by many. Another key aspect of the punk movement was the appearances of small, focused record labels, independent in their ethos and their business practices. Working with modest pressings and even more curtailed budgets, it was possible to put out a single from a brand new band without too much effort. Alternative distribution and a few sympathetic radio DJs like John Peel meant that a band could have a relatively fair hearing away from the mainstream. Again, this was a great boon to the young music-makers here.

Before this, Northern Ireland musicians had experienced what is commonly described as a cultural cringe. Many didn't feel confident of greater success and even if they did there were very few examples of homegrown players on international stages. Van Morrison was getting settled in America, and his accent had blurred to fit the landscape. It wasn't until *Veedon Fleece* in 1974 that Van came to reconsider his Celtic roots, just ahead of a three-year period of writer's block. So punk, with its Year Zero mentality, allowed the scene here to start afresh. Following the example of the Clash in London, bands were encouraged to write about social politics, about grim urban features. The American act the Ramones made a virtue out of three chord

Punk comes to town. The Outcasts at home in Belfast's Crown Bar.

songs played speedily. The Sex Pistols, who fronted the new regime, declared that you should never trust anyone over thirty. And thus began a period of significant activity in Northern Ireland. Rudi released the single 'Big Time' in April 1978, a song that mocked the aspirations of a shameless social climber. It was the first release on a label called Good Vibrations, an offshoot of the small record shop on Belfast's Great Victoria Street, a meeting place for many of the young tribes. The owner was Terri Hooley, a garrulous veteran of the 1960s scene, who connected with the new spirit. In the past, he had fraternised with the UK underground press. He appreciated the art of the 'happening', a situation that could provoke friction and dispute, even an amount of anarchy. So Terri became a trickster, a folk devil and a propagandist for the punk movement here.

Good Vibrations wasn't the only label – others included It and Rip-Off – but it had the best roster. In 1978 the label put out records by Rudi, Victim, the Outcasts, the Undertones, the Xdreamysts and Protex. Later it would deal with the Tearjerkers, Cruella de Ville, Andy White, the Moondogs and the Bankrobbers. Many of the records were heavy and poorly pressed. The sleeves consisted of an ingeniously folded sheet of A4 paper bearing the crudest of designs, but the product was often fabulous. With considerable media support, Good Vibrations released collectable artefacts. Hooley too had fun releasing his own record 'Laugh At Me,' and marketing a drinking game called Binge, helping to create a new perception of the place. Local magazines were typed or handwritten and photocopied, following the lead of London publications like *Sniffin' Glue*. This was fanzine culture: putting out opinionated and exultant copy in titles such as *Alternative Ulster, It's Your World, Plastic, Private World* and *Laughing Gravy*. Thus, the immediacy of events was telegraphed across the growing network. *Alternative Ulster*, one of the best of the lot, produced two strong writers; Gavin Martin and Dave McCullough. They were soon given staff jobs in London with *New Musical Express* and *Sounds* respectively.

Film-maker John T. Davis put together a great history of the time, *Shell Shock Rock*. A few of the bands he featured became well known, but some of the most exciting parts of the film are simple testimonies from born-again music fans, suddenly alive to the artistic possibilities around them. As with many other youth movements, punk provided easy access to self-expression,

Jake Burns of Stiff Little Fingers on stage at the Pound, 1978

and the participants often ended up in disparate parts of the creative media.

The Belfast act, Stiff Little Fingers, has left us with a contentious legacy. On the one hand, the band broached the subject of the Troubles headlong in songs like 'Suspect Device' and 'Wasted Life'. Singer Jake Burns delivered the words with a hoarse, righteous air that pleased many fans of the Clash. Certainly, this was one of the most successful bands of the era, selling 80,000 copies of its debut album *Inflammable Material* and touring abroad. However, some parties at home felt SLF's posturing was contrived – after all, hadn't its members formerly worked as Highway Star, playing heavy metal songs? And the influence of journalist Gordon Ogilvie was another tricky area. He was involved in writing the lyrics, which some felt were shamelessly tabloid, 'Barbed Wire Love' contains the worst pun ever: 'you set my armalite'.

The band gradually reverted to more traditional rock songs and the debate cooled. Stiff Little Fingers proved that success was possible. Unfortunately,

The Undertones in their native Derry

many record company scouts who were beginning to visit Belfast were look-ing for more of the same, and more worthy acts, who didn't care for politics, were sometimes overlooked. Having said that, other bands did voice opi-nions about burning issues. Rudi wrote 'We Hate The Cops' after an alterca-tion with the local constabulary before a punk gig. The Defects penned 'Brutality' about a supposed stay at the RUC holding centre in Castlereagh. Near the end of the punk spree, Stalag 17 imported the anarchist ideals of the English act Crass, attacking the racism that had infected the skinhead scene here, and developing a studio and rehearsal space in Belfast, fondly known as Giro's.

Punk was a highly judgemental era, even élitist at times. One of the bands that satisfied the harshest of tests was the Undertones. Their music was initially simple, but was based on a highly developed appreciation of 1960s music and American proto-punks like the Stooges. Despite their parka jackets, their Doc Martin boots and their urchin appearances, these boys were classicists. Their singer, Feargal Sharkey, had an astonishing, quivering style. The DJ John Peel was reduced to tears when he first heard 'Teenage Kicks'. He played the single numerous times on Radio One, which prompted a deal with Sire Records.

They set out their stall with the likes of 'Get Over You', 'Here Comes The Summer' and 'Male Model', releasing a self-titled debut in 1979 that was uniquely witty. Brothers John and Damian O'Neill played inventive, weaving guitar lines. The scheme deepened into 'My Perfect Cousin', which famously rhymed cabbage with University Challenge, reaching number nine in the UK singles chart in 1980. A year later and the mood had changed somewhat. The band released 'It's Going To Happen' during the republican hunger strike, and the lyric was a wry allusion to the situation at home. The band's last two albums, *Hypnotised* (1981) and *The Sin Of Pride* (1983) were maturing works, reflecting an interest in Motown soul and psychedelia, but record sales waned and the band split in 1983.

Many other acts from Northern Ireland have favoured bright melodies and crooning voices, often against the fashionable trend. Some day a musicologist may draw a connection between our folk song tradition and the pop equivalent. Perhaps there's a temperamental impulse at the heart of it. Van Morrison has put forward the Jungian explanation of race memory on at least one occasion. So while the London punk acts were rasping and grunting, and while the Dublin bands were mostly cerebral or bluesy, we had the big tunes. You found it with Derry act the Moondogs, a band which released some decent singles and fronted the TV show 'Moondogs Matinee' for Granada in 1981. The drift was evident with Protex and the Tearjerkers, bands which both promised a lot but were somehow frustrated, despite signing record deals abroad.

Even the menacing haircuts of Belfast act the Outcasts were accessorised by Greg Cowan's clear tenor. The Ruefrex, a north Belfast act also illustrated this tough-tender dichotomy. Allan Clarke warbled like a choirboy, yet he sometimes held the microphone stand at his shoulder like a firearm, miming an attack on the audience. The band regrouped in 1985 to release its most significant song, 'The Wild Colonial Boy', which took a pop at Americans raising funds for 'the struggle' in Ireland. The single sleeve pictured an arma-lite covered in wrapping paper, ready to send home to the 'auld sod'. Good Vibrations folded in 1982. Terri Hooley declared 'we'd rather be failures than owned' before closing the store, and while the label has been resurrected sev-eral times since then, it has never recaptured the epochal spark of 1978. More frustratingly, no other local label has managed to sustain such a strong roster or so appealing an ethos in the intervening decades.

There was, of course, an important sea change in the music industry in the 1980s. While punk had been obsessed with the dangers of 'selling out', Boy George from Culture Club flaunted the concept of 'selling in' – using the capitalist system to further his ambitions. This new decade was all about branding, design, visuals, irony and post-modernism. Duran Duran sailed the oceans in their videos. Expensive synthesisers and slick studio techniques were in heavy demand. The major record companies, with their deep finan-cial resources, were back in charge. In Manchester, independent acts like New Order and the Smiths, were responding to the new era with exquisitely designed record sleeves. They showed a deal of sonic adventure and impor-tantly, there was a school of talent around such acts, providing business and media advice, allowing the creativity to flourish. Similar plans were laid in places like Glasgow and Liverpool. In contrast, Belfast was back to the feast-or-famine syndrome. The scene withered.

During the punk years, bands had looked to Dublin with derision. The scene there was less vital but that perception changed in the 1980s as U2 began its astonishing ascent. Bono and his colleagues made a conscious decision to work from their hometown, thus building up a business infrastructure which has been hugely important in allowing Dublin to become an internationally recognised centre for music. The band's manager, Paul McGuinness, was a visionary dealer, securing important conditions for the band and allowing it the chance of a long, secure career. U2 made records that were airy and spacious, heavily dependent on the singer's charisma. In Glasgow, Simple Minds set out on a similar tack. A few acts from Northern Ireland – notably Silent Running – tried in vain. The Adventures were fronted by Terry

Sharpe, a former singer with The Starjets, who had made an impression at the commercial end of punk. Pat Gribben and his wife Eileen fleshed this new venture out. Their aesthetic dealt with highly polished harmonies, memorable tunes and a hint of melancholy. Singles such as 'Send My Heart' (1984) and 'Broken Land' (1988) were respected chart hits.

Feargal Sharkey guested with the Assembly, reaching number four in the charts with 'Never Never' in 1983. He went further in his solo career, topping the UK singles charts with 'A Good Heart' in 1985. The following year, he moved to Los Angeles and his recording career faltered. He took a music industry job in 1993 and has maintained a lower profile since. Two other Undertones, John and Damian O'Neill, based themselves in London and put together a more experimental act, That Petrol Emotion. With American singer Steve Mack on board, the music covered less expected sources such as Captain Beefheart and rap music. The band's finest moment was the 1987 single 'Big Decision' which pre-dated the UK boom in groove-orientated rock.

Not many pundits would be able to name the most commercial 1980s act with Northern Ireland connections. It was in fact Jive Bunny, a studio conceit which relied for much of its party appeal on the brass arrangements of John Anderson. The latter was already making a tidy living from his Glen Miller tributes, but now that he was spliced to a modern beat, his arrangements of party pleasers made it into summer discos and Christmas knees-up. In a rather more camp spirit, the Derry act Baltimora charted with 'Tarzan Boy' in 1985. Andy White wrote prickly songs in the style of Bob Dylan. Early 1980s releases such as *Religious Persuasion* were highly self-conscious, but Andy developed into a songwriter of note, plotting his migrations to London, Belfast, Dublin and then Switzerland. Energy Orchard was another London-based act, using past members of Ten Past Seven and the Bankrobbers. Singer, Bap Kennedy, was an unashamed fan of Van Morrison's *Astral Weeks* and tried to develop the myth of his city on the likes of 'Sailortown'. Bap has become close friends with American songwriter Steve Earle, who brought him to Nashville to cut the impressive *Domestic Blues* album in 1999 with some excellent bluegrass players.

Bap's brother Brian was also in Ten Past Seven, one of the last Good Vibrations acts of note. After a brief stay with Energy Orchard, he took to a solo career, casting winsome ballads in the Joni Mitchell vernacular. Van Morrison appreciated his high tones and took him on several world tours. While Kennedy has had limited success outside Ireland – he performed for President Bill Clinton on a number of occasions and sang in *Riverdance* on Broadway for several months – he really needs the long-term support of a large record label to sustain his profile.

Van Morrison made a significant comeback in the 1980s. One important release was *Irish Heartbeat*, a collaboration with the Chieftains that witnessed Van singing a series of traditional airs and street songs, many of which harked back to his childhood. A brace of 'Best Of' compilations sold well and Van accepted a Brit Award in 1994 for Outstanding Contribution To British Music.

The lazy version of the Paul Brady story is that he was an innocent folkie who came into rock and roll through some vile Faustian deal. In truth, Paul was smitten during his formative years by the likes of Jerry Lee Lewis and Fats Domino. While he surely absorbed the traditional music that was around him, he played in a series of R&B acts during his college days at University College Dublin, fronting his own band, Rockhouse. He joined the Johnstons in 1967, a group that played folksy tunes by the likes of Ewan McColl, Leonard Cohen and Jacques Brel. The band also popularised some lesser-known Irish songs, and in its later records, Brady's song-writing skill became apparent, particularly on the winsome 'Border Child'. He was asked to replace Christy Moore in Planxty in 1974, but sadly, he didn't record with the act during his short stay. However, he maintained the creative heat with Andy Irvine when Ireland's first traditional 'supergroup' fractured. The pair released *Andy Irvine and Paul Brady* in 1976, a record which still sounds potent and full of new chances. One highlight was 'Arthur McBride', the drama about a recruiting sergeant which was faithfully recorded by Bob Dylan two decades later. At least Dylan had the good grace to call Brady a secret hero in the notes to his *Biograph* box set.

In 1978 Brady furthered the story with a solo record, *Welcome Here Kind Stranger*. The title was a line from a New Orleans song, 'The Lakes Of Pontchartrain', and Brady's version has once again become the definitive one. Yet in 1981 Brady surprised some of the traditional flame-keepers when he released *Hard Station*, a record that rocked out in places. This was an important shift. The record didn't sell in massive numbers, but it put Brady onto an international platform. In retrospect, it isn't such a drastic change of style. It is the sound of a man who liked a bit of Paddy Tunney *and* Ray Charles. Brady revealed a stereophonic notion of Irish culture, mindful of the local story but simultaneously into the wider view. Records such as, *Back To The Centre* and, *Primitive Dance* sounded mature, as a series of other artists came to record his songs. These have included Cher, Carlos Santana and Tina Turner. And Brady has continued to collaborate to useful effect. His most recent record album, *Oh What A World* (2000) finds him in partnership with Carol King and Ronan Keating.

Things got noisy again in the 1990s. At the head of the charge was Therapy?, citing hardcore American acts like Big Black as their inspiration. Andy Cairns from Ballyclare was the intelligent, wry front man who along with Michael McKeegan and Fyfe Ewing from Larne, dropped into an era getting ready for grunge and the new gospel of teen angst. Therapy? found credibility with the UK music press and avoided many of the pitfalls that had finished off their punk predecessors. Rather than waxing morbid about the situation in Northern Ireland, Therapy? sang ambivalent songs about serial killers and delivered 'Potato Junkie', a diatribe that boggled many minds with the chorus: 'I'm twisted, I'm bitter, James Joyce is fucking my sister'.

The band made a commercial run with the *Screamager* LP in 1994, which fielded a number of successful singles and was nominated for the Mercury Music Prize. By the end of that year the band had sold more than half a million records, with a strong following in Germany and other parts of Europe. The follow-up, *Infernal Love*, was gothic and peculiar, and brought a dip in sales. But Therapy? have prevailed through a series of misfortunes, outliving the faddish side of the business, periodically returning to the touchstone of punk.

The Limelight bar became the centre for new music in Belfast. An occasional event, Belfast Rocks, was hosted there, serving as a showcase for the renewed scene. Some acts chose to create their own momentum. Downpatrick act Ash put together some of their early gigs in a little bar called the Penny Farthing, before getting noticed by a London manager. Their aesthetic was a more tuneful and wistful variant of Nirvana and their American grunge travellers. Ash sustained an impressive run of singles while

Neil Hannon of the Divine Comedy

finishing off their A-levels. The timing was perfect, as the wider success of bands like Oasis and Blur created a UK demand for young bands with energy and attitude. The first Ash album *1977* debuted in the UK charts at number one in 1996. Ash staged their comeback in 2001 with the album *Free All Angels*. They covered their ground well in advance, playing venues across the UK that their fans had nominated by voting online, just one of the band's clever publicity ideas. The single 'Shining Light' combined a love story with the Christmas theme, another majestic stroke that was well received. Thus primed, the album arrived in the albums charts at number one, nicely ahead of Janet Jackson.

Acts like Butterfly Child, the Four Of Us, Snowball and Joyrider had some success down the years. The latter titled their album *Be Special*, a punning allusion to Irish history. D:Ream, headed by Peter Cunnah from Derry, topped the UK singles chart in 1994 with 'Things Can Only Get Better'. Three years later, the Labour Party adopted the song during its slick general election campaign.

Over in London, Neil Hannon from the Divine Comedy was building his reputation. He contrived a raffish persona, part Terry Thomas, Noel Coward and Michael Caine, hailed on the single 'Become More Like Alfie'. On the breakthrough 1996 album *Cassanova*, Hannon perfected his debonair warble, a self-conscious tribute to 1960s star Scott Walker. He seemed to enjoy the role, crooning over singles like 'The Frog Princess' and 'Something For The Weekend'. The media were interested in the fact that Hannon was son of the Bishop of Clogher and had been schooled at Portora Royal, alma mater of Oscar Wilde and Samuel Beckett, while Hannon himself played the erudite card when it suited – putting Wordsworth's 'Lucy' to music, hailing composer Michael Nyman and wilfully misquoting Seamus Heaney. On 1997's *A Short Album About Love* the music was more sumptuous and string-driven – in part the work of Divine Comedy keyboard player and occasional co-writer, Joby Talbot. *Fin de Siècle* followed in 1998, which was more open, less prone to posturing. It finished with 'Sunrise', a track that described the author's upbringing in Derry and then Enniskillen, remembering the

Steve Gullick

David Holmes

Cenotaph Bombing and ended with the hope that Northern Ireland could sustain a fragile state of peace. Neil Hannon signed to Parlophone Records ahead of the 2001 album *Regeneration*. The tone on this new record was surprisingly sombre and the shiny suits had been replaced by grungey T-shirts. In place of the lascivious Leslie Phillips impersonations, Neil was singing about spiritual vacuity and junk culture. Sales were less buoyant than before, but Neil and the band were more artistically resonant than ever.

Meanwhile, a home-grown dance scene was in ruddy health. House and techno music had come out of the clubs and studios of Chicago, Detroit and New York. The British club fraternity had sensed the potential early on, and had noticed how this allied to the feel-good atmosphere of the Balearic Islands. The idea was imported to cities like Manchester and London and so the most durable and popular youth culture was birthed. Two important figures in this process were Northern Ireland brothers Maurice and Noel Watson, who promoted many early house music events in London. As with punk, many of the early participants threw their own events in private halls and makeshift bars. This developed into regular nights such as the Sugarsweet nights at the Art College in Belfast. This was the work of DJs David Holmes and Iain McCready, who fostered such an enthusiastic mood that many clubbers came visiting from England.

Holmes, from the Ormeau Road in Belfast, was a fearless networker and a formidable record collector from the days of the mod revival, a decade earlier. As rave culture developed, he began remixing tracks by name acts. He was involved in a well-received release called 'De Niro' which paid homage to both the actor and the Morricone soundtrack to *Once Upon A Time In America*. He strengthened his profile with a series of film commissions, including *Resurrection Man* and the Hollywood thriller, *Out Of Sight*. Simultaneously, he was touring the world as a club DJ and working on his own albums. His *Let's Get Killed* album was a hurtling collage of on-the-scene quotes and sonic impressions of New York and was highly praised in 1998. Two years later he came up with a more ambitious effort, *Bow Down To The Exit Sign*. This time the music was created in a New York studio rather than based on record samples and he involved guest vocalists and poets. He was using the soundtrack to the cult film *Performance* as a guide, but also drawing in hints of Miles Davis, electronic German sources and the chilling post-punk of Public Image. The record was themed around a screenplay for a film which had yet to be made. With typical verve, Holmes is currently pitching the idea of the film to the United States. His ambition is unrelenting and at the time of writing he is the most progressive and reputable music maker in popular music here.

Electronic music is currently booming in Northern Ireland. Acts such as Agnelli & Nelson, Basic and Welt are causing interest beyond the island. Digital technology means that many of the new composers can work independently of the established recording studios. A profitable club culture now exists, as the likes of Lush in Portrush and Shine in Belfast draw some of the best-known international DJs. The only loser from all of this is regular rock music, which must now compete with the clubs *and* the publicans who favour sterile acts playing cover versions. It is currently very hard for an act playing original material in Northern Ireland to make any kind of a living. There are some helpful possibilities out there, such as the outline of a business infrastructure in Northern Ireland, with a few labels, managers and media players raising the standards at their end. The music industry has been recog-

Pacemaker Press

David Trimble, Bono and John Hume support the 'Yes' campaign at a peace concert in the Waterfront Hall, May 1998

nised as a bona fide asset to the economies of the UK and the Republic of Ireland, and government policy has also helped the local scene. Bodies such as LEDU have made some commitment to the business of making music, and a recognised music industry body is at the planning stage. At the same time, new media possibilities are making it easier for a new act to get noticed. With the help of a website and some downloadable MP3 files, a musician can find an international platform for his or her work. The major record companies, who tend to centralise their assets, may have a less dominant role in the future. This may also prove to be good news for everyone.

So the optimist looks to some physical achievements like the Nerve Centre in Derry and the Waterfront Hall in Belfast as emblems of a more hopeful time. There are keen, ambitious plans for the Cathedral Quarter in Belfast and a well-researched plan might indeed deliver some of the tourist and cultural impact of the Temple Bar district in Dublin. Smaller initiatives exist too, like BelFEST, a regular celebration of local music arranged over many Belfast venues, and the like-minded Gasyard Féile in Derry. Even Stormont, often the embodiment of a deadlocked political system, has been opened up for a few select concerts. The performers – Elton John, Pavarotti and Michael Flatley – may be disappointingly mainstream, but the symbolism is at least some comfort.

Rock music was a surprise political force on Tuesday 19 May 1998 when Ash and U2 played a special concert for sixth formers at the Waterfront Hall in Belfast. The bands were lending their support to the Good Friday Agreement. The referendum vote was looming and the pro-Agreement momentum was apparently faltering. The international kudos of U2 gave some positive media attention to the campaign, especially when singer Bono introduced the political leaders David Trimble and John Hume to the stage, and encouraged then to shake hands in public for the first time. Young people and pop music were important to the political agenda, albeit for a short time.

Popular music has sustained a great cultural vitality here over five decades. It has manifested risk and adventure with a youthful edge. It has delivered reliable fun, helping to normalise a place which in many ways is so conspicuously abnormal. And when things have been particularly bad, the rock and roll concept of an Alternative Ulster has been a rare comfort. As the guy from Derry once sang – things can only get better. They've certainly been a lot worse.

Arts Administration

IAN HILL

F ew areas of the arts have changed as much in the final decades of the twentieth century as arts administration. Originally the preserve of well-intentioned, earnest, middle-class academics and their wives, trading on their own
preferences for the traditional disciplines of chamber and orchestral music,
opera, Shakespeare and landscape painting, today, a caucus of Ulster's arts
mandarins claim to manage 'creative industries'. They are seen to be, among
other things, activists who argue that their primary duty is as social engineers,
massaging the cultural paradigms of the disadvantaged sectors of the
community. Certainly they are now more regulated, more heavily administered and more mono-policy-driven then ever before. Once upon a time, it
had all been so very, very different.

The impetus for the formation of the Council for the Encouragement of

Music and the Arts for Northern Ireland in 1943 – CEMA – came from the Joint Committee for Adult Education at Queen's University. It had lobbied for the promotion of 'music for the people' and the establishment of a Northern Ireland equivalent to the English CEMA. Joint matching funding of £1,500 per annum was pledged from the Pilgrim Trust and the Ministry of Education and on 1 February 1943 CEMA held its first meeting. From its earliest days it produced the slim, and now rustily stapled, annual reports still accessible in the Linen Hall and Central Libraries in Belfast. Of pictures there are none, but the yellowing pages reveal that the council's aims were to provide the province as a whole, including the smaller as well as the larger centres of population, with art exhibitions of first class work and dramatic and musical performances of the highest standard by professional and semi-professional artists. The focus was on the visual arts, drama and music. The association saw itself as the provider of the best its small budget could afford. No-one called this a mission statement in those days, but brief, encompassing and to the point, it would nonetheless define the state's arts policy for much of the following six decades. That broad thrust would remain the core of the general aims and aspirations as reflected in every annual report of CEMA and its successor, the Arts Council of Northern Ireland – ACNI – right up to the cusp of the new millennium, no matter how many expensive consultants were to come and go.

The appointment of CEMA's members was in the gift of Queen's University's Joint Committee and the Ministry of Education. Only much later was representation from Belfast and other local authorities included. The committee had a chairman, David (later Sir David) Lindsay Keir and nine members including one university professor (A. Macbeath), one major (J.A. Glen), one lieutenant colonel (J.F. Hunter) and the splendidly named Oliver de Selincourt, who was soon to take the Chair of Philosophy at Cardiff University. Working from the English model, advice was taken from a number of sub-committees. One such body was a visual arts sub-committee of nine members which included the acerbic socialist poet John Hewitt, the gentle sculptor Miss S. Rosamond Praeger, and the drama panel, where the flamboyantly eccentric art teacher, costume and set designer Mercy Hunter, was registered in the minutes – for such was the etiquette of the times – as Mrs George McCann. The music panel boasted another who retained, as was the imperial fashion of the day, his army retirement rank of captain (C.J. Brennan) and Mrs W.E. Trimble, wife of the formidable editor of Fermanagh's Impartial Reporter and mother to the talented composer/piano folk duettists Joan and Valerie Trimble.

In these early years CEMA's board changed regularly but, typical of the times, what did not change was its distinctly tweedy, west-Brit establishment feel. By 1945 the formidable Mrs (soon-to-be Dame) Dehra Parker OBE had been added to the complement, as had the gregarious Right Reverend Monsignor A.H. Ryan, and architect Dr Padraig Gregory. The budget of three thousand pounds was spent acquiring paintings (£117. 4s. 8d) or funding tours – World War II travel permits permitting, from 'across the water' – thus Sadlers' Wells played the Grand Opera House. The pattern was set. Still, although it would be twenty years before CEMA changed its name to the Arts Council of Northern Ireland and thirty more years before it became a policy-led statutory agency, even in these early days, one can recognise complaints common to the early reports.

The fifth report noted that with government grants so low, were it not for public-spirited individuals willing to billet 'strolling players' – a convention continued until the end of the twentieth century by the chattering classes of Belfast 9 – many events would not have happened. It was lamented, 'that many who will cheerfully pay a shilling or more for a cinema show or a football match, will not take an interest in good music and drama unless these are brought specifically to their notice.' Plus ça change.

Much of that same report was devoted to the expression of despair at the lack of 'first-rate' visiting performers, coupled with news of CEMA's own incorporation in 1947, under the Companies Act (N.I.) 1932, with a Board of Governors. It also discusses the renting – at 55a Donegall Place – of the Association's first art gallery and the perceived need for both a literature panel and of a logo devised by public competition, the winner to be paid a princely twenty-five pounds. By 1951 Dr (later Sir) Eric Ashby, Vice Chancellor of Queen's University had become Board Vice President, the felicitously named Professor Ivor Keys chaired the music committee and the eighth report complained testily of the workload occasioned by the Festival of Britain. By the late 1950s, CEMA had come to realise it was not its job to present the arts, but to fund others who might. Change was on the way and by the unanimous decision of an extraordinary general meeting held on 29 January 1963, CEMA became the Arts Council of Northern Ireland, without – to the chagrin of its many dedicated monarchists – the Royal Charter that had ennobled the same change in Great Britain. Simultaneously an ill-defined association of up to one hundred 'members' came into being, though this was later acknowledged in private to be little more than a toothless internal pressure valve and talking shop.

Still the establishment feel remained. The new Arts Council had as its first patron, His Excellency, the Lord Erskine of Rerrick, later replaced by His Excellency the Lord Wakehurst. The first report of the new Arts Council spoke pessimistically of the north's cultural isolation and aridity, suggesting the best Ulster could hope for was the occasional return of successful native talent. There was a faint call for a government policy White Paper on the arts, but no hint that the new Council itself had any particular sense of the policy it was following.

A new Director was appointed in the mid 1960s on the retirement of the formidable Mrs Wilfred Capper, who had risen from the accounts office to succeed John Lewis Crosby as General Secretary, and later Director. He was Michael Whewell whose background – Oxford; Queen's Royals; Intelligence Corps; principal bassoonist Bournemouth Municipal Orchestra – was not at all untypical. The choice symbolised the colonial provincialism which staffed many Ulster institutions of the era with imported, and often unsuitable, English adventurers. The calvinist entrepreneurial classes were uncomfortable with the arts altogether. The pillars of anglicanism deferred, as did the remnants of the landed titled gentry, to the superiority of the Home Counties in producing the management classes, while the catholic middle class, though brought up on the dramatic theatricality of their church, had not yet achieved sufficient self-confidence to challenge this custom. The revolution from the ranks of the working classes was still a long way off.

Whewell called for the promotion of the arts in the education system, funding for professional performing companies, a theatre for 'highbrow' and 'lowbrow' audiences and increased powers for the Arts Council – a heady manifesto even in the 1960s. Yet a full quarter of a century after CEMA's inauguration, The Most Honourable the Marchioness of Dufferin and Ava joined the art panel, as the Council asked itself if it gave the public value for money – and answered its own query in the affirmative. By the year ending April 1966 the former schoolteacher and already distinguished painter Brian Ferran, later to be Chief Executive and the man who would preside over the revolution of arts policy and administration at the very end of his career, joined the establishment as Senior Art Assistant Officer. When Ken Jamison became the Deputy Director a year later, the Board still boasted two professors, the art committee a countess and a marchioness, and the literature and orchestra committees another four Queen's professors between them.

At the beginning of the 1970s Ken Jamison was in place as Director, and the Council braced itself for the worst decade the arts in Northern Ireland would face. Reading the annual reports from the 1970s, one cannot but be struck by the increasingly dusty tone adopted by Ken Jamison in his foreword as Director, nor by how the real impact which civil unrest had on the arts world in Northern Ireland, was being handled. The delicate matter of major artists from England avoiding the Troubles-torn province was but hinted at. The Council determined that a policy of 'steady as she goes' was the best course of action. Some new initiatives were taken but in themselves they were too small and too fragmented to be considered as discernable new policies.

The arrival of direct rule, after the prorogation of Stormont, created a situation where executive responsibility for the arts passed to the Department of Education; the arts becoming just one further responsibility added to a long list of duties taken on by the relevant British Minister when he was parachuted into Ulster. This re-packaging, due historically to CEMA's emergence from the coupling of the Ministry of Education and Queen's University, meant arts policy was but an under-acknowledged child, its only guardians half a handful of civil servants within the much larger and politically sensitive Department of Education.

By the mid 1970s the Council itself moved to the arcane girls boarding school ethos of Riddell Hall in Stranmillis with its rolling lawns, wooded walks and tennis court. Corridors echoed, tiled floors smelt of wax and an open fire blazed in its lofty common room. Lunches were long, literary and rarely on unlicensed premises. Visitors spoke apocryphally of empty desks, bar a single brochure for some long distant chamber recital. The image of a remote Council was set. At the same time, an offer from the government allowed the Council to present itself with the Grand Opera House, though the pessimistic Jamison could not foresee its likely re-opening. An internal paper entitled 'The Arts in Community Life' avoided using the term community arts which the Director reckoned too restrictive on an assessment of its aspirations. A policy proposal to share the professional costs of the Ulster Orchestra, was accepted. There were now eleven advisory committees and a new post of Film Officer taken by Michael Open, boss of the Queen's Film Theatre. The poet Ciaran Carson was Traditonal Arts Officer.

Having deemed in his 1977 report the firebombing of Belfast cinemas as, 'inexplicable, even in the zany cadre of Ulsterology', Jamison warned prophetically in 1978 in another almost impenetrable foreword, that, 'Community Arts, enslaved to any minority ideology, will simply cultivate yet another minority interest'. A Community Arts Committee was nonetheless

The many faces of Festival, including Robert Agnew, Michael Barnes and Betty Craig (left to right in the foreground), September 1981

Chris Hill, Belfast Festival at Queen's

promptly created. The Grand Opera House Trust was soon to face up to the government's decision to refuse to finance its running costs as it cut back the Council's funding at the end of the 1970s. By 1980 that Opera House decision had been de facto reversed, but the year itself was financially traumatic as attitudes to community arts were again reassessed. Government revenue funding was on standstill, despite occasional fire-fighting gestures of extra support. Dramaturge Denis Smyth became Youth Drama Director then Drama Director. Michael Barnes, seconded from Queen's University's History Department to run both the Grand Opera House and the Belfast Festival at Queen's, had an extraordinarily unfettered and prima donna-ish say in the prescription of the province's cultural diet.

One small step away from the concentration of remote arts administrators in Belfast, came in 1974 with the appointment by the Arts Council of regional officers east and west of the Bann. With the shake-up in local government around the same time, district councils were required to appoint recreation officers, an opportunity gingerly grasped by the Arts Council to prize in the thin edge of a provincial arts agenda. Only much later would a majority of local councils employ full-time arts officers, although with an abysmally low level of local authority funding often being directed towards the arts, the actual value of having these local arts officers was frequently hard to appreciate.

These were times of a peculiarly mixed economy for the arts. CEMA had started off selecting, funding, promoting and running what it could. Now, though the Ulster Orchestra and Arts Council Gallery were still dependencies and while dance and poetry tours were administered directly, there were also independent indigenous theatres and theatre companies hungry for cash.

The Thatcherite 1980s began with a freeze on public expenditure. Yet Northern Ireland has only just arrived at a stage of development long surpassed elsewhere. Small fluctuations in funding allowed the Arts Council to report the occasional crumb of good news in the 1980s, but in reality the Arts Council received a meagre slice from the cake and there was little change in the relative level of support. This is significant because it led to a situation where Arts Council structures and policies were barely examined never mind overhauled. The long delay in effecting change meant that when in the mid 1990s change was first mooted and then implemented, the shock was all the greater. Professor Alan Astin, the rather dry chairman of the Council for much of this time who was by day Professor of Ancient History at Queen's, regularly complained that increased financial stringency was jeopardising arts provision. More money arrived at the end of the 1980s when the Belfast-born Brian Mawhinney returned home as Westminster's Tory placeman and Minister of Education. Promoting the province in north America, he opportunistically held up the arts – and tourism – as a slender fig leaf to mask the otherwise unrelieved grotesquery of violence. But this increased government support came at a price – the arts as Ulster's 'good news story' used by politicians intent on fashioning the façade of a feel-good factor.

Nineteen ninety can be considered the fulcrum point in terms of the development of the modern Arts Council of Northern Ireland and with it, the establishment of a coherent arts policy with a single vision for how, where and by whom public money is spent. In June of that year Ken Jamison announced his intention to resign as Director after twenty-one largely unmemorable years. The 1990 report was his swansong and the 1991 report shows the urbane and diplomatic Brian Ferran in the post with not a mention of the desperate dark farce through which the Council had passed in the previous year. In that period not only had Michael Longley, a seasoned and

Brian Ferran, Chief Executive of the Arts Council of Northern Ireland 1991–2000

enterprising administrator as well as a poet of international standing, retired from his post as Combined Arts Director, but the Barbados-born Michael Haynes – formerly arts and entertainment officer with the London Borough of Hackney – had been appointed to be Jamison's successor over the favourite for the job, Brian Ferran. Writing before it was announced that Haynes would not in fact take up his post, the independent journal *Fortnight* with characteristic balance, wit, irony and stoicism assessed the situation: 'The good news is that the board has appointed a black Englishman. The bad news is that it hasn't appointed a Derry catholic.'

Mary Holland, a columnist for the *Irish Times*, argued that if the Arts Council was serious about reaching out to as broad a section of the community as possible it would be important to have somebody at the top who understands the sensitivities and prejudices that are part of the harsh realities of life in Northern Ireland. Detective work by concerned citizens, both within and without the Arts Council revealed that the Board – or its sponsor the Department of Education – had failed to confirm Haynes claimed qualifications, which in fact turned out to be false. Yet the Board's Acting Chairman, the librarian David Welsh, made no mention of the Haynes fiasco in his subsequent Annual Report, and Ferran himself was too much the diplomat to append the necessary historical footnote to this mephitic interlude.

It is pertinent to remember that in the main, the Arts Council *was* arts administration in Northern Ireland at this point. Local government was still largely unconvinced by the case for making a greater commitment to the arts, so the present raft of district arts officers did not exist; the local landscape was still plagued by violence so the Tourist Board's push for cultural tourism was a lone voice; and finally, devolution was still several years away, so local politicians had not assessed the old adage that there are no votes in the arts. Within months of Ferran's appointment a further minister with responsibility for the arts here, Lord Belstead, announced a review of arts structures with particular emphasis on the Arts Council itself. The review was to be conducted by Clive Priestley, Chairman of the New London Arts Board, assisted by the ubiquitous Maurice Hayes and Bryan Johnston. Priestley's final report, delivered in August 1992, was to usher in what on the surface *could* have been the biggest shake-up in arts policy here since 1943. He recommended that the existing arts administration be replaced by a smaller, streamlined body with representatives drawn from a much wider range of organisations. This he called an arts development board. Local government could support the arts and a complete overhaul of funding should also take place with a somewhat leisurely ten-year development.

Priestley further recommended the handing over of the Grand Opera House and the Arts Council Gallery to newly-formed management trusts to force these venues to work along more commercial lines. Finally, he argued for new theatres in Londonderry and Armagh, putting an end to what was seen as an artistic over-concentration on Belfast. He believed the scale of the province was such as to require the fewest and simplest structures possible. This meant eliminating duplication and overlap; and maximizing co-operation between players. The academic, ivory-tower stranglehold exerted by bodies which nominated members to the Board of the Arts Council was to be broken; Queen's University and the University of Ulster had at this stage three nominees each, the Department of Education had nine, and the Association of Education and Library Boards several more. The era of the relatively independent, gentlemanly, well-heeled, well-intentioned amateurs administering a burgeoning budget at the voluntary Arts Council was coming to a close. What Priestly should have foreseen was that its replacement would not necessarily bring about the improvements he proposed.

As the Council planned its modest fiftieth birthday celebrations in February 1993, an axe hung over the chivalrous and restrained Chairman, the French scholar Professor Colin Radford. He complained in print that a media led sound-bite culture failed to note the Council's resolute and steadfast ways, but his days were numbered and the announcement of his replacement was brutal. The following month the charismatic, polymathic, Maserati-driving Donnell Deeney QC was appointed Chairman, his appointment instantly raising the public profile of the arts. But more importantly it was simultaneously announced that legislation was to be enacted which would fundamentally re-configure the Arts Council as a statutory agency, thus transforming the essentially voluntary status it had enjoyed for fifty years.

There followed several years of dizzying change in this fustian yet fusty foundation. Brian Ferran was restyled Chief Executive Officer and both the Ormeau Baths Gallery and the Grand Opera House became, by legal prestidigitation, the creatures of two separate independent boards of trustees. The

Donnell Deeney QC, Arts Council Chairman 1993–1998

latter enjoyed the advantage of George Priestley as its Chairman, and he helped transform the organisation – in marked contrast to the former – into the most vibrant of the province's artistic enterprises. Michael Barnes, now OBE, took, as Deeney noted so succinctly yet elegantly, the opportunity of that 'natural caesura' to announce his retirement as head honcho of both Opera House and Queen's Festival. During the financial year ending March 1995, an Order in Council constituted the new statutory body of the Arts Council of Northern Ireland 1994 Limited. The new Council, its membership now reduced and appointed by central government, promised to maintain the arms-length principle of administration. It certainly looked a trifle younger and fresher and it was fashionably more sect and gender-proofed, though it was not necessarily any better equipped to change the hearts and minds of some staff ensconced in Riddell Hall. Its principal duties: to promote the arts; to advise the government on arts policy; to administer the annual budget; to consult district councils about spending and policy; and to administer Northern Ireland's share of Lottery funding.

ACNI Ltd began an internal reorganisation, imposing upon itself four directors: one each for the performing and creative arts and one each for planning/development and finance/personnel/administration – grist to the mill for outsiders' belief that bureaucratisation had gone ape. In preparation, decks were cleared: Deputy Director, and one-time Combined Arts Director and novelist John Morrow, Drama Director Denis Smyth, Central Services Director Bill Collins, Jazz Officer Brian Carson and the Grand Opera House's General Manager John Branch, were dropped or retired. On top of that the advisory panels, which had grown in number since 1943 to cope with the ever-greater range of arts activities, were similarly dropped. Yet this last move was but a three-card trick: recent annual reports detail four sets of advisory panelists, totaling forty-seven people.

As the prospects of peace and restyled political arrangements with the input of local politicians improved in the mid 1990s, questions began to be asked in public about how the Arts Council conducted itself. The perceived lack of genuine public accountability at how funding decisions were made – an issue that would continue to cause great concern over the years – was one issue regularly aired by the community arts pressure group in the news media. Another was the hidden cost of this new, more 'professional' Arts Council. In 1994 Lynda Henderson, lecturer in Theatre Studies at the University of Ulster in Coleraine, pointed out that the 1994 government grant to the council was £6,119,000 with the predicted costs for central services of £998,400 or 16.3 per cent. But, buried under a series of departmental expenses was a further £35,418 which, when added to a £95,000 allocation to strategy, gave a bill for 'running' the Arts Council of a staggering 18.4 per cent of its total budget. Countering the blithe optimism that smaller really meant better, she asked, since much of the real work was done by the arts officers, the full-time specialists, if we cannot have a democratic arts government, why not simply charge these people with producing an arts policy and acting upon it? It wouldn't be any worse. It might be a lot better. It certainly would be a great deal cheaper. And it would unequivocally place responsibility upon qualified persons.

Donnell Deeney's grand blueprint for the future was finally delivered, after nearly three years of consultation, in September 1995. *To the Millennium* weighed in at one hundred and thirty-two pages. Extensively illustrated with acres of designer white space, it became the Arts Council's bible for five years until it, in turn, was savaged by yet another report in 2000. The crowd-pleasing, feel good proposal that a dedicated arts facility of quality be sited within twenty miles of every person in Northern Ireland owes its origin to this report, a situation akin to half-a-dozen mountains each traveling to Mohammed. On funding, the report set out a laudable aim for parity per head of population with Scotland by 2001.

In the same year National Lottery funding for the arts topped £7 million, instantly overtaking the Council's own £6.9 million. This state of affairs that must have taken the pen pushers in Riddell Hall and the Department of Education off-guard, for the Lottery Unit was to have but four staff with four advisors, the Council thirty-six with forty-plus advisors. In the main, Deeney's legal expertise released Lottery funds in the unexpected direction of new arts commissions – such as publishing play scripts – while major capital tranches went to Belfast's Waterfront Hall and Londonderry's Verbal Arts and Nerve Centres.

After five headlining years, Deeney was replaced by the completely contrasting persona of Professor Brian Walker, Director of the Institute of Irish Studies at Queen's. Moreover, pedantic obscurantism was on the increase, most visible in the Annual Report for 1998/99, where the usual list of admirable achievement was absent from the Chairman's introduction. Instead, an uncredited author names the two main achievements of the period to be the 'establishment of an operational framework' and the 'foundation of a management information system'. These achievements, the number – and syntax – crunchers claimed, have underpinned the planning process, informed decision making and enabled the Council to set new standards of access, excellence and innovation. And that was in the year before Anthony Everitt came along and told the Council a high proportion of its planning processes were askew, duplicated, immeasurable and – therefore – unmeasured. Next come short statements under headings including Cultural Advocacy, Initiatives for Young People, Access to the Visual Arts, Co-operation with the Arts Council of Ireland, Relations with Local Authorities, Art and Disability plus Cultural Diversity. Only the statutory plea for more money reminds readers of the pre-cultural-revolutionary past. But of the specific artistic achievements of the year there is not a single descriptive note. Just a note of monies spent. The customary reports for each artistic discipline are absent, as are the names of the executive and staff – but not, significantly, of the Board and its advisors – in an unwelcome return to the arrogance of the long lost days of CEMA. And this from a Council promising openness and transparency.

Rita Duffy, who sat on the revamped Arts Council in the 1990s

Jim Maginn

And still with all this increased bureaucracy the arts here were still chronically underfunded. In 1998 the Department of Education listed the Arts Council's grant as 0.522 per cent of its total turnover of £1.4 billion. No wonder that, apart from the occasional personality clash, there has apparently been an almost total absence of power struggles between the top triumvirate of Chairman, Chief Executive and designated departmental official down the years. How could a power struggle at the top have existed when there was so little power to scuffle over? Central government allocations came and went, much as before. Year upon year they grew almost imperceptibly, lagging behind the rest of the UK in per capita terms. At half of one percent of the department's budget there can't have been all that much to discuss. Within those monetary constraints, what room was there for new policy initiatives? It is hardly surprising the original aims of CEMA were adhered to for so long.

But devolution has proven a watershed for the arts here. It has forced a re-examination of the arts – what it is, who it is for and how it should be funded. At the creation of the Department of Culture, Arts and Leisure – DCAL – the feminist painter Rita Duffy, urged the Minister to scrap the Arts Council, believing the arts would be better served with civil servants working directly to experts. Novelist Carlo Gebler urged the avoidance of an officious Stalinist arts bureaucracy which would gobble up money which should be spent on arts and artists. But community arts bureaucrats, tipped off as to which way the wind was blowing, were delighted. In the new dispensation

Roisín McDonough, appointed Arts Council
Chief Executive in October 2000

of a devolved legislative assembly with limited powers, the Department of
Education was to lose responsibility for the arts. In many European states the
arts portfolio is amongst the most desirable high profile ministries. Not so in
Northern Ireland, though, where the arts were unaccountably shoehorned
into the DCAL hotchpotch along with sport, inland fisheries, Ordnance
Survey, the Public Records Office and various other loose ends. Though
the Arts Council's share of the new Department's overall budget would rise
to around ten per cent of its relatively minute £70 million plus, the arts still
merited just three dedicated officials, much as had been the case under the
previous Department of Education regime.

The arrival of Roisín McDonough as Chief Executive in succession to
Brian Ferran in the summer of 2000 finally stirred the chattering classes.
Equally the packing of the Arts Council board with individuals who would
naturally be identified with the community arts lobby raised fearful eye-
brows amongst professional practitioners, and smiles on the faces of the
ever-growing ranks of community arts bureaucrats. A northerner by birth
and an economics, sociology and politics graduate of Trinity College Dublin,
Ms McDonough describes herself as coming from a radical political tradition.
Interviewed for BBC Radio Ulster shortly after her appointment, she acknowledged the tension between community and high arts and spoke of such

divisions as unhelpful. She refers to her layperson's delight and excitement in a broad range of arts activities when talking to the media – surprising perhaps in the light of the recruitment advertisement's demand for an intimate knowledge of the arts in Northern Ireland on the part of the new Chief Executive. Ms McDonough's appointment surprised experienced arts watchers, though in truth it should not have. Her background is in management with an emphasis on the voluntary sector and community regeneration, and social engineering aspiring to inclusivity has become by default and stealth the dominant mantra of the re-shaped Arts Council.

However the new Chief Executive had arrived amidst what can only be described as an *annus horribilis* for the Arts Council. For this was the year when Englishman, Professor Anthony Everitt, an arts consultant engaged by the Council's Board under its Chairman Brian Walker, had found the organisation more than wanting. Everitt's analysis concluded that the Arts Council had been largely wasting its time and therefore by inference, a hefty proportion of its millions of pounds of the taxpayers' monies, over the past half decade. The Council had used as its policy template the *To The Millennium* five-year plan. Though Everitt's analysis is rich in faint praise, at its core comes the observation that with ninety-eight objectives, the policy document had too many targets to provide direction or focus. Everitt concluded that thirty-eight per cent of the objectives were unclear, thirty-eight per cent were unquantifiable, half were not new and three quarters were not related to discernible outcome. Furthermore, one tenth were not acted upon, and in others, progress had been patchy. Most damning of all, perhaps, was a poll of client organisations showing that seventy-seven per cent found the rationale for ACNI decisions unclear, with an impenetrable veil of secrecy surrounding why their funding had been refused.

Professor Everitt inevitably recommended the commissioning of further consultancies, reviews and surveys, and indeed before long, the Council went on the road with a series of focus groups. By costly unquestioned duplication, so did DCAL itself. Then in January 2001 the Northern Ireland Assembly's Cultural, Arts and Leisure Committee recommended further public consultation. There is, however, no evidence to suggest that any of these meetings improve the odds for 'artistic excellence'. Indeed it can be argued they lead to a decline, for whatever costly consultations are conducted, it is invariably at the expense of the direct funding of artists themselves.

The fashion for these all but meaningless strategic reviews began with, *A Survey of Public Attitudes Towards the Arts In Northern Ireland*, published in 1991. By 1994, the Arts Council had spurred the formation of the Forum for Local Government and the Arts, convening a seminar and publishing *Partnership In Practice* which catalogued district councils by arts spending, by numbers of arts bureaucrats and even by the smallest, most barely used arts spaces. At almost the same time, John Myerscough had been working on *The Arts and the Northern Ireland Economy* for the Northern Ireland Economic Council. This dispassionate research monograph, researched through 1994/95 and published in 1996, ran to two hundred pages of text and table. Myerscough noted that arts policy was formulated by the Department of Education with the intent of improving the quality of life of the community by promoting a climate in which the arts in Northern Ireland can flourish. It was a bland and non-committal comment which could have applied to any developed economy in the western world, and it came as a ghostly echo of the aims CEMA had pencilled into its first ever annual report over half a century before.

Myerscough was not entirely without bite, however, for he did comment that the government of Northern Ireland had no cultural policy as a whole. He also raised the issue of the potential benefits of engaging in cultural tourism, an aspirational strategy soon to be discovered full of practical holes, as the Cultural Sector Summary of 1998 was to reveal. The then upcoming Ormeau Baths Gallery and Waterfront Hall, argued Myerscough, could address the low level of programming events. However, a 1500-seater theatre would still be needed for musical performances, along with another 500-seater space for touring and producing companies. There was also a recommendation that a new Northern Ireland Museum of Art be created. This was a plea made repeatedly first by Brian Ferran, then by Arts Council Chairman Brian Walker and in more concrete terms by Michael Houlihan, as the newly appointed Director of the Museums and Galleries of Northern Ireland.

Meanwhile through the late 1990s the rude mechanics of Council's management continued. In 1998 for example, publications detailing awards, bursaries, grants, codes of practice and protection of children poured forth. Also published for Belfast City Council was its *Review of Visual Arts Provision in Belfast*, though it was not well received at its publication when several practitioners, who despite being referred to in some detail in the review, claimed not to have been surveyed in person. The following year saw the publication of a three hundred and seventy-six page *Cultural Directory for Northern Ireland*, its editorial committee chaired by a top Arts Council bureaucrat. The directory claimed the expectation (of the arts) had never been higher, though, unfortunately, the directory was dotted with errors and had not the impact many had hoped it might have.

The annals of the Arts Council of Northern Ireland are awash with policy documents commissioned over the last decade. Most regurgitate elements of past reports which are appropriated from even older reports. Proposals put forward are rarely followed through. On the surface the argument for so many consultancies is that they will in the end increase effectiveness. But the reality is often quite different. They have created a paperchase of expensive, self-sustaining diversions in a self-perpetuating roundabout of reports, which consume quite a percentage of the Council's own budget. Consequently, more such monies are dedicated to producing marketing research and subsequent marketing strategies from highly paid public relations advisors, and the actual arts organisations – the so-called clients who produce the product – are prevented from seeing their annual budget allocations rise in the way that they otherwise might.

By March 2000 a new fifteen strong Council had been convened and another significant shift in local arts policy can be discerned in this year. The Board's membership reflected the newly aspirant alchemies, including representatives from the community sector, the world of cultural diversity, a campaigner for disability rights, an arts consultant, a local authority arts officer, plus a lone visual arts and design professor and an acting provincial theatre manager. The Council promised openness in decision making and transparency of process, but then astonished the arts community in January 2001 with the release of its spending plans for 2001/02. Roisín McDonough was a new Chief Executive who had already made clear her view that difficult funding decisions would have to be taken to ensure a more equitable distribution of public funds. She was in turn working with a Board well disposed towards the historically cash-strapped community sector. Finally, underpinning both Board and officers was DCAL, the government department determined to reverse the apparent funding decisions made under direct rule, and sensitive

Belfast Festival Director, Stella Hall

too to the fact that under devolution there was a heightened sense of public accountability.

For those pursuing high quality professional work in areas often seen to appeal to what used to be called the middle classes, the allocations proved a great shock. Their efforts were to be rewarded with either standstill or a decrease in funding, whilst community amateurs, particularly those in the troubled mono-sect ghettoes, welcomed massive increases to be administered by their particular brand of professional advisors. The Grand Opera House suffered a funding drop of £46,600. The Ulster Orchestra was down £48,000. The financially stretched Lyric Theatre – de facto our 'national' theatre and the province's only repertory house – received no increase. Moving On Music, the only Council supported professional agency importing internationally acclaimed jazz and world music to Belfast and the market towns, lost almost thirty per cent of its subsidy.

The Chairman's claim that the new priorities brought with them more

Ralph McTell, Betty Craig and Billy Connolly at the launch of the 1982 Belfast Festival

support to what are termed 'cutting-edge' arts, sat painfully at odds with standstill allocations to the most accomplished professional theatre companies, Prime Cut and Tinderbox. Opera Theatre Company, with its witty and critically applauded opera-for-all scheme was rewarded with a thirty-five per cent cut. The Fenderesky Art Gallery, which has repeatedly presented the best of contemporary painting, received standstill funding, as did Catalyst Arts and Proposition, both of which have launched the careers of major conceptual artists. This was particularly ironic as it stands at odds with the government's declared intention of boosting Belfast's Cathedral Cultural Quarter, where both are situated, as a major city centre focus. The Belfast Festival at Queen's, based in Belfast 9, which is surely at the very core of government plans to encourage cultural tourism – but for so long the bête noire of the vociferous community arts lobby in north and west Belfast – lost out by the rate of inflation too. The new market town theatres, whose growth had been condemned by Everitt, were quite rightly new beneficiaries for revenue funding – having given birth to them the Council could scarcely let them starve. What was missing though, was any measure to deal with the overall critical situation for theatre in Belfast, the north's major centre of population and home to the overwhelming majority of professional arts endeavour.

In its rush to faster community arts, the Council seems to have forgotten that without exposure to outside contemporary influences, generations of Ulster people – except those lucky enough to be able to afford to travel further afield – will be left in an artistic isolation, unaware of what the rest of the world is doing, becoming yet more and more 'provincial'. It is ironic in these circumstances that political correctness has itself become the new negative force in the arts. Much of the current crop of community art, rather than opening a window onto artistic and social enlightenment, pulls down the blind, leaving those inside to reinforce a bitter and divisive sectarian past, at their plays' core the mantra: '"a wee cup of tea in one hand and an armalite rifle in The other"'. Furthermore, in exercising this policy the Council has created an artistic *Animal Farm* where professional appears to equal Bad and where, by implication, distressed, ghettoised, socially deprived and amateur equals Good. Yet comparing standards in the majority of performances in the community sector to those in professional theatre is like rating players in county church league football against those in the English premiership. In tune with the New Labour government in Great Britain, the Arts Council substitutes focus group consultation as democracy. But who can afford to attend these lengthy consultational conferences? District council arts officers, civil servants, and state-funded community activists – yes; but hardly the individual artist or the already overstretched 'creative industries'. Some of the Council's aspirations to a PC heaven which have verged on the ludicrous, including a demand that grant aid applicants detail how many persons of Pakistani, Muslim, Caribbean, Chinese and Traveller ethnic groupings they have served. But not a mention of the truth which dare not speak its name – how many protestants, how many catholics, the divisional statistics on which every government grant is now decided.

So after nearly a decade of unstoppable change the artist's function has become socially and politically determined. Art must be tuned to the service of the state. That art's main function is to deliver a prescription to the socially, educationally, physically or mentally disadvantaged is, as many have pointed out, patronising to both practitioner and patron. And there still remain the unanswered questions: if the half decade of working under *To The Millennium* was so wilfully wasteful, why no apology? What makes the

Council so sure that in another five years, a different, expensively contracted, consultant will not say the same of the Everitt report? Who was it exactly who took the tiller and altered the course of the arts so decisively?

Thus far our MLAs at Stormont have demonstrated little interest in the arts, and much of what there is operates on a truly parochial level. Few politicians attend professional arts events, and there is a very real danger of funding battles being fought primarily on party lines – cultural ghettoisation cranked up a notch. Belfast's bid to be European City of Culture in 2008 is a dangerously two-edged sword. If the accolade is delivered solely on a sympathy vote we will wallow in the artistic morass, confident that we're the centre of the world thanks to an apparently irresistible fantasy constructed as we made world headlines for the long thirty years of the Troubles.

But that's the pessimistic prognosis. Optimists look at the role of honour and remember the artists who are the natural assets of this curious place. Debate the listings if you like, but the triumph of the artist over the administrator is that, in the end, bureaucracy will be no match in the long grass.

Reporting the Arts

GRANIA McFADDEN

Over the past thirty years the arts community in Northern Ireland has regularly levelled criticism at the media about the quantity and quality of its coverage. If the wider public is not made aware of arts events, so the central argument runs, then the arts world is increasingly ghettoised and any chance of enhanced coverage is further reduced because of what the press sees as a lack of interest. It's a downward spiral, say arts practitioners. Surely the media's role is to inform. If creative events are not publicised through the press, whose fault is it if no one turns up? As Gide said, 'the artist cannot get along without an audience'.

When compared to coverage of sporting and business events, the arts come a poor third in the media's overview of prevailing trends and future innovations, claim arts practitioners. As many people see a good play at Belfast's

Lyric Theatre in a week, for example, as cheer an average Irish League soccer team on a Saturday afternoon. So why isn't this greater interest reflected in the press?

Certainly before the late 1960s the arts had enjoyed a more comfortable relationship with the media. Local television was in its infancy but groups of academics gathered in radio studios, or on the pages of newspapers, to discuss the issues of the day: regionalisation, the role of the poet in contemporary society, new novels and the latest developments in the visual arts. Kate Pratt and her guests discussed community issues on the BBC's *Kate at Eight*. Edgar Boucher and Havelock Nelson set the agenda for musical life in the region, while others like John Boyd, who produced *The Arts In Ulster* for the Northern Ireland Home Service, and the *Belfast Telegraph*'s features editor, Tom Carson, encouraged audiences to consider the arts as part of daily life – a view reflected in the generous space given to a world beyond the news headlines. BBC Northern Ireland broadcast *Soundings*, a monthly arts review-programme, which was aired throughout the late 1960s, and all the main Belfast papers reviewed events taking place around Ulster, some even offering readers a poem a day to reflect upon.

But as the first bricks were hurled in Derry and the first bullets were fired in Belfast, the old order was swept away. News organisations cleared the decks for Northern Ireland's biggest story of all – the Troubles. The space once set aside for discussion and debate on the arts, was instead filled with the latest catalogue of bombings, shootings and sectarian attacks. After all, readers, listeners and viewers were more concerned about the 'big issues' and as wave after wave of violence engulfed Ulster, the opportunity for neat, non-contentious debates about identity and culture evaporated. Admittedly there was often little enough to report on as the Troubles took hold, but even with the curtailed range of events, lines had been drawn, and for many the arts were of little relevance in a country in turmoil. When murder stalks the streets there are more important things to discuss than the latest concert by the BBC Northern Ireland Orchestra. And so, like much of the rest of society, Northern Ireland's arts community hunkered down under the weight of the news agenda. Arts news found itself relegated to the 'and finally' slot, a position it would retain until very recent times – indeed some would say it is a position it still occupies all too often today. It fell to the arts community to provide some good news – theatre companies preparing new productions, authors publishing their latest books, painters at an exhibition were an occasional counterpoint to the daily dose of civil strife. Writers, artists and musicians struggled to keep culture's home fires burning as Belfast went up in smoke.

This was a not a new role for the arts community. In the early 1960s, Sam Thompson's drama *Over The Bridge* had prompted a massive public debate with its themes of sectarianism and class division, and a decade later the arts world was ready to reflect – and reflect upon – society's deep divisions. Individual artists sought opportunities to take a wider view, to find a place where the chaos on the streets could be translated into reasoned debate, where the unspeakable and inarticulate suffering of ordinary people could be given voice. The arts had the potential to offer a different way of seeing things by broadening out a debate stunted by bigotry, fear and narrow political self-interest. But those in charge of the news agenda were not interested. Northern Ireland was making world headlines and anyone seeking to promote an arts agenda was widely regarded as missing the big story. Graffiti of the day declared: 'The Malone Road fiddles while the Falls Road burns', and as 'closed for business' signs appeared all over Ulster, a shadow fell between the worlds of the media and the arts.

In the period immediately after internment in 1971, the Northern Ireland arts scene virtually dissolved. Certainly the performance arts were hard hit as venues disappeared and audiences stayed away from town and city centres after dark. But as the media was distracted by the bigger stories, the arts world began to respond to Northern Ireland's engulfing crisis. An outpouring of prose, poetry and plays - works by Jennifer Johnston, Brian Moore, Seamus Heaney, Derek Mahon, Paul Muldoon, Michael Longley and Brian Friel – demanded attention. Not all of these works related to the Troubles, but not all of them ignored it. At any other time, the media would have welcomed this regeneration of creativity and new talent. Now, however, it was squeezed between bombings, shootings and a seemingly permanent political intractability. An arts event could only win space at the front of a paper or the head of a programme if it made 'news'. Was this play politically biased? Could that poet be described as a nationalist and this one a unionist? Why, wondered the newshounds, was the orchestra, like the band on the *Titanic*, continuing to play as the ship sank?

Works that were spawned by Northern Ireland's divisions were themselves often interpreted by the media as divisive. Martin Lynch's controversial play, *The Interrogation of Ambrose Fogarty*, suggested that the country's police force might not always act with discipline and restraint. Brian Friel's *Translations* explored the historical Irishness of a nation that was in reality carrying out its own internal examination with bricks and bullets. Controversy became the key to publicity. The media, like any other business, is market driven. No editor in Northern Ireland would lead his or her news agenda with a story about how one Ulster artist has developed his own particular painting style or how one musician has won a new commission, however interesting and significant that might be to the artists concerned. Reports that a theatre has managed to fill seventy-five per cent of its seats for an entire season – headline news in the theatre world when it happens – have never persuaded editors to 'hold the front page'. Like the arts sector itself, the media operates a version of the 'bums on seats' policy. It's all about sales. If editors and producers believed they could increase their audiences by increasing their arts coverage they would have done it years ago. That an increase in sales or viewers or listeners might indeed follow such a move is an argument that falls on the arts community to prove. Stories about murder and mayhem, politics and paramilitaries will continue to dominate the news agenda. Only when statistics show that more people will tune in or turn on to arts news, will those who run our media organisations consider shifting ground. Until then, good news is generally no news. Exhibition banned – front page story. Moderately successful poetry reading – no story. Ulster Orchestra announces new programme – well, they do that every year, don't they? Ulster actor marries former IRA bomber – hold the front page!

So how has the arts community coped with having to fit into the straitjacket of Ulster's news agenda? Literature, suggested Ezra Pound, is news that stays news. So it follows that Ulster's writers might make the headlines, if critics could manage to find a convenient Troubles 'hook' on which to hang the work. But political controversy – for example in works by playwrights like Lynch, whose play *Dockers* caused a flurry of discomfort among middle-class sensibilities in audiences at the Lyric – wasn't the only way to make news. A conservative society is easily shocked. In the past three decades the merest hint of sex or blasphemy had tight-lipped protestors mounting pickets outside all sorts of arts events. Indeed, one of the few constants across the period, has been the very public indignation of fundamentalist protesters at all manner of productions, screenings and exhibitions. Among the earliest manifestations of this came in 1976 when groups of free presbyterians protested outside St Anne's Cathedral in Belfast, at plans by the theatre company Actors Wilde to stage a production of Andrew Lloyd Webber's *Jesus Christ Superstar*. The Belfast papers carried fulsome reports and photographs of the placard-waving protesters who claimed the show was blasphemous. The production, which featured the Belfast actor John Hewitt as Pontius Pilate, was a resounding success – helped in no small measure by the publicity provoked by the protests. Two years earlier free presbyterians had picketed the Lyric Theatre over the staging of the same musical. And they were back again in 1979 – this time outside the Arts Theatre, while inside the same show was playing to packed houses. The portrayal of Jesus as 'just a man' has never failed to shock a small minority here. In 1999 the *Belfast*

Theatre-goers brave a line of Free Presbyterian protestors at the opening night of the Lyric Theatre's production of *Jesus Christ Superstar*, January 1974

Belfast Telegraph

Telegraph reported that protestant evangelical groups publicly criticised Belfast's Grand Opera House for staging *Jesus Christ Superstar* - and no doubt they'll be at the door of the next production. The industrious free presbyterians have often gathered at Ulster's stage doors to picket against what they see as a threat to the moral well-being of Ulster, be it art that promises nudity, sex or homosexuality. In 1993 the Old Museum Arts Centre became the focus for protest when religious picketers demanded the banning of what they believed was 'a shocking new play featuring explicit bisexual love scenes' – the play in question was Welsh Volcano Theatre Company's L.O.V.E.

In May 2000, the Lyric's touring production of *The Butterfly of Killybegs* provoked an outcry amongst Down councillors when they learned the play contained swearing and nudity. 'There are hundreds of good plays to choose from', declared Councillor William Alexander. 'We don't want this kind of thing in the Down district.' The commentator Malachi O'Doherty later wrote in the *Irish News*, 'People who protest against art know nothing about it'. Many shows have faced similar protests over the past three decades prompting Alf McCreary to comment in the *News Letter* in 1999, 'There's nothing like a controversy to raise interest in a stage play'.

Of course, controversy hasn't been confined to the stage. Media headlines highlight the many attempts over the years to stop 'unsavoury' films being shown in cinemas here. 'Sexy film furore grows' – *Showgirls*; 'Blood rampage film cleared by censors' – *Natural Born Killers*; 'Michael Winner raps councillors over films ban' were just some of the headlines filling newspapers in the early 1990s. The mood of outrage was such that, in 1996, the *News Letter* reported that Strabane District Council had ruled that the controversial film *Kids* could not be shown in its area – even though there wasn't a single cinema in the town.

Sex and violence weren't the main objections either. When Jim Sheridan's film about the Guildford Four, *In The Name of the Father*, was released, the media aired public criticism at what was seen as its overtly political stance. Years earlier the comedy team Monty Python caused hackles to rise, with its 'blasphemous' film *The Life Of Brian*, and even books weren't safe from the self-appointed censors. The *Belfast Telegraph* reported in 1990 that the new graphic novel from the Ulster writer Garth Ennis had been 'withdrawn from sale after complaints by Christians that it was blasphemous'. Ennis' novel

Gerry Anderson, Rhonda Parisley and Eamonn Holmes,
the original presenters of *The Show*

centred on a man who burned down churches and cursed God.

Outrage is an art in itself. While controversy kept many away from arts events, some practitioners decided to use the shock factor to gain exposure for their works. A quick call to the media about a sprinkling of sex or swearing in a show, or a hint of nudity in an art exhibition, and protestors with placards would draw the punters in. The press was complicit in this role of agitator, after all it made for a good story. 'Should it be allowed?' asked the media. 'When does it open?' asked a curious public. 'Great box office!' said the organisers.

One of the clearest examples of just how deeply conservative a society Northern Ireland has been – and by implication how the media's reporting of the arts needs to take that conservatism into account – occurred in 1989 when BBC Northern Ireland launched its most ambitious investment in light entertainment. *The Show* was billed as a satirical programme, aimed at shaking the cobwebs from Ulster's funny bone. The brainchild of writer and BBC producer Martin Dillon, it was to be broadcast live each week. Even before its launch *The Show* was attracting mixed publicity, with its announcement that Rhonda Paisley – daughter of the DUP leader, Ian Paisley – was to co-present the programme with Eamonn Holmes, interviewing guests like Arthur Scargill and Fiona Richmond. Sinn Féin members warned they might picket the show, accusing the BBC of treating nationalists with contempt by choosing Ms Paisley to front the programme. The *Belfast Telegraph* noted that *The Show* was launched just days after a Broadcasting Standards Council survey revealed that bad taste caused offence to thirty-four per cent of viewers.

And the very first episode offended many. A comedy skit featured a mock minister preaching from a pulpit, urging viewers to 'gyrate for Jesus'. More than six hundred people phoned Broadcasting House. Just hours after her first appearance on the programme, Rhonda Paisley quit. A Belfast store cancelled a planned appearance by Eamonn Holmes. Senior BBC executives met to decide the future of the series. In the following week BBC Northern Ireland was inundated with phone calls and letters about the programme. Newspapers carried reports, features and editorials on the public's reaction. Ian Paisley demanded a meeting with BBC Northern Ireland's Controller, Dr Colin Morris, claiming his daughter was misled about the form and content of the programme before she agreed to appear in it. The *News Letter* reported that the BBC had announced a 'blackout' on the programme, with presenters like Gerry Anderson and David Dunseith forbidden from discussing *The Show* on air. The same thinking certainly didn't apply to the print media, which gravely pronounced the programme to have been a big mistake. An *Irish News* editorial declared: 'Vulgarity is not satire – *The Show* plunged unimaginable depths of tawdry and offensive material'. Unionists even tabled a House of Commons motion condemning the programme. *The Show* rumbled on for a couple of years, with new presenters and less inflammatory scripts, but it was pulled in 1991 after thirty programmes. Ulster evidently wasn't that keen to see the joke.

Aside from moral censure, new exhibitions, plays and books were studied in the light of surrounding events. Was the artist or writer turning a blind eye to events on the streets? Or perhaps the work in question drew inspiration from violence. Of course all art must be seen in the context of the community from which it emerges and a great deal of theatre, prose, poetry and even visual art created anywhere else in the world carries a political message. But for much of past thirty years almost everything was reviewed and analysed in the context of the Troubles, and as arts critics struggled to make their copy relevant to increasingly news-orientated editors, it was the party political or the partisan message that was sought.

Much has already been written elsewhere about the role of the media in the Northern Ireland Troubles, often with an eye on the debate about direct censorship and political propaganda. Not surprisingly, formal media censorship almost never affected the arts here, although paradoxically, Douglas Hurd's broadcasting restrictions of October 1988 did bring beneficial results for at least one section of the arts community. The legislation was designed to prevent the broadcasting of words spoken by representatives of eleven organisations, but in effect it was mainly Sinn Féin members who were affected and soon radio and television stations found a way to circumvent the restrictions. Occasionally the reporter merely repeated verbatim in the body of his or her report what the banned contributor had said, though that was inappropriate for lengthy pieces. Furthermore, while it did reflect *what* had been said, it did not satisfactorily reflect *how* it had been said, and in Northern Ireland politics that is equally important. Very quickly the broadcasters turned to a small cadre of local actors who were employed to speak the politicians' words. It became a lucrative business and with the right contacts some actors were able to earn considerable amounts of money 'dubbing' the voices of local politicians for local and national broadcasters. For some it was a steadier source of income than anything they could earn on the stage of any local theatre.

Still, no matter how top heavy the bombs and bullets news agenda became there were always some stories which broke through to become mainstream news. In 1981 five artists joined forces to form Field Day Theatre Company. They declared their intent to, 'avoid the populism of community theatre, the plebification of drama', but to deal instead with questions about cultural identity through plays about the north. The company's talk about creating a 'fifth province of the imagination' sparked debate, but Field Day was sufficiently influential to be included in Mary Robinson's inauguration speech in 1990, when she noted the company's aspiration to create a cultural state out of which the possibility of a political state might follow. The *Irish Times* accused Field Day of 'self-élitism and self-enclosure', a criticism reiterated after *The Field Day Anthology of Irish Writing* was published in 1992, ignoring the contribution of many women poets. Fintan O'Toole in the *Irish Times* declared: '*The Field Day Anthology* was symbolic of the company – an immense achievement of talent and organisation fatally undermined by inward looking exclusivity that could not even notice that there was a whole other world (in this case that of women) that was not dreamt of in its philosophy'. Nevertheless, Field Day did raise the level of artistic debate in Ulster. It was the first Irish drama group to present its work on the stage of the Royal National Theatre in London, it was nominated for a Laurence Olivier award and of course, it staged several great plays – though it also decided against staging others, including two of Frank McGuinness' best works. Media commentators watched the company's fracture and eventual demise closely, with the *Irish Times* suggesting that 'its failures, like its successes, were all of its own making'.

However, the media has often provided much less critical coverage, opting instead for the easier route of focusing on local talent which has succeeded on a wider stage. Jimmy Ellis, Liam Neeson, Kenneth Branagh, James Galway, Barry Douglas, Ruby Murray – shorthand for 'artistic' people, and famous enough to need little introduction – have been endlessly profiled, interviewed and snapped in a desire to celebrate local achievement. The current wave of popular, locally-born successes includes the actors Amanda Burton, Adrian Dunbar and James Nesbitt – the darlings of the local popular press.

In February 1977 Richard Francis, then Controller of BBC Northern Ireland, delivered a lecture to the Royal Institute of International Affairs, entitled, 'Broadcasting to a Community in Conflict – the Experience of Northern Ireland.' He acknowledged that because there was no political consensus in Northern Ireland, what many people wanted from the broadcaster was not so much reason or impartiality, 'but the reinforcement of their prejudices'. He went on to make the point, however, that 'more than eighty per cent of Radio Ulster's output was concerned with normality' and that the BBC was committed to covering such ventures as the Queens' Festival, the Belfast City Festival and the Derry Feis. As the arts scene became increasingly active, BBC television and radio – where the poet Paul Muldoon was engaged as a full-time arts producer – found space to reflect this resurgence. The corporation promoted programmes on musicians, writers and artists of the day, alongside radio and television dramas. The BBC considered such endeavour to be 'one way in which the BBC may play a constructive role in Northern Ireland's divided society'.

In particular, BBC Radio Ulster which was launched in 1975, offered more space to the arts. The station was able to broadcast a weekly fifty minutes arts review, along with monthly reviews of writing and music. The general drive throughout the period has been from monthly to weekly programming and Radio Ulster's core arts output is currently the daily programme *Arts Extra*. Other programmes familiar to regular arts listeners over the past two and a half decades would include *Auditorium, Saturday Review, The Good Arts Guide, All Arts and Parts, Evening Extra, Music Now* and *You're Booked*. While many in the arts fraternity have welcomed the volume of arts programming on the BBC, its scheduling has often proved puzzling.

The BBC's drama department in Northern Ireland was very productive throughout this period too. Graham Reid's *Billy* plays were a great success in the early 1980s, catapulting a youthful Kenneth Branagh onto the national stage. Later, under producer Robert Cooper, a clutch of television dramas pulled in sizeable audiences across the UK. *Amongst Women, Safe and Sound, Love Lies Bleeding* and *Eureka Street* all won critical acclaim. Later, the soft-centred, Sunday evening drama *Ballykissangel* became compulsive viewing

Brian Matthew (centre) presents a live edition of his BBC Radio 2 programme from the Belfast Festival's Harp Folk Club. Also pictured are Michael Barnes and Michael Palin.

for many and turned its picturesque location – the county Wicklow village of Avoca – into a tourist honey pot. More controversial were dramas like *Life after Life* and *Rebel Heart*, which once again raised complaints of political bias and insensitivity, charges the BBC rejected.

Throughout the 1960s and into the 1970s, Ulster Television – UTV – had regular and long-running series of music programmes such as *The White Line*, with jazz pianist Billy White, followed by *Black and White*. There were series on traditional music such as *From Glen to Glen*. In the early 1970s the arts series *Spectrum* began. It continued in various forms through to the early 1990s when UTV launched its hour-long teatime show *Live at Six*. The programme incorporated a number of key strands, including the arts, consumer issues and the environment. *Opening Nights* proved to be an interesting cross-border arts experiment in 1991 and 1992. UTV and RTÉ jointly commissioned the thirty minute preview and diary programme from Brian Waddell Productions in Belfast and the Dublin company Radius TV. After two series of the programme, however, UTV put its resources into the new *Live at Six* and RTÉ commissioned a third series on its own. UTV did commission a small number of one-off programmes and short series throughout this period – a profile on artist Roderick O'Connor, a short series on Irish cinema, several documentaries about the Belfast Festival at Queen's and a profile of the composer Shaun Davey – but it has been criticised for its lack of commitment to arts coverage in recent years.

By the mid 1990s there was talk of a post-ceasefire news agenda where the violence of the past quarter of a century would no longer dominate output. Producers and editors began to notice the more vibrant arts scene, with some parts of the media even playing a direct role in stimulating greater artistic involvement. In 1995 Downtown Radio's Derek Ray launched the first Belfast Radio Drama Festival, in collaboration with students and schools, which culminated in the broadcast of *All In A Day's Play*. BBC Northern Ireland, of course, had its Stewart Parker Award which helped turn the spotlight onto exciting new writers like Gary Mitchell, Joe Crilly and Daragh Carville. A *Belfast Telegraph*-sponsored initiative by the Creative Writers Network, which is now supported by Blackstaff Press, was a short story writing competition, in tribute to the late Brian Moore, where judges like the novelist Glenn Patterson panned for talent. The *Belfast Telegraph* had also sponsored the Entertainment, Media and Arts Awards which ran for four years in the early 1990s and sought to celebrate the achievements of the cream of Northern Ireland talent. But Ulster is a small place, and the same familiar faces who signified 'the arts' to the media, were nominated for the top awards time and again. The EMAs, although highly popular within the arts community, later gave way to the *Belfast Telegraph*'s annual sports awards.

The *Irish News*, under editor Tom Collins and features editor Colin McAlpin, launched a hugely successful initiative with the Lyric Theatre and the Belfast Festival, publishing a series of supplements to complement the theatre's production of *The Merchant of Venice*. The paper was later to collaborate with artists Yoko Ono and David Byrne to turn its news pages into works of public art. The *News Letter*, too, offered coverage of the arts through its colourful correspondent Charles Fitzgerald. Recognised by many as he strode the streets in his fedora and scarlet-lined cape, he was famous – or infamous – for racing to the front of the Grand Opera House stage to throw bouquets at visiting ballet troupes. Fitzgerald was a character whose eccentricities served to highlight the perceived difference between 'them' – the arts community – and the more normal 'us' – everyone else. For several years he was, in fact, the only full-time arts correspondent in Ulster. In the main, events were previewed and reviewed by a small core of enthusiasts who covered an increasing number of events for little more than the cost of their tickets outside their normal working hours. Caught between a rock and a hard place, they had the unenviable task of lobbying for more space from uninterested editors, while being dismissed as ineffective by an often cynical arts community.

Partly because of the quality of general arts coverage over the years, the arts community has turned to its own specialist publications for in-depth coverage. The *Honest Ulsterman* was founded in 1968. Its editor, James Simmons, claimed the magazine was taking the 'first steps in a revolution'. The *Honest Ulsterman* 'is a literary magazine', he told readers, 'but literature starts and finishes with men talking to men, and the most important thing for a man talking to men is to be honest'. Simmons expressed the hope that his magazine would provide a special opportunity for Ulster writers and readers, and that any profound effects it may have would be in Ulster. He carried works by John Hewitt, Brendan Kennelly and Seamus Heaney; profiles of Mary

O'Malley and Stewart Parker with drawings by Carolyn Mulholland – a feast for any arts lover.

The *Linen Hall Review*, a quarterly journal which started out in 1984, later climbed onto the shelves alongside the *Honest Ulsterman*. Editors John Gray and Paul Campbell announced that interest in our distinctive northern heritage was, in their view, flourishing as never before, and they hoped to tap into some of that expanding enthusiasm. The *Linen Hall Review* covered a wide terrain – articles, reviews and analysis of the latest fiction and poetry, paintings and theatre. Early editions of the magazine reflected the burgeoning market in Troubles publications. As one contributor noted: 'Since the Troubles began, we have had every Tom, Dick and Harry either writing novels with Belfast as the setting and our suffering as the action, or political pundits expounding on where we went wrong'. While two communities squabbled over which one held the copyright to the north's culture, the *Linen Hall Review* provided a sounding board for their struggles. One editorial read: 'Attempts to promote a new Northern Ireland culture stripped of all Irishness were a manifest absurdity because, no matter how much either may regret it, the experience of both planter and gael is inextricably mixed'.

As the arts reflected or rejected Ulster's increasingly vicious violence, there was no doubting the importance culture played in many people's lives: 'We look to our writers for truths which cannot be refuted and need not be defended, words that will help us go on living', wrote the journalist Susan McKay. It was a philosophy similar to the one that prompted the formation of Ulster's leading political magazine, *Fortnight*, in 1970. Primarily a publication that kept its readers up to speed with current affairs, it also carried a significant arts section, with reviews of the visual arts, theatre, film and fiction. Fortnight's coverage of culture has sometimes been spasmodic, but arguably its greatest legacy has been the poetry pages, where ample space was often provided for new writing. While many of the magazine's arts critics chose to encourage rather than criticise, some were determined to speak as they saw – theatre critic Seamus McKee, for example, incurred the wrath of the Lyric's Mary O'Malley on more than one occasion with his no-holds-barred reviews. There were topical articles about the state of the arts, too. In one issue in 1970, Mary O'Malley complained that the Lyric's new home in Ridgeway Street was 'too big', for instance. 'You can't fill more than two hundred or so seats at present. And the disturbances haven't helped.' One writer described the previous weekend's queues to see the Ulster Orchestra, and then referred to the even bigger queues for that night's wrestling – a depressingly familiar story, and grist to the mill of those journalists who favoured sport over art.

Other arts magazines came and went: *North, Belfast Review, Theatre Ireland, Krino* – all played a part in encouraging readers to explore the arts and, more importantly, perhaps, to question them. In its first issue in December 1988, *Rhinoceros* declared itself to be 'the first of an endangered species'. It set out its manifesto thus: '*Rhinoceros* aims to give breathing space to both writer and reader, room to stretch the legs of the imagination and the intelligence, by publishing long poems and sequences, extended interviews and critical articles that aren't bound by the constraints of reviewing. We want to question orthodoxies of taste and interpretation, to protest against the inflexibility of habits that see themselves as traditions, and to draw in good work from outside the mainstream'. With poems from Gary Geddes, Colin McGookin and John Kelly, and an interview with Roy McFadden, the magazine showed how much more was on offer than the mainstream media could ever hope to reflect.

This was a role the press couldn't afford to play, yet some form of analysis was clearly needed. The Troubles clearly affected arts activity and arts coverage in the province. But should all art be political? Seamus Heaney was often accused of failing to take a political stance, for example. Others, like Stewart Parker and Frank McGuinness, used the Troubles in their work. The media owed it to audiences to discuss these trends, and specialist publications offered the best forum for such discussions.

The Troubles also affected the range of arts events staged in Northern Ireland. Quite understandably, few artists clamoured to come to a country where bombs exploded indiscriminately, but throughout these troubled times the Belfast Festival refused to shut up shop. Each November, audiences who were for the other eleven months of the year starved of the range of events that would be staple in Belfast's equivalent British cities, could come and feast at Festival's table. Amongst the offerings would always be the Royal Shakespeare Company. Festival was seen as hugely important for members of the arts-going public – a sign of faith and better things to come.

Although little notice was taken of the event by anyone outside Northern Ireland, the Northern Ireland Office occasionally flew in an English critic or two to cover an opera or a play deemed important enough to make it to the pages of a London broadsheet. To be fair, the local media gave generous coverage to Festival throughout the years that it was seen as a beacon in a sea of darkness. For three weeks a year newspaper editors were prepared to concede that something artistic was afoot in south Belfast. The *Belfast Telegraph* annually devoted several pages daily to Festival coverage, and the BBC, UTV and the commercial station Downtown, broadcast regular preview and review programmes and updates throughout Festival's run. The Troubles only occasionally dented the festive spirit. In 1987 the *Belfast Telegraph*'s Neil Johnston wrote in his Festival Diary: 'My thought turned to Anthony Wormwood (sic) Benn, and his pronouncement that we are in a state of civil war. I heard the applause and the laughter and I stopped thinking about Mr Benn. I found it very easy to do so.' Uncomfortable echoes of Malone fiddling while the Falls was burning, perhaps, but the press was more often than not glad of the light relief provided by Festival for three weeks in the year.

In 1989 the *Irish News* noted: 'The bleak month of November is always brightened immeasurably by the arrival of the annual cultural feast of the Belfast Festival at Queen's. Through the worst years of the Troubles the festival has provided a beacon of normality, and has inspired a province-wide revival of the arts. Local festivals are now held in many towns across Northern Ireland'. The *Belfast Telegraph* summed it up as '19 days of crack, diversion and culcher (sic) around the old campus'. The *News Letter* suggested that 'when they leave, the stars' experiences of their stay help convince the world that all the media vultures who distort the real truth about this province are wrong'. As the *News Letter* hinted, the media was often seen as the Banquo at the Festival's feast. Heralding the launch of the 1988 event, the *Irish Times* claimed: 'the jaundiced view of the Northern Ireland press was not shared by the public'. Yet over the years virtually uncritical press coverage became Festival's right.

Some of the most objective analysis came from the *Irish Times*, which noted in 1987: 'For a theatregoer this did not feel like a festival – theatres half full on opening night. Classical music is still the darlin' of the festival and its audiences. Has a safety first policy for the Malone Road set reaffirmed conservative tastes and turned younger people off?' That was the year that Festival marked its 25th anniversary.

The Troubles came closest to disrupting Festival in 1993. In May of that year, an IRA bomb had ripped through Belfast's Grand Opera House, forcing the cancellation of the Moscow City Ballet's planned visit. Just days before Festival opened its doors for business, the Shankill bombing and Greysteel murders cast a dark cloud over Ulster. Festival's assistant director, Robert Agnew, said it would be understandable if people decided that the city centre in the evening was not a safe place to be. But the show must go on. There were 'audible sighs of relief emanating from Festival House that the feared commercial disaster, precipitated by three weeks of horrific sectarian violence, has not materialized', reported the *Irish Times*. The *Belfast Telegraph* noted that 'after the dark days of October, Belfast Festival serves as a welcome reminder of an alternative state of life in Northern Ireland'.

Saturation coverage continued through the 1990s, until some critics began to argue through the pages of newspapers and on radio arts programmes that perhaps audiences should be asking if everything sanctioned by Festival was necessarily a good thing. Damian Smyth, then *Fortnight*'s assistant editor, wrote to the *Irish Times* in 1993, to complain about an article headlined. 'Belfast unites to support festival'. He claimed that Festival was 'in no sense a civic event', and that no efforts had been made over a period of thirty-one years to make it so. 'It is unlikely that a violin playing in the Senior Common Room at Queen's will produce a metaphysical uplift in the Anderstonstown or Rathcoole estates', he continued. This was just the sort of public debate on the arts that Ulster needed. A week earlier the *Irish News* had reported Smyth's comments that a turbulent political backdrop to Festival served to stifle such analysis and discussion about its merits and demerits. 'Because it's tied in with the feel-good baggage, you're basically not allowed to say anything bad about it', he declared. As his remarks filtered through the arts community, the media began to take a more robust view of Festival. In 1994, the year the long-standing Festival Director Michael Barnes retired, relinquishing his hold on an event he had made very much his own, the *News Letter*'s Charles Fitzgerald asked readers: 'Was this the year the festival lost touch? Spread itself just a mite too far?' He called for Festival organisers to 'pull back to campus environs and look again for its roots as a classic arts festival rather than a hodge podge of hoi-polloi entertainment'.

The same year the *Irish Times* published a pullout supplement previewing Festival events. It asked six different people to react to the programme – including Damian Smyth, who said, 'There has always been a therapeutic feel to festival. It's not a civic event, so it shouldn't get civic funds'. A community worker from the Shankill Road asked the *Irish Times*: 'What the hell does the RSC have to say to us?' Sinn Féin's Tom Hartley declared that 'on the whole, the festival has no impact on my community'. Bernadette McAliskey put the case for those living outside Festival's small catchment area: 'There's much in the festival that interests me. People in rural areas are forgotten about', she declared, highlighting the difficulties of buying tickets and travelling distances to see events. Media discussions embraced the arguments for and against a more inclusive festival or, as the *Irish Times* described it, 'that old chestnut of the ongoing struggle between populism and arts'. It's a discussion that's still going on as newspapers carry rival columns arguing the relative merits of community arts versus the professional or high arts. What many people in the media who are not familiar with – or not interested in – the arts often fail to appreciate, is that when the arts community complains that not enough space is devoted to its activities, it is not that it wants coverage that amounts to acres of uncritical, free advertising. In fact all that theatre practitioners, painters, musicians and writers want is space for an intelligent debate. In short it is not just the quantity of that debate that matters, it is its quality too.

When Londonderry-born Sean Doran, took over the programming of the Festival in 1998, he produced what many critics believed to be the best event ever. Doran had already staged several hugely successful arts events in his native city – Impact '92 and Octoberfest, which pushed forward the boundaries of Northern Ireland's artistic experiences. At his invitation, international artists like Robert Wilson and Merce Cunningham visited Ulster, and audiences were encouraged to dip their toes into unknown territory. Doran soon departed for Australia, where he had been invited to programme events for Perth's festival. While the press clamoured for more of the same, Festival House pursed its lips, pointed at the huge costs and outstanding bills, and reverted to type.

Doran had given Belfast audiences a glimpse of a cutting-edge, international arts world which was much stranger and more daring than the annual offerings from the RSC, welcome though they had been down the years. Festival would not get away with serving up reheated dishes from previous years' menus any more.

So, the arts were back on the agenda – and the arts community was starting to ask for a bigger bite of the media cherry. At the end of the 1990s, community arts groups began to flourish. Unhappy with what imported and professional arts practitioners had to say to grassroots communities here, the groups sought to relate more directly to 'ordinary' people and their 'ordinary' lives. One theatre company which immersed itself in one local community was Dubbeljoint. It staged a series of dramas – the poorly received *Hang All The Harpers*, Marie Jones' massive hit, *Christmas Eve Can Kill You*, Terry Eagleton's provocative *The White, the Gold and the Gangrene*, with its Marxist examination of 1916, and an adaptation of Gogol's *The Government Inspector*. But it was Marie Jones' *A Night In November*, featuring a virtuoso performance from actor Dan Gordon, which really set the media alight. Set against the backdrop of sectarian hatred during the Republic's 1993 football match against Northern Ireland, the play looked at one man's journey along the road from prejudice to inclusiveness. The production caught the public's imagination; the media enthusiastically reflected the success.

The company, led by the formidable talents of writer Marie Jones and director Pam Brighton, continued to stage a wide range of productions. Furthermore, instead of opening them in leafy south Belfast, Dubbeljoint brought its brand of theatre to the Whiterock Road in the west of the city, drawing in new audiences as well as luring traditional ones away from their more comfortable haunts. Comedies like *Women on the Verge of* HRT and the internationally successful *Stones In His Pockets*; classics like *A Moon for the Misbegotten*, artistic disasters like Eddie Bottom's *Dream*, and political dramas like *Binlids*, helped raise the company's profile locally, nationally and indeed internationally.

Binlids, which aimed to portray a condensed version of life in west Belfast during the Troubles, created waves when it was first staged as part of the West Belfast Festival in 1997. The media gave voice to critics who condemned it as republican propaganda, although the *Irish Times*' Mic Moroney claimed it was really 'classic, left-wing agit-prop theatre'. The *Irish News* carried director Brighton's explanation of the thinking behind the play. *Binlids*, she argued, was not seeking a balance within the piece itself, but rather a balance in the overall perception of what makes west Belfast tick. More controversy was to come when Dubbeljoint teamed up with JustUs, a theatre group founded by former political prisoners. With productions of *Just A Prisoner's Wife* and *Binlids* behind them, the companies set about their next major project - *Forced Upon Us*. The drama looked at the role of the RUC in Northern Ireland and its effect on those who lived in west Belfast. Unforgiving, hard-hitting and contentious, the play hit a wall of controversy when it opened in 1999 – not least for the scene which depicted the rape of a catholic woman by a protestant man. Blasting *Forced Upon Us* in the *Belfast Telegraph*, commentator Malachi O'Doherty asked, 'What is the point in going to a community and affirming its most venomous prejudices?' His views formed part of a wider, and sometimes intense, debate about the two companies and their work.

The 1994 Féile an Phobail Carnival Parade gets underway on the Falls Road

The Arts Council of Northern Ireland decided to withhold a portion of Dubbeljoint's funding – some £18,000, after the company's sell-out run in west Belfast, describing the play as 'clumsy propaganda' which did not meet ACNI's artistic standards. Pam Brighton accused the Arts Council of censorship, claiming its decision was politically motivated. The press, in the main, looked on artistic developments in west Belfast with suspicion and apprehension. While events in the south of the city were familiar and – very often – unchallenging, the burgeoning festival in west Belfast posed problems for the media, which was not always comfortable with the detail of the internal arts community debate on the subject.

The West Belfast Festival – Féile an Phobail – was set up in the aftermath of the train of events set off by the Gibraltar killings in March 1988. At the funerals of the three IRA members killed by the SAS in Gibraltar, the loyalist Michael Stone ran amok in Milltown Cemetry killing three mourners and injuring several more. Three days later at the funerals of those killed by Stone, two army corporals were seized and killed by a mob in west Belfast. 'A few people got together and decided that we needed to take control of the image of west Belfast', Féile director Deirdre McManus told the *Irish Times* in 1995. 'We wanted to give a more reflective image of what was happening in the area.' Later, another Féile director, Catriona Ruane, was to declare, 'We don't hide our politics, we are a political community and . . . we believe politics is a part of life'.

Described by one critic as a 'republican wolf dressed up as community sheep', the Festival aimed to emphasise its roots in the republican struggle rather than stressing artistic merit, according to the *Irish Times*. The paper went on, 'It could be argued that Féile an Phobail is not about bringing people to west Belfast, but more about reaffirming the political values of those already there'. Nevertheless, the Festival soon became one of the biggest community festivals in Europe. While several sections of the media went for the standard 'imparting brightness and lightness' line used to describe the Belfast Festival at Queen's, there has been a reluctance to embrace fully what has been seen to be an overtly political event.

Féile garnered publicity through the big box office names it attracted. In 1997 the film *Wilde* was premiered at the festival, and actor Stephen Fry came to address audiences. Two years later the American actor Martin Sheen, a supporter of Sinn Féin, attended the Festival. Such appearances were noted by the mainstream media, but any whiff of controversy surrounding Féile guaranteed greater interest. In 1997 a row broke out when the then Taoiseach, Albert Reynolds, was pictured beside the Sinn Féin President Gerry Adams at the Festival launch. In 1999 Ruth Dudley Edwards criticised the political content of Féile. The *News Letter* reported her view that 'claptrap abounded', and her criticism of *Forced Upon Us* as a 'hate-fest about the RUC' and her questioning of the Northern Ireland Tourist Board's sponsorship of the entire event.

In the same year Belfast City Council voted to delay a decision on its £25,000 grant to the Festival, and organisers suffered a further blow when one of Féile's invited guests, Sinead O'Connor, withdrew after a row over punishment beatings – an issue she had intended to speak about during her Festival appearance. The *News Letter* was quick to show its feelings about the row. O'Connor, it suggested 'has learned that in some communities there is no such thing as free speech. If she has been the victim of blatantly censorial behaviour, shouldn't the sponsors and backers of the festival be wondering if this is the sort of event they want to support in future?' The media continued to air the 'politics versus art' debate. In February 2000 Damian Smyth, once such a critic of the Belfast Festival at Queen's, used the pages of the *Irish News* to criticise Féile an Phobail. Smyth, in his role as press officer for the Arts Council of Northern Ireland, wrote: 'No one is going to mistake Féile's Old Crocks Football Challenge, Bus Run to Butlins, Sooty's Disco or W.B. Yeats Guider Grand Prix as specifically artistic experiences'. Perhaps not, but the community of west Belfast apparently relished such events just as much as it did the theatrical, musical and artistic productions staged in Féile.

As the arts community grows in spread and stature, so the indigenous media continues to follow its progress, albeit from several steps behind. Yes, the arts have received considerable coverage in the media over the past turbulent three decades, but that coverage has been patchy and frequently ill-informed. If considered analysis of events has been relatively hard to come by within Ulster – coming instead from, in particular, the *Irish Times* in Dublin and the *Guardian* in London – and only rarely from within these borders – in particular from the *Irish News* and the BBC – this is perhaps a reflection of the poor value placed on the arts by society itself, rather than by the media. It is

Arts Minister Michael McGimpsey launches *Face to Face:*
A Vision for Arts and Culture at the Ormeau Baths Gallery, June 2001

only in recent years that the BBC and the *Belfast Telegraph* have appointed full-time arts correspondents, though even now these journalists combine their arts duties with other work. Furthermore, their brief appears to be less to analyse the arts, and more to reflect the sector's headline news.

As we move into the twenty-first century and Northern Ireland's arts agenda takes on a very different slant from that explored by the academics and writers of thirty years ago, perhaps we will see the media reflect the arts as an integral part of our society, rather than a self-contained world somehow detached from everyday life. If health, education, business, environmental and sports issues can make it onto today's news agenda, should not cultural and arts-related matters be given equal prominence?

Perhaps, too, the chronic introspection that has been such a hallmark of life in Northern Ireland – and which some parts of the print and broadcast media often appear to have helped perpetuate – will wane as political stability returns. That introspection has often worked to the detriment of proper arts coverage both within and without Northern Ireland. For example, in March 2001, a conference examining the part played by arts and culture in post-ceasefire Belfast was held at the Institute of Contemporary Arts in London. Entitled *Belfast – Are We Nearly There?* it presented a flavour of some of the artistic endeavour to emanate from Britain's most troubled city to an interested, cosmopolitan London audience. The event received widespread coverage in the arts pages of the national broadsheets, though it was almost completely ignored by the media at home.

Speaking at a performance by Replay Productions, Northern Ireland's only theatre-in-education company, in March 2001, the Arts Minister, Michael McGimpsey, said, 'Arts and culture is not an add-on, it's an integral part of the society we are striving to create'. At last politicians are beginning to get the message. Surely then it is time for the media and the arts community to appreciate their common purpose in persuading society that art does not exist for art's sake alone – it is an essential part of all our lives. If Belfast manages to secure the crown of European City of Culture for 2008 it will be one of the best news stories in this part of the world in half a century. The potential dividend for the north is immeasurable, but if the city of Belfast is to achieve that goal it will need the media to play its part. Meantime, of course, if the local media hopes to be in a position to report effectively on such a huge artistic jamboree on its doorstep in just seven short years, it needs to begin to give the arts community the status it deserves. The time to start building bridges has come.

Further Reading

Theatre

BELL, SAM HANNA, *The Theatre in Ulster*. Gill & Macmillan Ltd, 1972

BYRNE, OPHELIA, *The Stage in Ulster from the Eighteenth Century*. Linen Hall Library, 1997

GRANT, DAVID, *Playing the Wild Card, Community Drama and Smaller-scale Professional Theatre*. Community Relations Council, 1993

JORDAN, EAMONN, *Theatre Stuff, Critical Essays on Contemporary Irish Theatre*. Carysfort Press, 2000

MENGEL, HAGEL, *Sam Thompson and Modern Drama in Ulster*. Verlag Peter Lang, 1986

O'MALLEY, MARY, *Never Shake Hands With the Devil*. Elo Publications, 1990

RICHTARIK, MARILYNN J, *Acting Between the Lines: The Field Day Threatre Company and Irish Cultural Politics. 1980–1984*, Oxford University Press, 1994

ROCHE, ANTHONY, *Contemporary Irish Drama from Beckett to McGuinness*. Gill & Macmillan, 1994

Poetry

CARSON, CIARAN	*The Irish for No*, Gallery Press, 1987
	Belfast Confetti, Gallery Press, 1989
	First Language, Gallery Press, 1993
	Opera et Cetera, Gallery Press, 1996
	The Twelfth of Never, Gallery Press, 1998
	The Alexandrine Plan, Gallery Press, 1998
DUGDALE, NORMAN	*Collected Poems 1970–1995*, Lagan Press, 1997
FIACC, PADRAIC	*Ruined Pages: Selected Poems*, (ed.) Gerald Dawe & Aodán MacPóilin, Lagan Press, 1994
	Red Earth, Lagan Press, 1996
	Semper Vacare, Lagan Press, 1999
GREACEN, ROBERT	*Collected Poems 1944–1994*, Lagan Press, 1995
	Protestant Without a Horse, Lagan Press, 1997
HEANEY, SEAMUS	*Opened Ground: Poems 1966–1996*, Faber, 1998
	Beowulf, Faber, 1999
	Electric Light, Faber, 2001
HEWITT, JOHN	*The Collected Poems of John Hewitt*, (ed.) Frank Ormsby, Blackstaff Press, 1991
LONGLEY, MICHAEL	*Poems 1963–1983*, Salamander Press, 1985
	Selected Poems, Cape Poetry, 1998
	The Weather in Japan, Cape Poetry, 2000
MacNIECE, LOUIS	*Collected Poems*, Faber, 1966
McFADDEN, ROY	*Collected Poems 1943–1995*, Lagan Press, 1996
McGUCKIAN, MEDBH	*Selected Poems*, Gallery Press, 1997
	Shelmalier, Gallery Press, 1998
MAHON, DEREK	*Collected Poems*, Gallery Press
MONTAGUE, JOHN	*Collected Poems*, Gallery Press, 1995
	Smashing the Piano, Gallery Press, 1999
MULDOON, PAUL	*New Selected Poems 1968–1994*, Faber, 1996
	Hay, Faber, 1998
	Poems 1968–1998, Faber, 2001
PAULIN, TOM	*Selected Poems 1972–1990*, Faber, 1993
	Walking a Line, Faber 1994
	The Wind Dog, Faber, 1999
RODGERS, W.R.	*Poems*, (ed.) Michael Longley, Gallery Press, 1993

SIMMONS, JAMES   *Poems 1956–1986*, Gallery Press, 1986

Mainstream, Salmon Poetry, 1995

The Company of Children, Salmon Poetry 1999

Poetry Anthologies

CARR, RUTH, TOBIN, GRAINNE, WHEELER, SALLY and ZELL, ANN, (ed.), *Word of Mouth*, Blackstaff Press, 1996

FIACC, PADRAIC, (ed.), *The Wearing of the Black: An Anthology of Contemporary Ulster Poetry*, Blackstaff Press, 1974

ÓDUILL, GREAGOIR, (ed.), *Filíocht Uladh 1960–1985*, Coisceim, 1986

ORMSBY, FRANK, (ed.), *Poets from the North of Ireland*, Blackstaff Press, 1979, second edition 1990

ORMSBY, FRANK, (ed.), *A Rage for Order: Poetry of the Northern Ireland Troubles*, Blackstaff Press, 1999

SWIFT, TODD & MOONEY, MARTIN, (ed.), *Map-Makers' Colours: New Poets of Northern Ireland*, Nu-Age Editions, 1988

Fiction

CAHALAN, JAMES, *The Irish Novel: A Critical History*, Gill & Macmillan, 1988

FOSTER, JOHN WILSON, *Forces and Themes in Ulster Fiction*, Gill & Macmillan, 1974

HARTE, LIAM and PARKER, MICHAEL, (eds.), *Contemporary Irish Fiction: Themes, Tropes, Theories*, London: Macmillan, 2000

HUGHES, EAMONN, (ed.), *Culture and Politics in Northern Ireland, 1960–1990*, Milton Keynes: Open University Press, 1991

IMHOF, RUDIGER, (ed.), *Contemporary Irish Novelists*, G. Narr, 1990

KIRKLAND, RICHARD, *Literature and Culture in Northern Ireland since 1965: Moments of Danger*, Longman, 1996

PELASCHIAR, LAURA, *Writing the North: The Contemporary Novel in Northern Ireland*, Edizioni Parnaso, 1998

SMYTH, GERRY, *The Novel and the Nation: Studies in the New Irish Fiction*, Pluto Press, 1997

The Visual Arts

ANGLESEA, MARTYN, *Portraits and Prospects: British and Irish Drawings and Watercolours from the Collection of the Ulster Museum, Belfast.* Ulster Museum and Smithsonian Institution Traveling Exhibition Service, 1989

ANGLESEA, MARTYN, *Royal Ulster Academy of Arts: the Diploma Collection.* Royal Ulster Academy, 2000. Foreword by Richard Croft PRUA

ANGLESEA, MARTYN, *The Royal Ulster Academy of Arts: A Centennial History*, Royal Ulster Academy, 1981

ARNOLD, BRUCE, *A Concise History of Irish Art*, Thames and Hudson World of Art Library, 1969. Second edition 1980

BELL, SAM HANNA, (ed.), *The Arts in Ulster*. 1951. Chapter on *Painting and Sculpture in Ulster* by John Hewitt

CATTO, MIKE, *Art in Ulster 2: a History of Painting, Sculpture and Printmaking 1957–1977*, with selected biographical notes by Theo Snoddy, Blackstaff Press 1977

CROOKSHANK, ANNE, *Irish Sculpture from 1600 to the Present Day*, Department of Foreign Affairs, 1984

CROOKSHANK, ANNE and the KNIGHT OF GLIN, *Irish Portraits 1660–1860*, Dublin, National Gallery of Ireland, August–October 1969; London, National Portrait Gallery, October 1969–January 1970; Belfast, Ulster Museum, January – March 1970. Catalogue published by the Paul Mellon Foundation for British Art, 1969

CROOKSHANK, ANNE and the KNIGHT OF GLIN, *The Painters of Ireland c.1660–1920*, Barrie & Jenkins, 1978

DUBOSE, DAVID, *Northern Ireland Printmaking Struggles with Under-funding, Seacourt Bulletin*, February–March 2001

FINLAY, SARAH, *The National Self Portrait Collection of Ireland. Volume 1. 1979–1989*. University of Limerick Press, 1989

HEWITT, JOHN, *Art in Ulster 1: Paintings, Drawings, Prints and Sculpture for the last 400 years to 1957*. With biographies of the artists by Theo Snoddy, Blackstaff Press, 1977

KELLY, LIAM, *Thinking Long – Contemporary Art in the North of Ireland*. Gandon Editions, 1996

KENNEDY, S.B., *Irish Art and Modernism*, Institute of Irish Studies, 1991

LONGLEY, MICHAEL, (ed.), *Causeway: the Arts in Ulster*, ACNI and Gill & Macmillan, 1971. Chapter on *Painting and Sculpture*. by Kenneth Jamison

MCAVERA, BRIAN, *Art, Politics and Ireland*, Open Air, 1989

PYLE, HILARY, Irish Art 1900–1950. Rosc Exhibition, Cork, Crawford Municipal Art Gallery, 1975

SNODDY, THEO, *Dictionary of Irish Artists: 20th Century*, Wolfhound Press, 1996

SNODDY, THEO, *The UTV Art Collection. A Catalogue of Works chiefly by Northern Irish Artists, Plus Detailed Artists' Biographies*, Ulster Television, 1999

STEWARD, JAMES CHRISTEN (ed.), 'When Time Began to Rant and Rage', *Figurative Painting from Twentieth Century Ireland*, Berkeley Art Museum, University of California, 1998

Film

HILL, JOHN, McLOONE, MARTIN, and HAINSWORTH, PAUL, *Border Crossing, Film in Ireland, Britain and Europe*, Belfast and London, Institute of Irish Studies/QUB in association with the University of Ulster and the BFI 1994

MCILROY, BRIAN, *Shooting to Kill: Filmmaking and the Troubles in Northern Ireland*, Flicks Books 1998

MCLOONE, MARTIN, 'A Little Local Difficulty ? Public Service Broadcasting, Regional Identity and Northern Ireland' in Harvey, Sylvia and Robins, Kevin (eds) *The Regions, the Nations and the BBC*. BFI, 1993

NORTHERN IRELAND FILM COUNCIL, *Strategy Proposals for the Development of the Film, Television and Video Industries and Culture In Northern Ireland*. NIFC, 1991

OPEN, MICHAEL, *Fading Lights, Silver Screens*, Greystone Books 1985

PETTITT, LANCE, *Screening Ireland*, Manchester University Press 2000

REGAN, JOHN, (ed.), *John T. Davis*, Gandon Press 1993

ROCKETT, KEVIN, GIBBONS, LUKE, and HILL, JOHN, *Cinema and Ireland*, Routledge 1998

Classical Music

ACTON, CHARLES, *Irish Music and Musicians*, Irish Heritage Series, No. 15, Dublin 1978

ARTS COUNCIL OF NORTHERN IRELAND, *To the Millennium: A Strategy for the Arts in Northern Ireland*, Belfast 1995

BARDON, JONATHAN, *Beyond the Studio: A History of BBC Northern Ireland*, Blackstaff Press, 2000

BASHFORD, CHRISTINA and LANGLEY, LEANNE, *Music and British Culture 1785–1914: Essays in honour of Cyril Ehrlich*, Oxford, 2000

BOYDELL, BRIAN (ed.), *Four Centuries of Music In Ireland*, BBC 1979

CATHCART, REX, *The Most Contrary Region: The BBC in Northern Ireland 1924–1984*, Blackstaff Press, 1984

JOHNSTON, ROY, *Here We Sit: The Creation of the Ulster Hall*

JOHNSTON, ROY, *Music in Northern Ireland 1921–80*, [*A New History of Ireland, Vol 7*], OUP *awaiting publication*

MUSIC NETWORK (comp), *Irish Music Handbook, 2nd Edition*, Dublin 2000

NELSON, HAVELOCK, *A Bank of Violets*, Belfast 1993

Traditional Music

BELL, DEREK and O'CONCHUBHAIR, LIAM, (ed.), *Traditional Songs of the North of Ireland*, Wolfhound Press, 1999

CARSON, CIARAN, *The Pocket Guide to Irish Traditional Music*, Appletree Press, 1986

FELDMAN, ALAN and O'DOHERTY, EAMONN, *The Northern Fiddler*, Blackstaff Press, 1979

GRAHAM, LEN, *Harvest Home*, Arts Council of Northern Ireland, 1993

MOULDEN, JOHN, *Songs of the People. An edited selection of songs from the Sam Henry*

Collection, Blackstaff Press, 1979

O'BOYLE, SEÁN, *The Irish Song Tradition*, Gilbert Dalton Press, 1976

O HALLMHURAIN, GEAROID, *Irish Traditional Music,* O'Brien Press, 1998

SHIELDS, HUGH, *Shamrock Rose and Thistle*, Blackstaff Press, 1981

TUNNEY, PADDY, *The Stone Fiddle*, Appletree Press, 1979

VALLELY, FINTAN, *The Companion to Irish Traditional Music*, Cork University Press, 2000

Popular Music

BAILIE, STUART, *The Ballad Of the Thin Man: The Authorised Biography Of Phil Lynott And Thin Lizzy*, Boxtree, 1997

CLAYTON-LEA TONY and TAYLOR, RICHIE, *Irish Rock*, Gill and Macmillan, 1992

COUGHLAN, JOHN, (ed.) *The Swingin' Sixties*, Carrick Communications, 1990

DUNPHY, EAMON, *Unforgettable Fire: The Story Of U2*, Penguin, 1988

POWER, VINCENT, *Send 'Em Home Sweatin'*, Kildanore Press, 1990

PRENDERGAST, MARK J, *Irish Rock: Roots, Personalities, Directions*, O' Brien Press, 1987

ROGAN, JOHNNY, *Van Morrison*, Proteus, 1984

TRELFORD, GUY and O' NEILL, SEAN, *It Makes You Want To Spit: Punk In Ulster '77–'82*, The Punk Appreciation Society, 1998

TURNER, STEVE, *Van Morrison: Too Late To Stop Now*, Bloomsbury, 1993

Arts Administration

The Agreement (For the Government of the United Kingdom of Great Britain and Northern Ireland – For the Government of Ireland), Belfast, 1998

Annual Reports 1–19 (CEMA 1–19, 1943–44 till 1961–62)

Annual Reports, 20–56, (The Arts Council of Northern Ireland 1962–63 till '98–99) No Reports published for 1999–2000 **to come in September 2001 *National Lottery Fund Annual Reports* (Arts Council of Northern Ireland 1996–97, 1997–1998, 1998–1999)

The Arts – Inspiring the Imagination, Building the Future Five Year Arts Plan 2001–2006, Arts Council of Northern Ireland

Client Report Form 1999–2000, Arts Council of Northern Ireland, 1999

Community Arts Directory for Northern Ireland, Community Arts Forum, 1999

Cultural Directory for Northern Ireland, Arts Council of Northern Ireland et al, 1999

The Cultural Sector – A Development Opportunity for Tourism in Northern Ireland, Edmund, Johnston & Maklin, Northern Ireland Tourist Board, Arts Council of Northern Ireland et al, 1998

Face to Face – A Vision for Arts and Culture in Northern Ireland, Department of Culture, Arts and Leisure, 2001

Unlocking Creativity – Making It Happen, Department of Culture, Arts and Leisure, Department of Education, 2001

Devolving Power to the People of Northern Ireland, Executive Information Service, www.northernireland.gov.uk 1999

The Employment and Economic Significance of the Cultural Industries in Ireland, Temple Bar Properties, Dublin, 1994

EVERITT, ANTHONY AND JACKSON, ANNABEL, *Opening up the Arts: A Strategic review of the Arts Council of Northern Ireland,* Arts Council of Northern Ireland 2000

MARKET RESEARCH AND CONSULTANCY (IRELAND) LTD, *A Survey of Public Attitudes Towards the Arts In Northern Ireland,* Market Research and Consultancy (Ireland) Ltd, 1991

MYERSCOUGH, JOHN, *The Arts and the Northern Ireland Economy,* Northern Ireland Economic Research Council 1992

PRIESTLEY, CLIVE, *Structures and Arrangements for Funding the Arts in Northern Ireland,* Department of Education for Northern Ireland, 1992

Partnership In Practice, Arts Council of Northern Ireland, 1994

QUB, *Creativity at Queen's,* Centre for Creative Industry, Queen's University Belfast, 2001

To the Millennium – A Strategy for the Arts in Northern Ireland, Arts Council of Northern Ireland, 1995

A Strategy for Distribution 1999–2002, Arts Council of Northern Ireland, 1999

Smart Moves – A Good Practice Guide, Belfast City Council, 2000

Reporting the Arts

BARDON, JONATHAN, *Beyond the Studio: A History of BBC Northern Ireland,* Blackstaff Press, 2000

CATHCART, REX, *The Most Contrary Region: The BBC in Northern Ireland 1924–1984,* Blackstaff Press, 1984

Back catalogue of published *Fortnight, Honest Ulsterman* and *Linen Hall Review* magazines and *Belfast Telegraph, Irish News, Newsletter* and *Irish Times* newspapers.

Notes on Contributors

Martyn Anglesea

Martyn was born in north Wales and studied fine art and art history at the Universities of Leeds and Edinburgh. He came to Belfast in 1972 as curator of the watercolours, prints and drawings collections of the Ulster Museum. He served as Honorary Secretary of the Irish Museums Association 1981–85, and subsequently as Chairman, 1993–95. In 1987 he was Visiting Fellow in the Yale Center for British Art, New Haven, Connecticut. He was Chairman of the Association of Irish Art Historians 1987–91. In 1994 he was appointed Keeper of Fine Art in the Ulster Museum, now the National Museums and Galleries of Northern Ireland.

Stuart Bailie

Stuart is a freelance music journalist and broadcaster. Formerly the assistant editor of the NME (1993–96), he has subsequently written for Q, *Mojo*, *Hot Press*, *Uncut*, the *Times* and the *Sunday Times*. He currently presents a Friday evening show on BBC Radio Ulster and edits the Irish music website *www.ohyeah.net*

Ophelia Byrne

Ophelia is the Curator of the Linen Hall Library's Theatre and Performing Arts Archive. Educated at Cambridge and Trinity College Dublin, she was awarded a Cultural Traditions Fellowship in 1996 and wrote *The Stage in Ulster*. She has since edited educational theatre material and organised events, conferences and performances on the theatre in Ulster including *State of Play?* an exhibition on theatre and cultural identity in Ulster.

Mike Catto

Scots by birth and educated at Glasgow University – as an Art Historian – and at Glasgow School of Art – as a Graphic Designer – Mike has lived in Belfast for over thirty years, lecturing at the School of Arts and Design. His publications have been divided between work on art in Ireland and the mass media, especially film. He has been broadcasting regularly on radio and television as a film critic for over twenty-five years.

David Grant

David has worked extensively in theatre throughout Ireland as both a director and critic. He has been Programme Director of the Dublin Theatre Festival, Managing Editor of *Theatre Ireland* magazine and Artistic Director of the Lyric Theatre in Belfast. He currently teaches in the new School of Drama at Queen's University Belfast.

Ian Hill

Educated at Portora Royal, Ian graduated twice from QUB, first as an anatomist, yet emerged a journalist. An arts critic for the *Guardian, Irish Times, Belfast News Letter*. BBC, UTV and RTÉ, he sits on the executive committees of L'Association Internationale des Critiques de Théâtre and Ulster Historic Circle, and on the boards of the Historic Buildings Council, Cathedral Quarter Arts Festival and Ulster Theatre Company. He pursues parallel careers as *Belfast Telegraph* colomnist and travel writer with a dozen associated books to his name, including *Northern Ireland* (Blackstaff Press).

Dr Eamonn Hughes

Eamonn was educated at St Malachy's College in Belfast, Birmingham Polytechnic and the University of Leicester. He currently lectures in the School of English at Queen's University Belfast, specialising in Irish writing. He is the editor of *Northern Ireland: Culture and Politics 1960–1990* and has published widely on Irish literary and cultural studies including *Last Before America* (Blackstaff Press).

Tony McAuley

Tony is a broadcaster with many years experience in both radio and television. An acknowledged authority on Irish and Appalachian music and song, he was for many years a BBC producer and has worked closely with many of Ireland's best-known singers, songwriters and musicians. He has travelled extensively as a speaker and performer both here and in the USA. He writes and broadcasts regularly on Irish music and related topics.

Grania McFadden

Grania was born in Belfast. She was educated at Richmond Lodge School and studied journalism in Wales. She currently works as a sub-editor, and is also drama and literary critic for the *Belfast Telegraph*. She regularly contributes to arts reviews and discussions on BBC Radio Ulster.

Dr Joe McKee

Joe has been Director of Music at Methodist College Belfast since 1991 and was appointed Head of the Faculty of Creative and Performing Arts in 2000. Previously he has been Head of Music at the Royal School in Armagh and a radio producer for BBC Northern Ireland. Music Critic of the *Irish News* since 1994, Joe has served as a member of the Arts Council's Performing Arts Panel and is a Director of the Tyrone Guthrie Arts Centre at Annaghmakerrig.

Frank Ormsby

Frank was born in Enniskillen. He has published three collections of poems, edited four poetry anthologies and was editor of the *Honest Ulsterman* magazine from 1969–1989. He works as Head of English at the Royal Belfast Academical Institution.

Index